BIRDS OF PREY

Predators, Reapers and America's Newest UAVs in Combat

Bill Yenne

specialtypress
PUBLISHERS AND WHOLESALERS

Specialty Press
39966 Grand Avenue
North Branch, MN 55056
Phone: 651-277-1400 or 800-895-4585
Fax: 651-277-1203
www.specialtypress.com

Edit by Mike Machat
Layout by Sue Luehring

ISBN 978-1-58007-153-6
Item No. SP153

Library of Congress Cataloging-in-Publication Data

Yenne, Bill
  Birds of prey : predators, reapers and America's newest UAVs in combat / by Bill Yenne.
    p. cm.
  Includes index.
  ISBN 978-1-58007-153-6
  1. Uninhabited combat aerial vehicles--United States.
  2. Drone aircraft--United States. I. Title.
  UG1242.D7Y463 2010
  358.4--dc22
                                    2010011859

Printed in China
10 9 8 7 6 5 4 3 2 1

On the Front Cover:
The menacing maw of an MQ-9 Reaper greets the camera as heat waves from the aircraft's turbine exhaust obscure the manned cargo aircraft in the background. Armed with precision weapons, this Reaper is ready for action." (US Air Force photo by Brian Ferguson)

On the Front Flap:
Northrop-Grumman's RQ-4 Global Hawk is the world's first unmanned high-altitude surveillance aircraft, capable of reaching denied territory, loitering, and then returning to its base after more than 30 hours in the air. (USAF photo by George Rohlmaller)

On the Title Page:
An armed MQ-9 Reaper sits on a ramp in Afghanistan in October 2007, just after it was announced that the "new hunter-killer unmanned aerial vehicle" (as the Air Force described the Reaper) had already completed a dozen successful missions. (US Air Force)

On the Facing Page:
General Atomics MQ-1 Predator flares for landing at its home base after successfully flying another patrol mission over Iraq. Note that this Predator has fired one of its two AGM-114 Hellfire missiles. (US Air Force photo by Suzanne Jenkins)

On the Back Cover, top:
Just as today's UAVs are manufactured using advanced digital design methodology, this photo was produced by skillfully incorporating scale model photography with that of a real aerial background to create dramatic virtual imagery of an MQ-9 Reaper. (Digital Illustration by Erik Simonsen)

On the Back Cover, bottom:
Capt. Richard Koll (left) and Airman 1st Class Mike Eulo, of the 46th Expeditionary Reconnaissance Squadron, perform function checks after launching an MQ-1 Predator in August 2007 at Joint Base Balad in Iraq. (US Air Force by Steve Horton)

Distributed in the UK and Europe by
Crécy Publishing Ltd
1a Ringway Trading Estate
Shadowmoss Road
Manchester M22 5LH England
Tel: 44 161 499 0024
Fax : 44 161 499 0298
www.crecy.co.uk
enquiries@crecy.co.uk

TABLE OF CONTENTS

ABOUT THE AUTHOR

Bill Yenne is the author of more than two dozen books on military, aviation, and historical topics, and has been a contributor to encyclopedias of both World Wars. *The Wall Street Journal* described his book *Indian Wars* as having "the rare quality of being both an excellent reference work and a pleasure to read." *The New Yorker* wrote of *Sitting Bull*, his biography of the great Lakota leader, that it "excels as a study in leadership."

His works in the aviation field include *Convair Deltas: From SeaDart to Hustler;* his dual-biography of Dick Bong and Tommy McGuire, *Aces High: The Heroic Story of the Two Top-Scoring American Aces of World War II; The Story*

of the Boeing Company; and histories of other important American planemakers, including Convair, Lockheed, McDonnell Douglas, and North American Aviation.

Mr. Yenne worked with the legendary U.S. Air Force commander, General Curtis E. LeMay, to produce the recently re-released *Superfortress: The B-29 and American Airpower in World War II*, which *Publisher's Weekly* described as "an eloquent tribute." Meanwhile, *FlyPast*, the United Kingdom's leading aviation monthly, said that his *The American Aircraft Factory in World War II* "knits a careful narrative around the imagery."

His website is www.BillYenne.com

A pair of Northrop Grumman X-47B unmanned attack aircraft on a maritime strike mission deep in enemy territory. (Northrop Grumman)

INTRODUCTION

As recently as the beginning of the twenty-first century, unmanned aerial vehicles were just a footnote in the annals of military history. The concept and the hardware had been around in one form or another since World War I, but their names were certainly far from being household words.

In listing the important aerial weapons of twentieth-century wars, including the Cold War, hardly any historian or combat commander would have ranked unmanned aerial vehicles among the remotely significant.

Suddenly, with the Global War on Terror, all this changed. Beginning with Operation Enduring Freedom in 2001, unmanned aerial vehicles suddenly had a role to play—not only an important role, but a vital role. As far as popular culture is concerned, unmanned aerial vehicles may actually have been the signature new weapons system of the Global War on Terror battlefield.

Even among military commanders, the perception of unmanned aerial vehicles has changed radically since 2001. A large part of the change in perception since 2001 is in the idea of unmanned aerial vehicles being used in combat.

Back in the twentieth century, many predicted that unmanned aerial vehicles could and would be invaluable in a reconnaissance role in such places as the mountains of Southwest Asia, but few would have imagined them as the ideal warplanes for this environment.

In the high-tech twentieth century, "stealth" technology meant strange airframes that were "low-observable" by radar. In the mountains of Southwest Asia, "stealth" means a quiet killer riding the thermals high above the mountain valleys that have stymied Western armies since the time of Alexander the Great.

By the second decade of the twenty-first century, warfare has evolved to the point where Lieutenant Colonel Lawrence Spinetta of the 11th Reconnaissance Squadron, a former F-15 pilot, could speak of a day in which unmanned combat air vehicles could form the centerpiece of the largest and most technologically adept air force in the world.

The use of unmanned aircraft in combat has been part of a long evolution in both technology and tactical doctrine, but this evolution has moved very quickly since the turn of the century. This is the story of how this has happened.

A composite photo of an MQ-8B Fire Scout unmanned aerial rotorcraft over the frigate USS McInerney *(FFG-8).* (Northrop Grumman)

General Atomics Aeronautical Systems contractors refuel an MQ-9 Reaper at Creech AFB, home of the 432nd Air Expeditionary Wing, the first U.S. Air Force wing dedicated to unmanned aerial vehicles, including both reconnaissance and attack aircraft. (U.S. Air Force photo by Lance Cheung)

An MQ-1 Predator goes through post-flight mainte-nance at a base in Iraq. The unmanned Predator provided American and coalition forces with integrated intelligence, surveillance, and reconnais-sance capabilities, as well as close air support. It was the first routinely deployed unmanned aircraft with an attack capability. (U.S. Air Force photo)

A ground crew secures the Global Hawk unmanned aerial vehicle for towing to a secure hangar at Andersen AFB, Guam. The aircraft has a wingspan of 116 feet and is designed to cruise at extremely high altitudes for long periods of time. (U.S. Air Force photo by Senior Airman Miranda Moorer)

A composite illustration of an MQ-8B Fire Scout unmanned aerial rotorcraft supporting American ground troops in urban combat. (Northrop Grumman)

A bad guy's eye view of a Northrop Grumman X-47B releasing a laser-guided bomb (LGB). (Northrop Grumman)

Through the years, there have been many terms to describe these aircraft that became household words in the twenty-first century. At one time, around the third quarter of the twentieth century, they were correctly referred to as Remotely Piloted Vehicles (RPV). Toward the end of the twentieth century, they officially came to be called Unmanned Aerial Vehicles (UAV), a term used generically in this book.

During the 1990s, officialdom flirted with the notion of calling them *Uninhabited* Aerial Vehicles (UAV) to imply that the pilot who was not actually *in* the vehicle was not always a "man." This idea was short-lived, a victim perhaps of someone pointing out that aerial vehicles are never really "inhabited."

Since the turn of the century, the Pentagon has transitioned to using the term Unmanned Aerial System (UAS) or Unmanned Aircraft System (UAS), a term that references the doctrine of the acquisition of these craft as "systems." This systems concept not only referred to the flying vehicles, but also to maintenance, ground control, and related support entities. This term

has had incomplete acceptance by industry and the media, especially when referring specifically to the vehicle itself. The acronym UAS is used sparingly throughout this book, often in conjunction with UAV.

The term Unmanned Air Combat Vehicle (UCAV) originated for a specific program, but has become a widely used generic term and acronym for armed UAVs. In 2003, the Pentagon superseded these with Joint Unmanned Air Combat Systems (J-UCAS), but ended this program in 2006. The baseline requirements for the combat aircraft once defined under J-UCAS are seen as the benchmark for future armed UAVs, even though "UCAV" became generic and "J-UCAS" refers only to a canceled project.

In the media, the term "drone," implying an external form of control, is often used. Like RPV and UAV, it is literally correct—most of the time. As these vehicles become more and more capable of autonomous operation, the term "drone" is no longer accurate.

The generic term, "unmanned aerial vehicle" is as literally accurate as any, and it is the one used in this book.

TWENTIETH-CENTURY EVOLUTION

A Ryan BQM-34 Firebee painted bright orange to make it easy to see for the pilot who will use the drone for target practice. (Northrop Grumman)

The story of remotely piloted aircraft goes back many centuries to the day when Leonardo da Vinci, or someone like him, first controlled the flight of a hand-held winged contraption with the flick of his wrist. By the early nineteenth century, people such as William Henson and John Stringfellow were tinkering with winged flying machines powered by steam engines. The idea was to build such a machine to carry a person or persons, but in their having built small models, these men were actually pioneers in the field of unmanned aerial vehicles.

In the early twentieth century, after Wilbur and Orville Wright proved that powered, heavier-than-air machines could carry people, the art and science of remotely piloted aircraft was sidelined to the world of toys and amusements. It was the milieu of paper gliders and rubber band–powered miniatures. Serious airmen—and airwomen—concerned themselves with aircraft that were flown by someone in them. That was the point of aircraft, after all. Right?

Another part of the reason that remotely piloted aircraft were relegated to the periphery of the aviation world was because it was technologically a lot harder to remotely pilot an aircraft. You could tweak the airfoil of a paper airplane and get a pretty amazing flight, but rarely was a toy airplane able to fly for minutes rather than seconds. As in Leonardo's day, guidance was still in the wrist of the ground-bound "pilot."

Guidance is the key word in discussing remotely piloted aircraft or unmanned aerial vehicles. It is the pivotal feature that separates such vehicles from simply being a projectile. A marksman can put a rifle bullet into a distant target, just as a good artilleryman can calculate the trajectory that can put a round on a pin-point target beyond the horizon. However, neither can make the projectile deviate from the course that is prescribed by the physics of the trajectory.

Anyone who has seen a really good thrower of paper airplanes has seen how the pilot of the remotely piloted vehicle uses aerodynamics rather than ballistics to apply control to the flight path of his creation. It is, as they say, all in the wrist—or rather, it was. Given the parallel strides in radio technology that were also unfolding at the turn of the century, it was only a matter of time before someone figured out how to communicate guidance data to his airplane while it was in flight. In fact, radio guidance had been applied to toy airships in the late nineteenth century.

As with so many other stories of the development of aircraft technology, great strides were made during World War I. It was between 1914 and 1918 that many aspects of aviation came of age and demonstrated the potential that would define the rest of the century.

Bugs and Larynxes

Changes that affected and supported the evolution of remotely piloted aircraft included advances in both engines and the use of radio guidance. As with the Wright brothers and their people-carrying aeroplanes, there were gifted tinkerers and inventors who tackled the problem of large-scale unmanned aerial vehicles. In the United Kingdom during World War I, Harry Folland built one, while Professor A. M. Low experimented with television guidance and produced a radio controlled rocket. In the United States, Dr. D. F. Buck built a piston engined biplane designated "AT" for Aerial Torpedo.

Meanwhile, Charles Kettering of the Delco company built a similar vehicle that he called the "Bug." With a range of over 60 miles, it was quite advanced for its era. Unlike other early such craft, it was also designed to be recoverable and reusable. It also won a serious government contract. The U.S. Army Air Service ordered and tested large numbers of Kettering Bugs in 1918 and was planning to send them into combat as precursors to modern cruise missiles. However, the war ended and the project was shelved.

During the 1920s, Britain's Royal Aircraft Establishment built and tested the oddly-named Larynx, a monoplane with a 100-mile range that was powered by a Lynx engine. Ironically, much of the testing of this remotely controlled airplane took place in the deserts of Iraq, over which twenty-first century unmanned aerial vehicles would develop their enduring reputation.

The Bugs and Larynxes were isolated projects that had no successors. The idea was there, but the roots of the Unmanned Aerial Vehicle family tree were still a decade away from being planted. In the two decades that followed World War I, the aviation world was characterized by a great deal of tinkering by private individuals with unlimited imaginations, but limited budgets. Numerous small companies came and went. Some survived to become industry-dominating giants, others disappeared. You have to look at the future and follow the evolutionary threads back in time to their beginnings.

As noted earlier, as piloted aircraft technology was developing in the early twentieth century, remotely piloted aircraft were sidelined to the world of toys. After World War I, this trend continued, although the craft were more sophisticated. Radio guidance had come of age, and the radio-controlled (RC) aircraft hobby was born.

Ironically, it was out of the RC hobby that the family tree of modern military unmanned aerial vehicles would grow. In tracing the roots of this tree to their origin, I open the page to a story so unthinkable that it would be rejected as fodder for a Hollywood movie. However, it begins in Hollywood.

Radioplanes, Loons and Other Drones

The improbable father of the first generation of military unmanned aerial vehicles was actually a B-movie actor named Leigh Dugmore Denny. Born in Britain in 1891, he had immigrated to the United States after World War I and had made his first Hollywood picture by 1919.

Hollywood film star Leigh Dugmore "Reginald" Denny pursued an interest in radio-controlled model airplanes in his spare time. In the 1940s, Reg Denny had formed his Radioplane Company, and was spending more of his time at the factory where he made drones for the U.S. Army Air Forces, than on the back lot at Paramount Studios where they filmed his famous "Bulldog Drummond" pictures. (Author's collection)

The Radioplane Model RP-4, designated as OQ-1, was first delivered to the U.S. Army Air Corps in November 1939. It was the harbinger of a family of drones for which Radioplane would earn short-lived notoriety as a footnote to World War II. Reg Denny delivered 50 of these drones to the Air Corps, but this order was followed by much larger orders for OQ-2s and, later, similar types. (Author's collection)

With dashing, leading man good looks, he appeared in nearly two dozen short silent films during the 1920s under the name Reginald Denny. With the advent of the "talkies," he earned numerous roles as the stereotypical aloof Englishman in drawing room comedies, and stardom as Algernon Longworth in Paramount's long series of "Bulldog Drummond" films in the late 1930s.

When he was not on the back lot, Reginald Denny indulged his passion of radio-controlled model airplanes. He even went so far as to open a hobby shop on Hollywood Boulevard. In 1934, he founded Denny Industries to manufacture radio-controlled model planes. As with many makers of full-size airplanes during the 1930s, this maker of models imagined that there was a military application for his radio-controlled planes, so a year later, he formed the Radioplane Company to build larger RC aircraft. The RP-1, with wings spanning a dozen feet, was demonstrated to the U.S. Army, but there was no interest.

In 1938, Denny began working with Walter Righter, a fellow tinkerer—and a graduate of CalTech in Pasadena—who was making miniature piston engines in his back yard shop in Burbank, about a half hour north of Hollywood. The result was a very sophisticated flying model called the "Dennymite."

Early in 1938, the Army was ready to take a second look. It was not, however, the Air Corps. It was the Artillery Corps! Colonel C. M. Thiele at Fort MacArthur in San Pedro, about a half hour south of Hollywood, asked for a demonstration. He saw the value of RC models for use as target practice for anti-aircraft gunners. In May 1938, Reg Denny and Walter Righter were summoned to the Air Corps research and development center at Wright Field, Ohio. They came away with a contract for three experimental RC aircraft of a type that could be used as aerial targets. In 1940, the Air Corps contracted with Reg Denny to construct large numbers of radio-controlled aerial targets. He opened a factory in Van Nuys, near Burbank, to manufacture

The Radioplane factory in Van Nuys, California, with OQ-2As on the line, circa 1942. (Northrop via Author's collection)

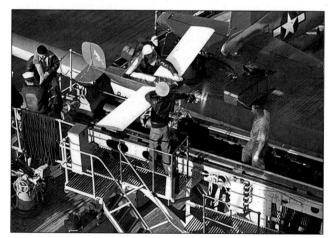

The U.S. Navy equivalent to the USAAF Radioplane OQ-2 was designated as TDD-1 for "Target Drone, Denny." The TDD-2 was roughly equivalent to the OA-3. Seen here is a TDD-2 aboard the USS Wyoming *in May 1945.* (U.S. Navy)

them and brought Walter Righter in as the chief engineer on the project. Righter soon returned to his own company, but this firm, the Righter Manufacturing Company, was acquired by Radioplane in 1945.

In the beginning, the Air Corps (U.S. Army Air Forces after June 1941) had planned to use the letter "A" to designate the RC aerial target aircraft, but this was obviously confusing because attack aircraft were also designated with this letter. By the beginning of 1942, the U.S. Army Air Forces (USAAF) discovered this and the letter "Q" was added to its system of nomenclature to identify all unmanned aircraft—or "drones"—that were radio-controlled or remote controlled. Initially, the Army would designate its drones as "OQ." This meant "radio controlled model" rather than "observation drone," as the use of these aircraft as observation platforms was still over the horizon for Army planners.

The first Radioplane Model RP-4 aerial target officially ordered by the USAAF was designated as OQ-1, and the initial production series of Model RP-5s, were designated as OQ-2s. Each was powered by a 6.5-hp Righter engine.

Even before the United States entered World War II in December 1941, the quantity numbers on the purchase orders for all types of aircraft mushroomed. For Reg Denny and Radioplane, this would mean thousands of radio-controlled aircraft. During 1942, so many orders poured in that Radioplane's Van Nuys plant could not handle them, and the USAAF turned to the Frankfort Sailplane Company of Joliet, Illinois, to build thousands of aircraft based on Radioplane RP-5 designs. Various detail differences between production blocks were incorporated, leading to designations through OQ-14, although not all went into large-scale production. Many were transferred to the U.S. Navy under the designation "TD" for "Target Drone." Radioplane itself built more than 8,550 radio-controlled aircraft during the war, mostly OQ-3s and OQ-14s, while Frankfort built 5,429 of these three types.

This first generation of American military unmanned aerial vehicles varied in length from 8 feet 8 inches to 9 feet 3 inches. The wingspans ranged from 12 feet 3 inches in the OQ-2 to 11 feet 6 inches in the OQ-14. The speed increased from 85 mph to 140 mph as

The Radioplane Model RP-8 was acquired by the USAAF as OQ-14, and by the Navy as TDD-3. With a wingspan of nearly 12 feet and a weight of more than 130 pounds, it was larger and faster than its predecessors. More than 5,000 were built, and they continued to be used until the late 1940s. (Northrop via Author's collection)

The U.S. Navy's official caption read "Small Target Drone Aircraft Falling in flames, after being shot down by USS Makin Island (CVE-93) during gunnery practice off Wakanoura, Japan, 1 October 1945." It was probably a Radioplane TDD-2. (U.S. Navy)

the models incorporated larger and larger powerplants. The OQ-14 had a 22-hp engine. Each type had a flight time of about an hour in duration.

There were also numerous experiments with arming winged vehicles without pilots aboard during the war. Germany produced and deployed the world's first operational cruise missile, the Fieseler Fi.103. This unmanned aircraft would be better known as the "V-1," with the letter standing for Vergeltungswaffe, or "Vengeance Weapon." The jet-propelled V-1s wreaked havoc on southern England during the summer of 1944, but they were simply terror weapons. They couldn't be used against specific targets because they lacked precision guidance.

Meanwhile, the Americans also experimented with wartime cruise missiles. These included the Republic JB-2/KVW-1 Loon, which was based on the V-1, and the Northrop JB-10 Bat, an original concept. Neither became operational. As it was for the Germans, precision guidance was a problem. Indeed, resolving this dilemma would delay the deployment of truly reliable cruise missiles for more than three decades. However, once this problem was solved, it opened a new world of possibilities upon which the UAVs of the twenty-first century are drawing.

The USAAF created a class of hybrid secret weapons that were launched as normal manned aircraft, but which became crude cruise missiles when the pilot bailed out, turning control over to a pilot in another aircraft who guided the aircraft remotely on its one-way target run. In designating these "guided bomb" weapons, the letter "Q for drone" was combined with the "B for bomber"

nomenclature and applied to a series of aircraft during World War II. Most were small single-engine aircraft, but the BQ-7 Aphrodites were about two dozen converted B-17 Flying Fortresses, and the BQ-8 Anvils were several B-24 and PB4Y-1 Liberators. Both the Anvil and Aphrodite aircraft were manned by a crew who flew the ship part way to the target. The BQ-8s carried 25,000 pounds of Torpex high explosives, giving them what is probably the largest non-nuclear payload of any missile in history. The first BQ-8 mission was flown in August 1944 against a German V-3 weapon site near Calais in France by Lieutenant Joseph Patrick Kennedy, the son of the former United States ambassador to the United Kingdom, and the older brother of John F. Kennedy, the future president. Apparently, when Kennedy set the fuses in preparation for abandoning the BQ-8, they misfired and the Torpex exploded in midair. This was the first violent death in a series of such that would plague the Kennedy family for over half a century. Three weeks later, a BQ-8 mission successfully obliterated a German base in Heligoland.

World War II ended without the U.S. military having developed a tactical doctrine for using its thousands of unmanned aerial vehicles for anything other than one-way missions. They were deployed either as cruise missiles to destroy themselves while destroying, or as target drones whose reason for existing was to be destroyed.

Even the term "drone" is implicit of their being like hive insects. Just as thoughtless drone insects that inhabit beehives or anthills are controlled by the whims of their mistress, remotely piloted aircraft drones were directed by an external source of control. The idea that they could be used routinely for observation purposes would not evolve as a tactical doctrine until later.

After the war, as the U.S. Army Air Forces were divorced from the U.S. Army as the independent U.S. Air Force in 1947, the development of high performance, remotely piloted aircraft led to the first generation of winged cruise missiles. These preceded vertically launched ballistic missiles based on the German V-2 by several years. The winged cruise missiles included shorter range tactical missiles such as the Martin B-61 (later TM-61) and B-76 (later TM-76) Mace, as well as the intercontinental Northrop B-62 (later SM-62) Snark.

Meanwhile, the U.S. Air Force established a Pilotless Aircraft Branch and initiated a new series of remotely controlled drones, which were used mainly as aerial targets. Through the 1950s, these were assigned the letter "Q" as their primary designation letter. After 1962, the letter was relegated for use as a prefix to primary designation letters, but in 1997, the Department of Defense formally readopted "Q" as a primary designator.

The original Q-1 was a pulsejet-powered target drone built by Radioplane and designed to be air-launched by a Douglas B-26 (formerly A-26). It had a landing gear that allowed it to land after a mission for reuse. Only 28 experimental XQ-1s were built before the program was terminated, but the engineering work later evolved into the GAM-77 Crossbow air-launched anti-radar missile. The XQ-1A was 20 feet long, and the XQ-1B was 18 feet 4 inches long. Both had straight wings spanning 14 feet 5 inches. As with Radioplane's wartime aircraft, their duration aloft was about an hour.

Firebees

In 1948, the Q-2 designation went to the aircraft that would evolve into the most successful jet-propelled American drone of the twentieth century—the Ryan Firebee. More than 6,500 would be built over the ensuing decades.

The Ryan Aeronautical Company had been founded in San Diego in 1934 by T. Claude Ryan. Born in Kansas in 1898, Ryan learned to fly in the U.S. Army Air Service during World War I. He relocated to San Diego in 1922, where he started the first of many companies that would bear his name. He operated airlines and flight schools, and he built airplanes. Among the most famous of these was the Ryan NYP, better known as Charles Lindbergh's *Spirit of St. Louis*. During World War II, Ryan built more than a thousand primary trainers under the PT-20 and PT-22 designations, all of which were based on his prewar Model ST sport plane. Late in the war, as jet propulsion technology began to evolve, Ryan built the U.S. Navy's first hybrid fighter aircraft, combining both piston engine power with an auxiliary jet engine. Only 69 of these FR-1 Fireballs were built, but the exercise got Ryan started with jet aircraft.

The Q-2 was a jet-propelled target drone designed originally for both surface-to-air and air-to-air gunnery training. The first flight of the XQ-2 came early in 1951, and the Firebee entered production as the Q-2A for the Air Force and as the KDA-01 for the U.S. Navy. It was 17 feet 3 inches long, with swept wings spanning 11 feet 2 inches. Powered by either a Continental J69 or a Fairchild J44 turbojet engine, it had a top speed of Mach .9 and a range of 400 miles. Its duration was just under an hour and it was capable of operating above 50,000 feet.

Operationally, Firebees could be air launched, or surface launched with an Aerojet General X102 solid-fuel rocket booster engine. Unlike the wartime remote-controlled OQ aircraft, it was not recovered through the use of landing gear on a runway, but rather with a remotely deployed parachute system.

The larger Q-2C Firebee (Ryan Model 124) made its first flight in December 1958. It was 22 feet 11 inches long, with a wingspan of 12 feet 11 inches. Powered by an improved Continental J69, it had a range of 800 miles, double that of the Q-2A, and could operate above 60,000 feet. Like the Q-2A, its speed was just short of supersonic. The Q-2C Firebee's signature feature was probably its distinctive engine intake, which looked like a laughing mouth beneath the long, sharply-pointed, shark-like nose.

In 1962, two years after the Q-2C entered production, the Defense Department nomenclature system was reorganized. At that time, the "Q" for drone prefix was merged with the "M" for missile and drones were renumbered in the missile lineage. (The "Q" designation would be re-instituted in 1997, with the Predator as the new Q-1.) Under this new nomenclature, the Air Force's Q-2C became the BQM-34A, while the U.S. Navy's KDA-1 and KDA-2 Firebees became BQM-34B and BQM-34C. Those Firebees used by the U.S. Army

The U.S. Air Force 99th Strategic Reconnaissance Squadron operated this array of Ryan Firebee drones in Vietnam. Seen here at Bien Hoa AB, they include a Model 147J configured for low-altitude day photography (left); an extended range Model 147H used for high-altitude missions (rear); a Model 147G, which was essentially a basic Model 147B with a larger engine (right); and a Model 147NX, used as a decoy or medium-altitude day photo-reconnaissance drone. (Al Lloyd collection via Bill Yenne)

would be designated as MQM-34D. As used here, the "B" prefix implied that a particular drone operated from multiple launch platforms, not that it was a bomber.

The natural next step in Firebee evolution was the supersonic Ryan Model 166, which was ordered by the U.S. Navy in 1965 under the designation BQM-34E. Known officially as the Firebee II, it made its first flight in January 1968 and became operational in 1972. The U.S. Air Force ordered the Firebee II in 1969 under the designation BQM-34F. It was similar to the

An AQM-34M Firebee riding on a 99th Strategic Reconnaissance Squadron DC-130 is flying in formation with a manned U-2R reconnaissance aircraft over Southeast Asia. It has been said that maximum results were achieved by teaming U-2Rs with Firebees that were equipped with LORAN (Long-Range Radio Aid for Navigation). (Al Lloyd collection via Bill Yenne)

BQM-34E, but was designed to be retrieved in mid-air by a helicopter as it was descending by parachute. This scenario was first tested in 1971.

The Firebee II aircraft were 29 feet 2 inches long, with a wingspan of 8 feet 11 inches. They were powered by a Continental J69-T-406 turbojet and had a top speed of Mach 1.1. The range was nearly 900 miles, with a ceiling of 60,000 feet. The endurance was more than an hour. The range could be extended through the use of a conformal external tank, but this limited the speed to less than Mach 1. There would be 50 Firebee IIs built before production ended in 1980.

While the Firebee originated as a target drone and long continued to be used as such, it was also one of the first recoverable unmanned aerial vehicles to be widely used in a reconnaissance role. In the 1960s, the U.S. Air Force took a first step toward the widespread use of adapting its unmanned aerial vehicles for use as something other than just target drones.

Ryan had originally experimented with Firebees in a reconnaissance role as early as 1959, and after the high-profile losses of manned U-2 and RB-47 "spy planes" over the Soviet Union in 1960, the U.S. Air Force and the Central Intelligence Agency (CIA) were ready to talk. The idea of an aircraft with the minimal radar cross section of a Firebee, especially one that put no crewmember at risk, was very appealing. Under the project codenamed Fire Fly, the Air Force ordered a reconnaissance variation of the Firebee in 1961.

Ryan retrofitted a BQM-34A with new navigation and surveillance equipment and additional fuel capacity, and this aircraft was first flight tested between April and

Seen here at Bien Hoa AB in April 1966, a Ryan Model 147J Lightning Bug low-altitude day photographic aircraft is suspended from the Number 3 pylon of a 99th Strategic Reconnaissance Squadron DC-130A. (Al Lloyd collection via Bill Yenne)

August 1962 under the non-military designation Model 147A, and the official name "Lightning Bug." Apparently, no Bug overflights were conducted in Soviet air space, but a small number of missions would be made over southern China during the summer of 1964.

The Lightning Bugs were, however, widely used in Southeast Asia from 1964 to 1975, controlled by both the U.S. Air Force and the CIA. The latter was responsible for the design and management of specific equipment packages. The U.S. Navy, meanwhile, operated the Model 147SK. Launched with a rocket booster from the aircraft carrier USS *Ranger* (CVA-61) in the South China Sea, the Navy Bugs were operational between November 1969 and June 1970.

For the first three years of their Southeast Asia deployment, most Lightning Bugs were used for high-altitude photo-reconnaissance missions. These were conducted between August 1964 and the end of 1965 by Model 147Bs, which had been specially modified with an enlarged wing. These aircraft were succeeded by the longer Model 147G, which remained in action until August 1967. Between them, these two types conducted 161 missions. In the meanwhile, aircraft designated as Ryan Models 147D and 147E were used for a small number of CIA electronic intelligence missions in 1965 and 1966.

The U.S. Air Force Bugs were assigned to the 100th Strategic Reconnaissance Wing of the Air Force Strategic Air Command. In the autumn of 1968, the Air Force began using the AQM-34 designation, rather than BQM-34, to classify its reconnaissance Lightning Bugs operating in Southeast Asia.

The first Air Force Lightning Bugs operating in the theater to be assigned the AQM prefix were the AQM-34Gs, which were manufactured and deployed under the Air Force Compass Bin and Buffalo Hunter programs that succeeded the earlier Combat Angel radar jamming program. The AQM-34Gs were configured to aid manned strike aircraft by conducting electronic countermeasures and laying radar-confusing chaff ahead of them as they entered enemy airspace. The night-time reconnaissance Bug, designated as AQM-34K, flew 44 missions between November 1968 and October 1969.

The Lightning Bugs were air-launched from DC-130A and DC-130E drone director "mother-ships," of which at least 15 were converted from Lockheed C-130 Hercules transport aircraft. Having been air launched, the Lightning Bugs were recovered by parachute. In some cases after 1969, these descending Bugs were snatched in mid-air by helicopters outfitted with the Mid-Air Retrieval System (MARS).

After 1967, the majority of Lightning Bug operations were low altitude, mainly photo-reconnaissance missions. These aircraft got down and dirty at as low as 500 feet where the antiaircraft gunners did not see them until they were practically gone. Manufactured and deployed under the Air Force Compass Bin and Buffalo Hunter programs, the AQM-34L aircraft flew 1,773 low altitude mis-

sions between January 1969 and June 1973. Most of these were photo-reconnaissance flights, but 121 missions, flown after June 1972, involved real-time television imaging. This made the AQM-34L RPV a true precursor of twenty-first century unmanned aerial vehicles.

The capabilities of twenty-first-century Unmanned Aerial Vehicles were responsible for reviving signals intelligence. In the mid 1960s, the Airborne Command & Control Center (ABCCC) activity (the predecessor of today's AWACS) was located aboard Lockheed EC-121 Constellations, operating in conjunction with other electronic warfare assets under such operational code names as College Eye and Big Eye. Their job, like today's AWACS, was to patrol the Gulf of Tonkin, monitoring North Vietnamese radio frequencies. It was dangerous work for an unarmed manned aircraft operating so close to enemy territory. When an EC-121 was lost, the Air Force decided to use a drone for this mission. The Combat Dawn project led to production of specially configured AQM-34Q electronic surveillance aircraft. These were operational on 268 missions from February 1970 to June 1973, providing real-time electronic intelligence.

For the Lightning Bug fleet, the reconnaissance mission continued even after the Paris Peace Accords of 1973 ended major United States military involvement in Vietnam. Until April 1975, when North Vietnam successfully conquered South Vietnam, 183 low-level real-time imaging missions would be flown by AQM-34M Lightning Bugs (Model 147H). The AQM-34Ms had earlier been used to fly 138 high-altitude photo-reconnaissance missions between March 1967 and July 1971. The AQM-34Ms occasionally operated at altitudes as low as 200 feet.

When the AQM-34Q Combat Dawn signals intelligence aircraft were phased out, they were superseded by the longer range AQM-34R aircraft, which flew 216 missions between February 1973 and June 1975 with a 97 percent success rate.

Three decades before RQ-1 Predators were armed for offensive operations during the Global War on Terror, the U.S. Air Force experimented among its Firebee/Lightning Bug aircraft for missions in Southeast Asia. Under the Have Lemon project of 1971, Firebees were armed with various types of ordnance, including Hughes AGM-65 Maverick ground attack missiles, and Rockwell GBU-8 "Stubby Hobo" glide bomb units. The first live fire test of a guided air-to-surface missile launched from an American Unmanned Aerial Vehicle came on 14 December 1971 when a Firebee flown by the 6514th Test Squadron at the Edwards AFB Flight Test Center scored a direct hit with a Maverick on an old retired radar van parked on the test range. A second Maverick test one week later was also successful, as were two Stubby Hobo tests in February 1972.

Like the Firebee itself, both the Maverick and the Stubby Hobo were electro-optically guided, meaning that the controller at a remote control station could watch their progress on television as though he was aboard. When the weapon was launched, he could then switch screens from the drone to the weapon and guide it to the target.

In theory, this combination of unmanned aerial vehicles and air-to-ground ordnance would have been ready for action by the time of the Operation Linebacker I offensive in May 1972, but they were never deployed. The most dangerous and highest-value targets assigned to the Have Lemon drones were enemy air defenses, and with 1972 imaging technology, it would have been hard for the operator to identify and react to such well camouflaged targets with the split second timing that was required.

As a reconnaissance platform, however, the Firebees and Lightning Bugs received high marks. The combat record of America's longest-serving twentieth century unmanned aerial reconnaissance aircraft was remarkable. Without the peril of losing a pilot, the Lightning Bugs could penetrate into the most dangerous of places and they did. Between 1964 and 1975, the Lightning Bug fleet flew 3,435 operational missions in Southeast Asia. More than half of these were by AQM-34Ls.

These Bugs lasted an average of 7.3 missions before they were lost, but one AQM-34L, nicknamed *Tomcat*, successfully returned from 67 missions before being lost on its 68th. Certain missions had higher success rates. As may have been expected, more than half of the Lightning Bugs used as decoys and for especially dangerous night missions were lost on these missions. On the high-altitude missions during the early years of the war, only six in ten returned from such operations. However, the later low-level reconnaissance missions counted on a better than 90 percent success rate.

When the final Southeast Asia operations wound down in 1975, the U.S. Air Force suspended its use in a reconnaissance role, although experiments in other operations continued. The Air Force revisited the old Combat Angel project, by contracting with Ryan to retrofit approximately five dozen existing Lightning Bugs with electronic radar jammers and such equipment as AN/ALE-38 chaff dispensers. Redelivered under the designation AQM-34V, these aircraft were supplement by an additional 16 factory fresh aircraft. The

An artist's conception of a BQM-34 Firebee target drone that is about to be destroyed by an air-to-air missile launched from an F-16. (Northrop Grumman)

Repainted in battlefield gray, this well-guarded BQM-34 Firebee is one of those that would see service during Operation Iraqi Freedom in March 2003. (Northrop Grumman)

Loaded aboard a DC-130 and bound for action in the skies over Iraq, this BQM-34 Firebee carries a handwritten message for Saddam Hussein. For him, the handwriting was also on the metaphorical wall. (Northrop Grumman)

AQM-34Vs were tested between 1976 and 1978, but then withdrawn from service.

Other Lightning Bugs that survived the Vietnam War went into long term storage or continued to be used as aerial targets for missile development tests. About 33 were transferred to the Israeli Air Force, where they were known as the Mabat. These aircraft were successfully deployed as decoys to divert antiaircraft fire from manned bombers during the Yom Kippur War of 1973. Since the 1970s, the Israelis have continuously been using unmanned aerial vehicles as reconnaissance aircraft.

Firebee production continued until 1982, and was resumed in 1986 under the Reagan Administration, with the additional aircraft being produced under the BGM-34 designation. Meanwhile, in 1969, Ryan Aeronautical was acquired by Teledyne, becoming Teledyne Ryan. Three decades later, in 1999, it became part of the Northrop Grumman Corporation.

In 2003, four decades after their first combat deployment, Firebees were back in combat. As a fitting curtain call to their distinguished combat career, the little drones were used during the opening phase of Operation Iraqi Freedom. These vehicles were used on the first night of the war to lay chaff corridors through Iraqi air space to shield cruise missiles and manned aircraft on strike missions to Baghdad and other targets deep inside Iraq.

Chukars

While pointing out that the Lightning Bugs were the signature reconnaissance drone of the 1960s, it is important to make reference to the continuing lineage of Radioplane, the place, where operational military unmanned aerial vehicles were born. Northrop Corporation acquired Radioplane in 1952, eventually renaming it as the Ventura Division. In 1953, this entity began work on the Q-4, a jet-propelled remotely piloted aircraft that was intended to be capable of supersonic speeds. The XQ-4A was 33 feet long, with a wingspan of 11 feet 1 inch. First flown in 1961, the Q-4B was about 28 inches longer, with a 19 inch greater span. A total of 25 examples of the two types were built, but the program was terminated before these became operational.

A decade later, Northrop Ventura proposed its Model NV-105 to meet a U.S. Navy requirement for an aerial target for anti-aircraft gunnery and missile training. The original delta winged design of 1964 was superseded by a straight-winged NV-105A a year later. This vehicle was ordered for production by the Navy under the designation MQM-74A. Powered by a Williams J400-WR-400 turbojet engine, the MQM-74A was designed to be launched from a ship using a rocket assist system. The MQM-74A was 11 feet 4 inches long, with a wingspan of 5 feet 7 inches, and it weighed 425 pounds. The first one was delivered to the U.S. Navy in 1968, the year after Reginald Denny passed away.

The test launch of a Ryan BQM-74C, circa the 1970s. (Northrop Grumman)

This U.S. Navy vessel is a target-rich environment as crews prepare to launch BQM-74E drones during an exercise at sea. (Northrop Grumman)

The MQM-74 unmanned aerial vehicles were officially named "Chukar," for a ground dwelling game bird found in the Midwestern United States. Contrary to what the name suggests, the MQM-74A and all of the subsequent Chukars were capable of operating at altitudes as high as 40,000 feet.

New BQM-74E target drones take shape on the factory floor. (Northrop Grumman)

The Chukar's inflight tracking was passive, meaning that the "pilot" had to either be able to see the Chukar's flight path, or track it on radar. If a particular vehicle was to be recovered rather than expended on a mission, a remotely operated parachute could be commanded to be deployed.

An improved MQM-74B was evaluated, but not produced in large numbers, but the U.S. Navy started taking delivery of the improved MQM-74C Chukar II in 1974. It was 12 feet 8 inches long, with a wingspan of 5 feet 9 inches. It weighed in at just under 500 pounds and had a range of nearly 400 miles, half again more than the MQM-74A. Powered by a J400-WR-401 turbojet, it had a top speed of 575 mph, again a marked improvement over its predecessor.

In the meantime, Northrop proceeded with the BQM-74C for the U.S. Navy, of which a sizable number were produced during the 1980s. The BQM-74C was also known as the Chukar III, and the Chukar III name was used by Northrop as the principal designation of the export version of this drone. First deployed by NATO countries in Europe in 1984, the Chukar III was still in service at the turn of the century with France, Spain, and the United Kingdom, as well as Japan, Taiwan, and Singapore. The company produced more than 1,150 Chukars for its international customers.

A good close-up view of a BQM-74E target drone at NAS Point Mugu in California. A DC-130 loaded with four BQM-74Es prepares for takeoff in the background. (Northrop Grumman)

The BQM-74C Chukar III was 12 feet 11 inches long, with a wingspan identical to that of its predecessor. This variant incorporated an optional onboard video system for reconnaissance missions, and was designed to be air-launched as well as surface launched. The lighter, air-launched version had a range of more than 500 miles. As with the Firebees, the Chukar IIIs were air launched from Lockheed DC-130 mother-ships. During Operation Desert Storm in 1991, BQM-74Cs, as well as Firebees, were used with reported success as decoy aircraft, drawing Iraqi anti-aircraft fire away from manned strike aircraft. (These BQM-74Cs were launched as a diversion for the second wave of air attacks following the F-117 stealth fighters and cruise missiles, and were ground launched in groups of three in specified waves. The USAF "Big Safari" team was responsible for this important operation.)

By the late 1970s both the U.S. Army and the U.S. Air Force studied the Chukar II for possible adaptation as top secret reconnaissance vehicles. The Army version was to have been designated as BQM-74D, but a production model was apparently not produced. The Air Force version was evaluated under the Tactical Expendable Drone System (TEDS). As with the Army's BQM-74D, this secret project is believed to have been terminated.

Beginning in 1992, the U.S. Navy began taking delivery of the BQM-74E Chukar. The same size as the BQM-74C, the new drone has a top speed of 620 mph and a range of nearly 750 miles.

An estimated 3,200 MQM-74A and MQM-74C drones were produced, and through the turn of the century, about 2,000 BQM-74C and BQM-74E vehicles had been delivered.

An artist's conception of a BQM-74F Chuckar target drone in flight. (Northrop Grumman)

A BQM-74E drone is launched from the flight deck of the guided-missile frigate USS Robert G. Bradley *(FFG-49) in October 2003 during Exercise UNITAS 45-04. Hosted by Argentina, this South Atlantic Ocean exercise also included naval forces from Brazil, Peru, Spain, Uruguay, and the United States.* (U.S. Navy photo by PH2 Robert Taylor)

As the company explained, "Fielded in eleven countries around the world, the Chukar III is based on the U.S. Navy's BQM-74 which has been used for over 80 percent of the Navy's target missions since 1978." (Northrop Grumman)

In 2003, after the BQM-74s were used, along with Firebees, as chaff dispensers during Operation Iraqi Freedom, plans for a further improved BQM-74F were accelerated under a U.S. Navy System Development and Demonstration (SDD) contract. The BQM-74F has improved speed, range, maneuverability, and endurance characteristics as well as increased payload capability. As the company describes the maneuverability feature, the BQM-74F can conduct "aggressive all-axis weave maneuvers down to 7 feet."

Higher, Faster and Top Secret

Even as the Lightning Bugs were proving the concept of using unmanned aerial vehicles for high-priority reconnaissance missions, specialized manned reconnaissance aircraft were coming of age. The aerial reconnaissance types within the U.S. Air Force and the CIA were working with the Lockheed's Advanced Development Projects component, better known as the "Skunk Works," to develop two unique aircraft that were the epitome of what were known during the Cold War as "spy planes." With its long, glider-like wings, the U-2 was optimized for long-duration flights at high altitudes. Meanwhile, the Mach 3.2 SR-71 (originally designated as A-12) Blackbird was the fastest air-breathing aircraft known to have flown during the twentieth century.

As the operational careers of these manned aircraft were unfolding, the U.S. Air Force initiated programs that would involve the development of unmanned aerial vehicles that generally had parallel characteristics to the U-2 and SR-71 and could be used in situations where the pilot's life might come into serious danger from enemy action. The Lockheed Skunk Works developed the D-21, the super high-speed unmanned analog to the SR-71, and in fact, this drone was designed to be used in conjunction with the Blackbird.

The D-21 was the fastest of its kind known to have flown during the past century. Unlike the subsonic Lightning Bugs of the Vietnam era, or the lumbering UAVs of today, the D-21 was capable of flying at three times the speed of sound. The idea for the D-21 program originated with Skunk Works boss Clarence "Kelly" Johnson, who saw it as a natural extension of the SR-71 program. He could see the value of a Mach 3 reconnaissance drone that could be air launched by the Mach 3 A-12/SR-71 aircraft. No aircraft in the world was fast enough to catch either one, so they could operate with virtual impunity in any hostile airspace.

The CIA, Lockheed's original customer for the A-12, showed little initial interest in the Mach 3 Unmanned Aerial Vehicle, but in October 1962, it finally authorized the project under the code name Tagboard. As with the A-12/SR-71 program, the Tagboard drone originated as a CIA project, but in both programs, the U.S. Air Force would ultimately emerge as the dominant player.

A Lockheed M-21 (A-12) carrying a D-21 drone approaches the refueling boom of a Boeing KC-135Q Stratotanker. The first successful launch of a D-21 from the back of its mothership occurred on 16 March 1966—more than one year after the pairing had begun flight test. Code-named Tagboard, the first flight of these mated aircraft took place on 22 December 1964 at Lockheed's secret test facility at Groom Lake in southern Nevada. (Lockheed)

After the loss of the second M-21 mothership in a mid-air collision with its D-21, the Boeing B-52H was selected as the D-21 launch aircraft. This rare photo shows the now-rocket-boosted D-21B moments after separation from the B-52. Photo was taken by remote camera in the B-52's launch pylon. (Lockheed)

Originally, Lockheed referred to its new drone aircraft as the Q-12, implying that it was to be a drone associated with the A-12. In 1963, as the two aircraft evolved as a joint weapons system, the A-12 carrier aircraft were redesignated with an "M" for "mothership," and the Q-12 was designated with a "D" for drone, or "daughter-ship." To avoid confusion with other A-12s that would not be used with Tagboard, the numerals were also inverted. Thus it would be a D-21 drone aboard an M-21 mother-ship.

The wind tunnel and other tests took place during 1963, and the first D-21 was completed in August 1964. The debut flight of a D-21 mated to the top of its mothership occurred at Groom Lake (Area 51) in Nevada in December 1964, and the first air-launch and free flight of a D-21 followed in March 1966.

This artist's concept shows an operational QM-94A Compass Cope UAV in tactical markings. The mottled blue-and-gray camouflage scheme was one of several that was considered by the U.S. Air Force as it transitioned away from the brown-and-green Southeast Asia markings. The blue-and-gray was also used on the Northrop YF-17 prototype. (U.S. Air Force)

The first three launches were successful, but a D-21 malfunction on the fourth flight resulted in the loss of both drone and mother-ship as well as of one of the mother-ship crewmen. In the wake of this incident, Kelly Johnson proposed that they switch to using a B-52H as a mothership. This new launch scenario would be code named Senior Bowl, and the drones themselves would be modified and redesignated as D-21B. In the Senior Bowl operations, the launch would be made at subsonic speeds and a rocket booster would propel the craft to ramjet-operable speeds above Mach 2, but the D-21B could be mounted under the wings of the mother-ship, and hence could be dropped rather than having to be launched from the top of another aircraft. After a series of failed launches, the first successful Senior Bowl launch of a D-21B from a B-52H occurred in June 1968.

After more testing, the CIA and the Air Force requested and received presidential authorization to use the D-21B on an operational photo-reconnaissance mission over North Vietnam. In November 1969, the first such deployment failed when the data link failed and the D-21B "vanished." Three further operational missions between December 1970 and March 1971 were all deemed as failures when the camera modules were lost or damaged in recovery.

The Tagboard/Senior Bowl/D-21 program was officially canceled in July 1971, although its existence would remain classified until 1977.

The Unmanned Aerial Vehicle that was analogous to the large winged U-2 evolved somewhat later than the D-21. The concept was first formalized in the Compass

Cope program of 1971. As with the U-2, Compass Cope was intended to be a slow aircraft—certainly relative to the D-21—with an emphasis on very long endurance (up to 24 hours) at very high altitudes above 70,000 feet. As with modern UAVs, Compass Cope would be controlled by way of a real-time television data link to a ground-based operator. In addition to reconnaissance, the platform could be tasked with communications relay and atmospheric sampling. Like the earlier Radioplane drones, the Compass Cope would be intended to takeoff and land on runways, rather than being air-launched like Firebees or D-21s.

Though Boeing was originally considered as the single-source for the Compass Cope aircraft, Teledyne Ryan, makers of the Firebee family, also received a contract to build a prototype. Boeing's Model 901 was designated as the YQM-94A Gull (Compass Cope B), while the Teledyne Ryan Model 235 entered flight test as the YQM-98A Tern (Compass Cope R). While the Boeing Gull would be an all-new aircraft, the Tern had its roots in the Teledyne Ryan Model 154, which had been built for an earlier Air Force project code-named Compass Arrow. The Model 154 aircraft itself was code-named Firefly, which infers a relationship with Operation Fire Fly, the version of the first Ryan Model 147A Firebee adapted for use as a reconnaissance aircraft in 1962. Not unlike Compass Cope, the idea of the Compass Arrow project had been for a high-altitude photo-reconnaissance aircraft capable of a deep penetration into Chinese airspace. Such a mission was beyond the range of the Firebee or Chukar families and too dangerous for a manned U-2.

Compass Arrow was initiated in 1966 and the Model 154 made its debut flight in June 1968. Officially designated as AQM-91 in 1970, the Firefly was powered by one General Electric J97 turbojet engine. It was 34 feet 2 inches long, with a wingspan of 47 feet 8 inches. It had a service ceiling of 78,000 feet and a range of 4,370 miles. Like the Lightning Bug drones then active over Southeast Asia, it was air-launched from a DC-130 and it was recovered with the Mid-Air Retrieval System. Nearly two dozen production series AQM-91s were built, but they were reportedly scrapped without having been used operationally as a result of a change in U.S. relations with China in the 1970s ending reconnaissance overflights.

Both Compass Cope aircraft, like the U-2, had long wings like those of a sailplane, which made for extended range and endurance. This feature continues to be an important characteristic of twenty-first century UAVs, such as the RQ-4 Global Hawk, which itself originated as a Teledyne Ryan program.

The debut flight of the prototype Boeing YQM-94A Gull came in July 1973, but the prototype crashed a few days later on its second flight. The flight test program continued, with the second YQM-94A, until November 1974. The Gull was 40 feet long with its nose probe, and had a wingspan of 90 feet. It was powered by a General Electric TF34 turbofan, which was, like the engine in the

Tern, mounted above the fuselage. During the flight test program, the YQM-94A demonstrated an endurance of more than 17 hours.

Meanwhile, the Ryan YQM-98A Compass Cope R made its first flight in August 1974, and went on to set a world endurance record for an unmanned, unrefueled aircraft—28 hours 11 minutes. The twin-tailed Tern was powered by a Garrett YF104 turbofan engine, which was mounted on its back to reduce its radar signature. It was 37 feet 4 inches long, with a wingspan of 81 feet 2 inches.

The Boeing YQM-94A was chosen over the competition in August 1976, and a contract was issued for a series of YQM-94B production aircraft. Having produced what it felt was a superior (albeit more expensive) aircraft, Teledyne Ryan lodged a protest. It was a moot point, as the Air Force canceled the whole Compass Cope project in July 1977 before any further aircraft were built.

The respective airplane makers would go on to bigger and better things in the world of unmanned aerial vehicles—Boeing to the Condor and Ryan to the Global Hawk. While the Global Hawk earned a spot as one of the most important American UAVs of the early twenty-first century, the Condor had but a brief career in the 1980s.

Battlefield Drones

Throughout the late Cold War period, the United States military establishment showed an interest in unmanned aerial vehicles that could be deployed on strategic reconnaissance missions, but that interest was fleeting. Among pilots, there was a natural bias against airplanes that did not carry a pilot onboard. Among the "techies" of the reconnaissance world there was a bias toward the increasingly amazing capabilities of spy satel-

Preparing a Lockheed YMQM-105A Aquila for a test flight. The first launch of an Aquila took place at Fort Huachuca, Arizona, in July 1982 and flights continued into 1987. The rail-launched UAV was intended to provide the U.S. Army with an easy-to-use UAV for a variety of tasks, including reconnaissance and target designation. (Lockheed)

lites and high-resolution digital imaging. The D-21 was canceled, the Lightning Bugs were mothballed, and Compass Cope was stillborn. A few projects would be discussed during the last decades of the Cold War, and some research work done, but unmanned aerial vehicles in the service of strategic reconnaissance had few friends in high places in the 1970s and 1980s.

As for the tactical reconnaissance requirements of battlefield units, there were a number of interesting small unmanned aerial vehicles that were developed during this period. The first major foray by the U.S. Army into such aircraft was the Lockheed MQM-105 Aquila (Eagle) program, which was initiated in the early 1970s under the Target Acquisition, Designation & Aerial Reconnaissance (TADAR) program. While the idea of TADAR was to provide battlefield commanders with a light, easy-to-use observation platform, the U.S. Army also wanted to use its drone as an over-the-horizon artillery target designator so that it could pick targets for laser-guided Copperhead 155mm artillery shells. The Defense Department had been working with Ford Aerospace on such a project, code named Prairie, since 1973, but the Army wanted this capability incorporated into Aquila.

The full-scale Aquila development contract went to Lockheed Missiles & Space Company in 1979, and a 17-flight test program involving the YMQM-105 prototype occurred at Fort Huachuca, Arizona, during the summer and fall of 1982. The Aquila was powered by a single, small gasoline engine driving a pusher propeller, but that is where the similarity in appearance ended. Aquila had swept wings and no tail. It was 6 feet 10 inches long, with a wingspan of 12 feet 9 inches.

The Aquila Unmanned Aerial Vehicle had no landing gear, being catapult-launched from a truck and recovered aboard a truck using a large nylon net. It also carried a parachute for emergency landings. The truck recovery system for the Aquila was built in Germany by Dornier, which would have helped make acquisition of the drone system by the German government a potentially attractive proposition.

It was equipped with a Westinghouse electro-optical payload that included a stabilized laser artillery designator. However, problems with the systems and systems integration led to delays, and ultimately to the cancellation of the program. The U.S. Army had originally planned to achieve an initial operating capability with the first of 995 MQM-105s by 1985, but this didn't happen and the program was terminated in 1987. Lockheed's plans for an export version of the Aquila, known as Altair, also died along with the YMQM-105 program.

As with the U.S. Army's YMQM-105, the U.S. Air Force YCQM-121 Pave Tiger was a small, compact tailless drone with swept wings and a pusher propeller. Boeing had initiated the 1979 in-house project as the BRAVE-200 (Boeing Robotic Air Vehicle). Unlike the contemporary reconnaissance unmanned aerial vehicles, BRAVE was an attack drone. Actually, its mission profile made it a cross between a cruise missile and what we'd expect in a twenty-first century Unmanned Combat Air Vehicle. Like a cruise missile, it destroyed its target by running itself into it, but like a UAV, it was recoverable and it could also fly non-lethal missions such as radar jamming.

The Air Force ordered the BRAVE-200 in 1983 under the designation YCQM-121A assigned the Pave Tiger name. The plan at the time was to deploy as many as 1,000 of them into Germany by 1987 for defense against a potential Warsaw Pact invasion. However, after limited flight testing, the Pave Tiger program was canceled by the United States in 1984. The problems in the program were said by the Air Force to have been due to "underestimating the complexity" of integrating the airframe and the targeting system. This phrase could easily have been worked into the cancellation explanation for a lot of programs during the Cold War.

The German government, meanwhile, continued to look into using the Pave Tiger as an anti-radar system, and it was evaluated—unsuccessfully as it turned out—against the Messerschmitt-Bolkow-Blohm Tucan Unmanned Aerial Vehicle.

Meanwhile, during the 1980s, Teledyne Ryan initiated its Scarab and Peregrine small battlefield drone projects. The former program involved 56 Model 324 reconnaissance drones delivered to Egypt between 1984 and 1992. The Peregrine was created in response to a 1988 Department of Defense request for a joint-service Unmanned Aerial Vehicle that could be either air or surface launched and could be used as an aerial target or as a reconnaissance platform. This program, designated as Unmanned Aerial Vehicle, Medium Range (UAV-MR), selected Teledyne Ryan in May 1989 to proceed with the Model 350 Peregrine, a derivative of its Model 324, under the designation BQM-145A. The debut flight came in May 1992, but UAV-MR was canceled 17 months later when both the Navy and Marine Corps dropped out. Only six of a planned 500 production Peregrines were built, and they were not flown until 1997.

While the United States drifted from program to program for two decades without putting a home-grown tactical reconnaissance UAV into production, another country was taking them very seriously.

Israel's experience in the 1973 Yom Kippur War led battlefield commanders to crave an "over-the-horizon" reconnaissance system, and this planted a seed that would, in time, grow into a new generation of UAVs.

During the 1970s, two small Israeli UAVs emerged. First was the Mastiff, created by Tadiran Electronics, followed by the Scout, developed by Israel Aircraft Industries (IAI), the country's major planemaker. Both were roughly the same size as Reg Denny's early Radioplane drones, and like the Radioplane drones, they were powered by a single, simple gasoline engine. The relative wingspans were 13 feet 11 inches for the Mastiff and 16 feet 3 inches for the Scout. They both had straight wings, a tail mounted on twin booms, with a pusher prop between the booms on the rear of the fuselage. Surveillance equipment centered on a small video camera with a real time data link to an operator on the ground. Like the Radioplane UAVs, they had landing gear to facilitate runway operations.

These little Israeli UAVs experienced their baptism of fire during the 1982 conflict in Lebanon and proved themselves invaluable to battlefield commanders. Among other things, the UAVs successfully spotted—and facilitated the destruction of—more than two dozen Syrian surface-to-air-missile sites hidden in the Beka'a Valley.

The UAV paradigm of the 1980s had more in common with Reginald Denny's radio-controlled models from the 1940s than they did with D-21s and Firebees. The emphasis was, once again, on simplicity and economy over extreme high performance. Indeed, the success of the small Israeli drones was not lost on battlefield commanders in the United States, who had been through their own recent battles in Lebanon and Grenada in the early 1980s. The next generation of American UAVs would be the offspring not of the American initiatives of the 1960s, but the Israeli initiatives of the 1980s that led to the Hunter UAV, which was developed by Israel Aircraft Industries (IAI) and which evolved into the widely used Pioneer.

The Hunter was the winner of the Defense Department's Unmanned Aerial Vehicle, Short Range

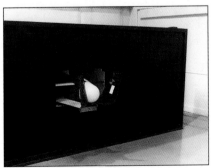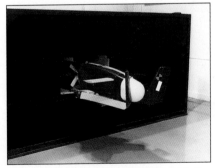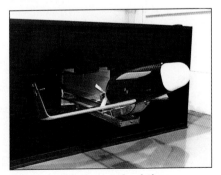

The unique storage module designed for housing Boeing YCQM-121A Pave Tiger attack drones had the appearance of something like the coin lockers at a bus station, or perhaps like a morgue. The UAVs were designed to be packed into a 15-locker module and shipped to Central Europe. If World War III had started, they would be unpacked, unfolded, and launched as a swarm to attack Soviet air defenses. (U.S. Air Force)

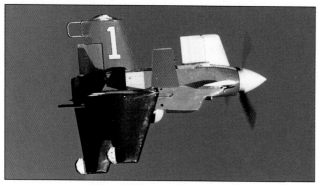

The Sparrow Hawk VTOL UAV was developed in a "Rapid Prototyping" demonstration by Sky Technology Vehicle Design & Development Company. It was designed under contract with McDonnell Douglas as a VTOL craft to minimize the need for launch-and-recovery equipment. Two were built and test-flown for the U.S. Army and U.S. Marine Corps at the Yuma Proving Grounds in 1992. (McDonnell Douglas)

The Northrop Grumman Model 324 was an autonomous, long-range reconnaissance unmanned aerial system providing electro-optical and infrared imagery. Designed to meet Egyptian Air Force requirements, it was produced from 1984 to 1993 and was first flown in 1988. The company reports that 56 were produced and delivered. In the first decade of the twenty-first century, Egypt was discussing a modernization program with the company. (Northrop Grumman)

Sergeant. R. W. Lewis, left, and Lance Corporal H. B. Davis of the 1st Remotely Piloted Vehicle (RPV) Company perform preventive maintenance on a Pioneer in October 1990 during Operation Desert Shield. (Defense Department photo by Lance Corporal J. O. Alvarado)

Flight crewmen from fleet composite Squadron 6 (VC-6), RPV Detachment 1, perform pre-flight maintenance on a Pioneer UAV on the deck of the battleship USS Iowa (BB 61) in September 1988. The aircraft was being tested aboard the ship as a basic gunfire support system with over-the-horizon targeting and reconnaissance capabilities. (U.S. Navy photo by JOCS James Guisti)

The McDonnell Douglas Sky Owl was typical of the twin-boom, pusher-prop UAVs of the late Cold War period. It was based on the R4E SkyEye. (McDonnell Douglas)

A Sky Owl is seen here during a December 1991 flight test. Though the vehicle was equipped with a center-line landing skid, the preferable means of recovery was by parachute. (McDonnell Douglas)

(UAV-SR) competition of 1991–1992 and officially ordered in February 1993. Designed by the Malat (formerly Mazlat) component of Israel Aircraft Industries (IAI), the Hunter would be assembled in the United States by TRW, which has since become a component of Northrop Grumman.

The losing finalist in the UAV-SR competition was the McDonnell Douglas Sky Owl, a derivative of the Lear Siegler SkyEye. The first ancestor of this Unmanned Aerial Vehicle had been created by Developmental Sciences—a company that later became the Astronautics Division of Lear Siegler—and first flown in 1973. The U.S. Army had actually flown operational surveillance missions with this aircraft in 1984 and 1985 along the Honduran border with Nicaragua from bases at Puerto San Lorenzo and Palmerola. The SkyEyes used low-light-level video systems to track guerilla infiltration along the border. The company also sold SkyEye UAVs to Thailand.

Several years later, McDonnell Douglas then adapted the SkyEye design for the Sky Owl project. This drone made its first flight in June 1991, an eight-hour endurance and a service ceiling of 15,000 feet. Like the Hunter, the Sky Owl was constructed with landing gear for takeoffs and landings from runways, but it was also configured for a catapult launch and a parachute recovery. It was radio controlled, but also had a programmable guidance system. This same system would be revisited in the X-45 UCAV after the McDonnell Douglas UAV team became part of Boeing in 1997.

Though the Sky Owl is occasionally mentioned in the same breath with the Defense Department designation YPQM-149A, this designation was probably never officially assigned. The designations YPQM-149A and YPQM-150A were reserved for the UAV-SR program, but neither was assigned. The Hunter was briefly designated as BQM-155A, but was redesignated as RQ-5 in 1997.

The initial Hunter order in 1993 was for seven

A Pioneer assigned to the Marine Corps' 3rd RPV Platoon sits at the bottom of its launch rail prior to a November 1990 flight during Operation Desert Shield. (Defense Department photo by Sergeant J. R. Ruark)

Marines retrieve a Pioneer Remotely Piloted Vehicle (RPV) after it lands on a runway following a flight of Operation Desert Storm in January 1991. (Defense Department photo)

An RQ-2A Pioneer on its twin rail catapult mounted on a 5-ton truck. This launch is conducted by the Cherry Point Marine Base, Squadron-2, part of Combined Arms Exercise (CAX) 5-97 at Airfield Seagle at the U.S. Marine Corps Air Ground Combat Center (MCAGCC) at Twentynine Palms, California, in April 1997. (Marine Corps photo by Lance Corporal Young)

A Pioneer is catapulted from a launching rail set up atop an M814 5-ton cargo truck in the Saudi desert on the eve of Operation Desert Storm in January 1991. This scene is highly remeniscent of Cold War–era truck-mounted missile launches such as the Douglas Honest John. (Defense Department photo)

A U.S. Marine Corps RQ-2A Pioneer conducts a daytime reconnaissance mission. (Marine Corps photo by Lance Corporal Andrew Williams)

Hunter "systems" of eight aircraft each, and the first of these were delivered to the U.S. Army by April 1995. A "system" in this context is a Defense Department term referring to the way operational UAVs were acquired and deployed. Rather than being ordered as individual aircraft, they were ordered as systems. A system includes a certain number of aircraft, such as eight in the case of the RQ-2 Pioneer or RQ-5 Hunter, plus support equipment. This equipment included operational crew shelters, ground data terminals, remote video terminals, and modular mission payload modules, as well as launch, recovery, and ground equipment.

In the meantime, both France and Belgium also each ordered a Hunter system. The Department of Defense had imagined an eventual procurement of as many as 52 systems, but after three crashes in close succession during August and September 1995, the Defense Department decided to terminate the Hunter program after the last of the initial seven systems was delivered in December 1996.

The RQ-5 Hunter is 22 feet 10 inches long, with a wingspan of 29 feet 2 inches. As with other twin-boom reconnaissance UAVs of Israeli origin, the Hunter has two engines; in this case two 64-hp Moto-Guzzi piston engines. They have an endurance of 12 hours and can operate up to 15,000 feet.

Operational gear includes data relay equipment and a dual low light television (LLTV) and forward looking infrared (FLIR) installation. Control is by way of a ground-based operator, but the Hunter can be pre-programmed for autonomous operations. The Hunter is equipped with landing gear for runway landings, and an arrestor hook for short field landings.

During the late 1990s, the Hunter program made numerous component quality improvements. For example, failures of the servo actuators, the leading culprit for the 1995 spate of crashes, were identified, and their relia-

bility was increased from 7,800 hours to 57,300 hours. Other key components, such as the datalink and engine were examined and improved. Before 1995, Hunters were experiencing a mishap rate of 2.55 per 1,000 hours, but in the 1996 to 2001 period, that rate dropped to 0.16.

The U.S. Army deployed a contingent of the UAVs to the Balkans in 1999 as the appropriately named Task Force Hunter. They operated extensively in the area, flying routine night-time reconnaissance missions along the mountainous and heavily-wooded Kosovo-Macedonia border monitoring infiltrations by rebel fighters.

During a June 2001 operation, Hunters maintained surveillance of a U.S. Army convoy as it moved through rebel territory, and guiding it toward a safe route to the American base. Captain Dan Dittenber, who was with General William David, Commander of United States forces in Kosovo, as they watched this in real time at the tactical operations center, said later that the general had described the Hunter as "worth its weight in gold."

Ironically, a program that had been curtailed because of reliability problems later became a standard of UAV reliability. Though the Hunter was replaced by the RQ-7 Shadow early this century, it was evaluated in 2004 by the Customs and Border Protection Bureau of the Department of Homeland Security for border patrol operations in an operation that saw the RQ-5 logging more than 300 flight hours. The "Q-5" designation was later assigned to the air-launched Northrop Grumman GBU-44 Viper Strike weapon system known as the MQ-5.

Like the Hunter, the RQ-2 Pioneer is a twin-boom, straight-winged drone with roots in earlier Israeli UAV technology. It was originally acquired by the United States in the mid 1980s as an interim UAV, the Pioneer remained in service in the twenty-first century, having been active in the Balkans and in both Gulf Wars. It is manufactured for the United States armed forces by Pioneer UAV, Incorporated, a Maryland-based co-venture of Maryland-based AAI Corporation and Israel Aircraft Industries (IAI).

The Pioneer is 16 feet 11 inches long, with a wingspan of 14 feet and a gross weight of 450 miles. It cruises at 92 mph and has a service ceiling of 15,000 feet. It has an endurance of up to 5½ hours. It is powered by a 26-hp twin-cylinder, rear-mounted engine driving a pusher propeller.

The RQ-2's surveillance gear centers around a gyro stabilized high-resolution MKD-200A low-light television (LLTV) system and an MKD-400C forward-looking infrared system (FLIR) for day and night operations, as well as meteorological and chemical detection sensors. It also boasts an integrated radio-relay package for VHF and UHF frequencies. Equipped with landing gear for runway operations, the Pioneer is launched with a rocket assisted takeoff pack from Navy surface ships, and it can be recovered with a net.

The Pioneer was initially used by the U.S. Navy as a ship-board UAV, the Pioneer has also been operated by the U.S. Marine Corps and the U.S. Army. The first system of eight Pioneer aircraft was delivered to the Navy in July 1986, and these shipped out aboard the battleship USS *Iowa* in December of that year. Three systems were delivered to the U.S. Marine Corps in 1987, and one to the U.S. Army at Fort Huachuca, Arizona in 1990. The Marines assigned part of their Pioneer fleet to ground-based units and part to units assigned to amphibious assault ships.

The RQ-2 had is baptism of fire with United States forces during Operation Desert Storm, flying long and short range patrols. They helped track Iraqi armor in the desert and they conducted reconnaissance operations in connection with the Marine assault on Faylaka Island. They were operational aboard both the USS *Missouri* (BB-63) and USS *Wisconsin* (BB-64), providing invaluable target selection and battle damage assessment in what were probably the last combat deployments by battleships in naval history. When the battleships sent their Pioneers on a low-level surveillance of Faylaka Island after pummeling its defenders with 16-inch gunfire, the surviving Iraqis were observed waving bed sheets in an effort to "surrender" to the UAVs. General Walter Boomer, the commander of the Marine Corps expeditionary force called the Pioneers "the single most valuable intelligence collector" in Operation Desert Storm.

The first missions flown over the Balkans by the Pioneer UAV involved flights from the USS *Shreveport* over Bosnia and Croatia in October 1995. These included missions to observe the effects of Serbian shelling of the United Nations sanctuary area at Mostar. In this case, Pioneers were able to identify which bridges had been destroyed and which had been repaired. The Pioneers from the USS *Shreveport* also surveyed Albania and supported actions ashore by U.S. Navy SEAL teams.

The Pioneer was used extensively by the U.S. Army and Marine Corps in Iraq, serving notably with units such as Unmanned Aerial Vehicle Squadron 1 of the 3rd Marine Aircraft Wing, especially during the intense fighting in the labyrinthine streets of Iraqi cities such as Ramadi and Fallujah. During Operation Phantom Fury in November 2004, VMU-1 conducted all-day and all-night operations, providing vital situational awareness to the Marines in Fallujah. In 2006, the Pioneer marked two decades of operations—including four wars—by completing 40,000 flight hours including more than 13,000 combat hours.

Paradigm Shift

For a number of reasons, the way that the United States' armed forces perceived unmanned aerial vehicles reached a crossroads in the last few years of the twentieth century. Part of this involved advancements in technical capabilities of the hardware itself. Another part, arguably a more important part, was in the way that top leaders had come to perceive unmanned aerial vehicles as part of tactical, and even strategic, doctrine.

The top brass had come to understand what the troops in the field had seen in combat, especially in the Balkans. By the middle 1990s, the promise and potential of unmanned military aircraft to the United States armed forces had progressed to the point where they could be considered to be fully integrated into American military doctrine. In no other country—except Israel, where the value of UAVs in military operations had been recognized a decade earlier—were unmanned aerial vehicles embraced with such enthusiasm for the work they had done and the potential they obviously had.

Army personnel position an RQ-5A Hunter for takeoff at Petrovec Airfield in Skopje, Macedonia, in support of Task Force Harvest. The mission of the task force was to collect arms and ammunition voluntarily turned over by ethnic Albanian insurgents, and, according to the Defense Department, to thereby help to build confidence in the broader peace process suggested by the President of former Yugoslav Republic of Macedonia. The Hunter looked for any changes in the local area that might hinder the peacekeeping mission. (U.S. Air Force photo by Sergeant Jocelyn Broussard)

An RQ-2 Pioneer of Marine Unmanned Aerial Vehicle Squadron 2 (VMU-2) stands ready for upcoming missions in Al Taqaddum, Iraq, in June 2006. (Marine Corps photo by Sergeant Jennifer Jones)

Above and below: This UAV, identified as a Hunter by DOD, actually a Pioneer, is seen in flight during a Combat Search and Rescue (CSAR) training exercise at Naval Air Station Fallon in Nevada, as part of exercise Desert Rescue XI. The exercise was a joint service training exercise hosted by the Naval Strike and Warfare Center. (DOD photo by Sergeant Reynaldo Ramon)

This paradigm shift had not been arrived at easily. There were many within the American defense establishment who had questioned the value of unmanned aerial vehicles as more than just a minor weapon in the arsenal. It was not unlike the prevailing attitude toward aircraft in general during the early years of the twentieth century. Especially among pilots, there had been a resistance, for obvious reasons, to the notion of integrating airplanes that *didn't need* pilots into the mix of front line aircraft.

To many, especially pilots of high-performance aircraft, the Hunter and Pioneer looked like toys. Many old hands who were around in the 1990s remembered when unmanned aerial vehicles *acted* like toys. The history of UAVs was filled with technical difficulties, especially with guidance and control, and that perception colored the opinions of many people in the armed forces. That is, after all, why they still called them "drones."

Because of secrecy and compartmentalization, few people still in the service in the 1980s were aware of the full dimensions of the Lightning Bugs, and of the Compass Bin and Buffalo Hunter operations in Southeast Asia. Those on the front lines in the Balkans, however, had learned newer lessons. They had seen and experienced the real capabilities of the Hunter and Pioneer—and those of a new contraption out of Southern California that was called a Predator.

Perhaps the most telling indication of the paradigm shift came when the U.S. Air Force officially embraced UAVs as real *airplanes*. The descriptive term Unmanned Aerial Vehicle was capitalized and the acronym UAV was formalized. As for the "U" in the acronym UAV standing for "Unmanned," there has been surprisingly little controversy over this "gender-specific" term. During the Clinton Administration there was a brief flirtation with political correctness in which alternatives were explored. The term "Unpiloted" was not applicable because the UAVs did have pilots in remote locations. They just don't have a man or a woman *aboard*. Briefly, the nomenclature was rewritten as *Uninhabited* Aerial Vehicle. However, it must have been pointed out that no aircraft are ever actually *inhabited*, even if we do fall asleep aboard one. It has also been accepted that the term "man" is used as a generic term for humans as well as a specific term for male people. Of course, a growing number of combat pilots in the American armed forces—including ground-bound UAV pilots—are *women*.

With UAV—whatever the exact wording—prescribed as an official term, the long-used acronym RPV, meaning Remotely Piloted Vehicle, faded from the official lexicon. For many, the RPV epithet was a relic from that bygone era when airplanes were airplanes, and drones were still drones.

It was in July 1995 that the U.S. Air Force took a step that was symbolic of the UAV finally coming of age. It officially formed its UAV squadron and equipped it with Predators. General Ronald Fogleman, the Chief of Staff from 1994 to 1997, officially authorized the reactivation of the 11th Reconnaissance Squadron at Indian Springs Auxiliary Airfield (Creech AFB after 2005) in Nevada as a UAV outfit. In August 1997, this unit was joined by another, the 11th Reconnaissance Squadron.

Many saw this squadron as an appropriate choice. With a lineage dating back to 1942, the unit had operated Firebee drones from 1971 until it was inactivated in 1979. Between 1991 and 1994, it had been briefly reactivated as an intelligence squadron, but with no aircraft assigned. Because Indian Springs was part of the vast Nellis AFB range, it was located in one of the largest and most restricted military operating areas in the United States. It was a perfect place for the Predators to drill without distraction.

In a 1997 interview with John Tirpak of *Air Force Magazine*, Lieutenant Colonel Steve Hampton, commander of the 11th, said that he saw his unit as a "prototype" for the UAV organizations that would follow.

"Our charter is to normalize the UAV business," he said. "We continue to work hard to make the rules [of the UAV squadron] look the same [as those in a typical squadron]."

Also in 1997, the Department of Defense formally readopted the "Q" as a primary designator, and UAVs in service from that date were designated thusly.

In his activation of the 11th Reconnaissance Squadron, Fogleman said, "The bottom line is that the U.S. Air Force will embrace UAVs and work to exploit their potential fully on my watch. We are committed to making UAVs successful contributors to our nation's joint war fighting capability."

An RQ-7 Shadow is inspected by Congressman Terry Everett, of Alabama's 2nd, as Rob Stone, division chief of the Shadow UAV system, points out the design and capabilities of the aircraft during a ceremonial first flight at the RT-3 test range on Fort Rucker, Alabama. (U.S. Army photo by Carlton Wallace)

An RQ-7 Shadow is launched during exercise Sudden Response at Camp Blanding, Florida. The exercise involves a Chemical, Biological, Radiological, Nuclear and high-yield Explosive (CBRNE) Consequence Management Response Force in support of local, state, and federal agencies. (U.S. Air Force photo by Tech Sergeant Dennis Henry, Jr.)

UNANTICIPATED WARPLANES

Crew members from the 11th Reconnaissance Squadron perform preflight checks on an RQ-1 Predator at Indian Springs prior to a training mission in November 2001. (U.S. Air Force photo by Technical Sergeant Scott Reed)

Having embraced UAVs as airplanes rather than as toys or ancillary hardware, the United States armed forces continued to explore the concept both from a technological point of view and from a doctrinal perspective.

Just as the perception of unmanned aerial vehicles morphed from novelty to legitimate airplane, a new generation of war fighters would soon bring them out of the cold as legitimate tactical aircraft. The next step toward becoming warplanes would happen much faster than the long-range planners of the 1990s could have anticipated.

The development of unmanned aircraft for long-range strategic missions would represent as big a leap from a conceptual perspective as from a technological perspective. Initially, these aircraft would be strategic reconnaissance platforms, but how far down the road were strategic *strike* missions?

On the technological side, the American armed services were all exploring various projects at the approach of the new century. Among the projects that were under study around the turn of the century were Micro-UAVs, a.k.a. Micro Air Vehicles (MAV), small, radio-controlled airplanes for military surveillance tasks. They are something with which Reginald Denny would have been familiar in 1936, although he would have been surprised—and delighted—by the way television cameras had been miniaturized. The initial thrust of the MAV program was to aimed at developing a reconnaissance aircraft smaller than 6 inches with a range of 6 miles and an endurance of 20 minutes that could be used by a squad. The idea was—and still is—to give a small unit useful, real-time combat information, especially in difficult terrain, such as in mountains and canyons, heavily forested areas with dense foliage, even inside buildings.

The turn-of-the-century MAVs included the tiny Lockheed Martin MicroStar and the AeroVironment Black Widow, which was developed in conjunction with UCLA and Caltech. The Black Widow uses a system of miniature gyroscopes and airflow detectors to measure speed and rate of turn. In turn, this is linked to a Global Positioning System unit to confirm its exact location. It can operate for a half hour with a combat radius of more than a mile, returning live color video from its tiny onboard camera.

Meanwhile, the Office of Naval Research (ONR) developed the Smart Warfighting Array of Reconfigurable Modules (SWARM) which was later used in Operation Iraqi Freedom. Flying in groups—or swarms—the SWARMs were envisioned as low cost, expendable UAVs that operate as a cooperative group, replacing individual losses by re-configuring the group to complete their mission. With a "plug-and-play" payload capability, the SWARM could be used for ground surveillance, sea search, battle damage assessment, data link relay, gunfire control spotting, chemical or biohazard aerial sampling, close air support, air defense decoy work, or clandestine "tailing" of surface contacts.

The SWARM project led to the Silver Fox, a mini-UAV that is built by Advanced Ceramics Research in Tucson, Arizona, from the ONR design. The 20-pound Silver Fox is 5 feet long, with two detachable 4-foot wings, and it looks like one of Reginald Denny's Radioplanes.

Strategic Reconnaissance

At the opposite end of the spectrum from the tiny MAVs are some of the largest aircraft in the world—and they fly with no beating human heart aboard. As noted above, the American military establishment finally accepted UAVs as airplanes because the evolution in technology, and the value of this technology in combat, was on an inescapable trajectory. One place where this trajectory has been so well demonstrated has been in the area of strategic reconnaissance.

Many years ago, during the heyday of Compass Cope, strategic planners talked of augmenting or even superseding the capabilities of the manned U-2 with an Unmanned Aerial Vehicle. It never happened back in the 1970s. Partly it was because of technology, but partly because of that well-known bias against airplanes without people and the bias of techies toward the "unlimited" capability of spy satellites.

Of course, as those who have so articulately mourned the retirement of the SR-71 Blackbird have pointed out, there are some things that aircraft can do better than satellites. One thing that UAVs certainly can do is loiter for many hours over a target, which is a capability that pushes a manned aircraft to the limit.

As noted previously, Compass Cope aircraft developed by Ryan and Boeing back in the 1970s led eventually to the Ryan (later Northrop Grumman) Global Hawk, and the Boeing Condor. While the Global Hawk earned a spot as one of the most important American UAVs of the early twenty-first century, the Condor had but a brief career in the 1980s.

During its flight test program, the Boeing Condor was retrofitted with ventral and dorsal radomes and super-charged engines. The big bird would set an altitude record for a propeller aircraft of 67,028 feet in a 1989 flight. (Courtesy John Kvasnosky, Boeing)

This is not to say that the Condor was an unremarkable aircraft. The project was specifically aimed at creating and flight testing an extremely high-altitude Unmanned Aerial Vehicle with extremely long duration.

The program was initiated by the Defense Advanced Research Projects Agency (DARPA), the DOD organization responsible for exploring and developing leading-edge technology. Founded in 1958 as the Advanced Research Projects Agency (ARPA), it had the "D for Defense" added to the acronym in 1972. (The "D" was dropped for three years between 1993 and 1996, but was restored.)

The Condor was built by Boeing with design input from Dick Rutan, who also designed the Voyager, the only airplane to circumnavigate the globe nonstop and unrefueled. As with most of the Rutan aircraft, the Condor was built primarily of carbon fiber composite materials. Its 200-foot wingspan, greater than that of a 747 jetliner, made it the largest Unmanned Aerial Vehicle built up to its time. The fuselage was 68 feet long, 52 inches high, and 34 inches wide. The gross weight of 20,000 pounds included 12,000 pounds of fuel and 1,800

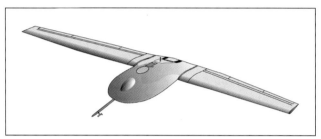

The Lockheed Martin RQ-3 DarkStar (Tier III Minus) UAV was a large, futuristic stealth aircraft. (U.S. Air Force graphic by Billy Smallwood)

The Northrop Grumman RQ-4 Global Hawk (Tier II Plus) UAV would revolutionize long endurance, high-altitude reconnaissance during the conflicts at the dawn of the twenty-first century. (U.S. Air Force graphic by Virginia Reyes)

pounds of instrumentation. It was powered by a pair of liquid-cooled Teledyne Continental engines, each delivering 175 hp. Its Delco Magic flight computers—dinosaurs by today's standards, but then state of the art—were programmed for autonomous operations.

The huge aircraft was unknown publicly before its March 1986 roll-out was reported in *Aviation Week*, but its debut flight did not take place until 9 October 1988. This launched two years of testing, which was to be conducted from big Boeing experimental facility at Moses Lake in central Washington state.

The Condor set an altitude record for a propeller aircraft of 67,028 feet in the spring of 1989. Its duration capability was demonstrated to exceed 50 hours, although it was believed capable of staying aloft for several days.

Fulfilling the brief given the project by DARPA, the Condor demonstrated the capability for strategic reconnaissance missions with video cameras or film cameras, mapping gear, synthetic aperture radar, and an interface with such other electronic reconnaissance aircraft as E-3 Airborne Warning And Control System (AWACS) aircraft or an E-8 Joint Surveillance Target Attack Radar System (J-STARS) aircraft. Such capabilities were said to have made the Condor attractive as an inexpensive alternative to spy satellites, but it is not believed to have been deployed as such.

Based in part on the experience from the Condor program, DARPA undertook the High Altitude Endurance (HAE) advanced airborne reconnaissance program in 1993.

Developed for the Defense Airborne Reconnaissance Office (DARO) in cooperation with the U.S. Army, U.S. Navy, and U.S. Air Force, HAE was a successor to DARPA's High-Altitude, Long-Endurance (HALE) program of the 1980s that had led to the development of the Condor. (The term High-Altitude, Long-Endurance, and the acronym HALE were later revived, and are still used.)

HAE was an Advanced Concept Technology Demonstration (ACTD) program developed outside the traditional defense acquisition system, and imposing minimum system requirements. The idea was a government-industry team empowered to accomplish an "innovative solution."

This solution involved two complementary aircraft, which were tested by the U.S. Air Force and classified by the "Tier" system adopted by that service. In the 1990s, the American armed services each developed a complex "Tier" system to classify their UAVs according to their capabilities and their intended mission parameters. Each service created its own different system, and to date they have yet to be integrated. Essentially the only commonality was that each had three tiers in which size and range increased from Tier I to Tier III, and MAVs were not classified in a numbered tier. The range of the UAVs in the higher U.S. Air Force had much longer range than those in the corresponding tiers used by the other services. Especially with respect to the U.S. Army, the Air Force considers long-range aircraft to be its turf exclusively.

To add further complexity to this brief discussion of the Air Force Tier System, the two ACTD aircraft were categorized not as belonging to Tier II or III, but to Tier II Plus and Tier III Minus. Initially, the specific aircraft were referred to by their Tier affiliations, but they were both soon assigned "Q-series" designator (with an "R" prefix for reconnaissance) and were given names.

Built by Teledyne Ryan, the Tier II Plus aircraft would be the RQ-4 Global Hawk, and the Tier III Minus bird would be the Lockheed Martin RQ-3 DarkStar. Both aircraft represented a quantum leap forward technologically and conceptually.

As precursors to the twenty-first century generation of UAVs, the DarkStar and Global Hawk were to be designed with completely programmable control systems for autonomous operations from takeoff to landing. The automated controls would use the differential Global Positioning System.

Both were designed to interface with a common mission ground control station. The payload systems for both would include Synthetic Aperture Radar (SAR) and Electro-Optical/Infrared (EO/IR) sensors. The types differed in that the Global Hawk was to be defined by extremely long endurance, while the DarkStar was optimized for a more moderate endurance, but it had low-observable, or "stealth," characteristics for operating in a high-threat environment. Both tiers were seen as having a role to play in U.S. Air Force operations.

Lockheed Martin was awarded the DarkStar contract in July 1994, with the Skunk Works responsible for the design and development of the fuselage, subsystems, final assembly and systems integration. Boeing, as the principal subcontractor, would have responsibility for the wing and for wing subsystem development and testing. Together, they completed the first RQ-3 aircraft in less than a year.

Seen here in June 1998, the second RQ-3 DarkStar UAV makes a fully autonomous touch-down approach at NASA's Dryden Flight Research Center using the differential Global Positioning System. (NASA photo by Carla Thomas)

The DarkStar prototype rolled out at the Skunk Works facility at Palmdale, California, on 1 June 1995.

The airframe was composed primarily of non-metal composites, and it had no vertical tail surfaces. It was only 15 feet from front to back, but its wing spanned 69 feet. The DarkStar had a gross weight of 8,600 pounds and was powered by a single Williams FJ-44-1 turbofan engine. It was rated with a top speed of 345 mph with an endurance of 12.7 hours or 8 hours above 45,000 feet. It had a service ceiling of 50,000 feet. As with most modern UAVs conceived since the 1980s, the DarkStar was equipped with conventional landing gear for runway operations.

DarkStar made its debut on 29 March 1996, taking off autonomously for a 20-minute flight. It completed a pre-programmed routine of basic flight maneuvers and reached an altitude of about 5,000 feet. On 22 April the second flight of the first DarkStar aircraft did not go so well. Scheduled for a nearly 3-hour mission, the DarkStar encountered problems just as it took off. The main gear lifted off the runway ahead of the nose wheel and the aircraft experienced a series of pitch oscillations. Ten seconds after it cleared the runway, the DarkStar

A good sense of scale is provided by this image of the Lockheed Martin RQ-3 DarkStar being inspected by NASA personnel on 14 September 1995, following its arrival at the Dryden Flight Research Center. (NASA photo by Tony Landis)

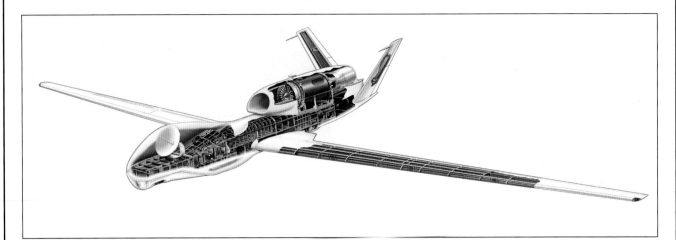

A detailed cutaway illustration showing the internal structure of the Northrop Grumman RQ-4 Global Hawk. Note the Electro-Optical/Infrared (EO/IR) and Synthetic Aperture Radar (SAR) systems, as well as the Rolls-Royce-Allison AE3007H turbofan engine. (Northrop Grumman illustration)

rolled to the left and crashed in a ball of fire. The composite structure was almost completely destroyed.

It was suggested that perhaps the DarkStar program ought to be terminated, but the Joint Requirements Oversight Council of the Joint Chiefs of Staff recommended against that. After 26 months of reworking the system, the second DarkStar made a 44-minute fully autonomous first flight on 29 June 1998. The second DarkStar had been modified with new landing gear and redesigned flight control software. Intensive simulations preceded the flight test. However, after just five successful flights by the second DarkStar, the Defense Department officially terminated the Tier III Minus program on 29 January 1999.

It seems that by the turn of the century, there was more interest in the potential usefulness of a long range Global Hawk than a stealthy DarkStar. However, rumors abounded that the Skunk Works was already at work on a super-secret successor to the RQ-3 that was dubbed "Son of DarkStar" by Internet blogs who make it their business to speculate about secret aircraft programs. Unidentified aircraft that were encountered during Operation Iraqi Freedom in 2003 are said to have been this aircraft.

As for the RQ-4 Global Hawk project, it was initiated in 1995 about a year after the RQ-3 DarkStar. As with the RQ-3, it was seen as an advanced concept technology demonstrator. However, unlike the RQ-3, it would become an operational aircraft type. The contract went to Teledyne Ryan, which was absorbed into Northrop Grumman in 1999.

The Global Hawk prototype rolled out in San Diego in February 1997, and the first flight occurred at Edwards AFB on 28 February 1998. In roughly the same size class as the manned Lockheed U-2, and more than twice the size of the DarkStar, the Global Hawk is the

The fourth RQ-4 Global Hawk deployed from Edwards AFB in California to Eglin AFB in Florida for six weeks in the spring of 2000. The aircraft made the transcontinental flight nonstop, setting a UAV endurance record of 31.5 hours nonstop. (U.S. Air Force photo by George Rohlmaller)

An RQ-4 Global Hawk over Edwards AFB during 2000, when the first Air Combat Command flight crews were being trained to fly the Global Hawk operationally. (U.S. Air Force photo)

A Northrop Grumman RQ-4 in operational colors on an evaluation flight. Global Hawks are capable of surveying an area the size of the state of Illinois, or 40,000 square miles, in just 24 hours. (Northrop Grumman)

The Global Hawk over Edwards AFB on 28 February 1998, during its first flight. Sensors onboard the aircraft provided ground teams with real-time data during the test program. (Department of Defense photo)

A new Global Hawk test aircraft arrives at Edwards AFB after its delivery flight. The new arrival joins the other Global Hawk UAVs undergoing flight testing as part of the engineering, manufacturing, and development phase of defense acquisition. (Photo by Carlos Rolon via Department of Defense)

largest military UAV known to have been operational at the turn of the century. It is 44 feet long, with a wingspan of 116 feet. It weighs 25,600 pounds when fully fuelled and has a range of 13,000 miles. The fuselage is constructed of aluminum, but fiberglass composites have been used for the wings, wing fairings, empennage, engine cover, engine, intake and the three radomes. The powerplant is a single Rolls-Royce–Allison AE3007H turbofan, delivering 7,600 pounds of thrust.

Starting in June 1999, the Global Hawk was evaluated in a series of Joint Forces Command exercises. In April 2000, the fourth Global Hawk aircraft deployed to Eglin AFB in Florida for a series of operations that would include the first transatlantic flight. In February 2001, the Global Hawk became the first UAV to be awarded the Collier Trophy for aeronautical achievement by the National Aeronautic Association. The range capability of the Global Hawk was demonstrated by a widely publicized, unrefueled, 7,500-mile flight across the Pacific Ocean from North America to Australia in April 2001.

Three months later, the Air Force chose Beale AFB in Northern California as the main operating base for the Global Hawk fleet. The base is remembered as having been the home base to the U.S. Air Force SR-71 Blackbird fleet during the Cold War, and it still serves as home to the U-2 and TR-1 reconnaissance aircraft.

Implicit in this move was the acceptance of a UAV as a member of the service's fleet of strategic aircraft. As Air Combat Command commander, General John Jumper put it, "Collocating Global Hawk with Beale's 9th Reconnaissance Wing and the U-2 mission will ensure Global Hawk transitions smoothly from initial beddown to full operational capability. It also ensures cultural issues associated with transitioning from manned to unmanned reconnaissance are in the hands of our current high-altitude reconnaissance experts at Beale. They are best suited to complete the transition with the least disruption to the mission."

At this time, no one involved with the program anticipated that by the end of the year, the Global Hawk would be sent to war. When the United States began Operation Enduring Freedom in October 2001, Global Hawks went to work in the air space over Afghanistan, providing battlefield commanders of all the armed services with near-real-time, high-resolution, intelligence, surveillance, and reconnaissance imagery.

From altitudes up to 65,000 feet, Global Hawks surveyed large geographic areas at better than 3-foot resolution. Using cloud-penetrating Electro-Optical/Infrared (EO/IR) and Synthetic Aperture Radar (SAR) systems, an RQ-4 could cover an area the size of Illinois on a single mission.

No mention of the endurance and performance capabilities of the Global Hawk is complete without an aside to a parallel, although unrelated, project that was ongoing at NASA around the turn of the century. The Environmental Research Aircraft & Sensor Technology

(ERAST) program, saw the development of Centurion and Helios, which were slow, remotely-operated aircraft that could perform long-duration, remote-sensing scientific missions at altitudes above 60,000 feet.

Centurion and Helios were the largest UAVs ever built, with wingspans greater than a 747 jetliner, and exceeding the 200-foot wingspan of the Boeing Condor UAV that was flight tested from 1988–1990. Ironically, they were developed by a company that was simultaneously developing some of the tiniest Micro Air Vehicles (MAV) ever built. AeroVironment of Monrovia, California, was founded by Dr. Paul MacCready, a pioneer in solar-powered aircraft. Among his early efforts were the Solar Challenger, Pathfinder, and Pathfinder Plus aircraft, which set an unofficial world altitude record for solar-powered aircraft of 80,201 feet in the summer of 1998.

Seen here near the island of Kaua'i, the Helios flying wing was built by AeroVironment as part of NASA's Environmental Research Aircraft and Sensor Technology (ERAST) program. Helios used its solar panels to power its 10 electric motors for takeoff and during daylight portions of its flight, and when sunlight diminished, Helios switched to the fuel-cell system to continue flight into the night. (NASA Dryden Flight Research Center photo)

Ground crewmen maneuver the AeroVironment's Helios prototype on its ground-support dolly during functional checkouts prior to its first flights under solar power from the U.S. Navy's Pacific Missile Range Facility on Kaua'i in April 2001. (NASA photo by Nick Galante)

Centurion, with its vast wingspan of 206 feet, was an awesome sight as it made its first flight in November 1998. However, it was soon trumped by the huge Helios, which made its debut flight on 8 September 1999 over the NASA Dryden Flight Test Center at Edwards AFB in California. Helios was essentially an enlarged version of the Centurion, with a wingspan of 247 feet.

In August 2001, flying from the U.S. Navy's Pacific Missile Range Facility at Barking Sands on the Hawaiian island of Kauai, Helios, set an unofficial world-record altitude of 96,863 feet, flying about 96,000 feet for the better part of an hour. In marked contrast to its extreme altitude capability, the solar-powered Helios had an extremely slow cruising speed of about 25 mph. It was also an extremely light aircraft, weighing just 1,600 pounds when fully fitted out with its onboard instrumentation.

The next step in Helios development had been a planned series of long-duration missions. Unfortunately the program came to an abrupt end in June 2003, when the aircraft was lost during a shakedown flight in preparation for a 40-hour mission planned for later in the summer. Helios crashed into the Pacific and sank before it could be recovered.

The loss of Helios would not be the end of high altitude solar aircraft research. In 2008, for example, DARPA was soliciting proposals under its Vulture program for a remotely operated solar-powered surveillance aircraft capable for staying aloft for *five years*. It will be only a matter of time before the lessons learned in the NASA ERAST program found their way into tactical UAV applications.

Enter the Predator

Predator drone.

It is hard to think of another airplane since the B-17 Flying Fortress of World War II whose name would

In January 1994, the Department of Defense awarded a contract for ten Predator aircraft to General Atomics Aeronautical Systems of San Diego, California, and the first Predator flew just six months later in July. Within a year, Predators deployed to Europe, where they proved their value in operations over Bosnia from July 1995 to March 1996. (Defense Department photo)

become such a household word that mere mention of the word conjured up, not just an airplane nor even a whole class of warplanes, but a revolutionary new concept in military operations.

Even people who could not pick a General Atomics RQ/MQ-1 out of a line-up have heard the phrase "Predator drone" in the media, and know what it means.

Few who would later regard it as a household name, of course, were aware of it during its formative years. New prototypes of small, slow military aircraft are hardly part of the currency of popular culture. The airplane that was destined to play the pivotal role in amending both official and public perceptions about the role of UAVs evolved from a contract issued to General Atomics Aeronautical Systems in January 1994.

This contract called for a Tier II Medium Altitude and Endurance (MAE) UAV that would fly reconnaissance missions under U.S. Air Force control on behalf of surface commanders of all the services.

Based in San Diego, California, General Atomics originated in 1955 as General Atomic Division of General Dynamics Corporation. Tasked with harnessing nuclear power for energy and propulsion, the division developed the TRIGA reactor, and worked on Project Orion, a study of nuclear pulse propulsion for interplanetary spacecraft. After being owned by a succession of oil companies between 1967 and 1986, General Atomics became independent. Retired U.S. Navy Admiral Thomas Cassidy, who joined the firm in 1987, established General Atomics Aeronautical Systems subsidiary.

The experience of General Atomics in the UAV field includes the Gnat-750, which itself had roots in the top secret Amber project that dates back to 1984. In that year, DARPA contracted with Leading Systems in Irvine, California—later acquired by General Atomics—to build a long-endurance UAV under the code name Amber. This aircraft, which had the general appearance, including the V-tail and pusher propeller, of the later Predator, made its first flight in November 1986. In turn, Amber demonstrated an endurance of at least 24 hours during tests in 1987. DARPA and the U.S. Navy (the service most interested the project) continued to study the aircraft through the end of the decade. The Amber I, an "evolved" reconnaissance version, made its debut flight in October 1989. Approximately 13 Amber or Amber I vehicles had been built by 1990 when the program was canceled for budgetary reasons.

The Gnat-750 originated as a simpler export version of Amber which first flew in 1989. When General Atomics acquired Leading Systems in 1990, the Gnat-750 project continued. Both the Turkish government and the United States CIA expressed interest in the Gnat's capabilities, and eventually, the Gnat-750 would see service in the Balkans as a precursor to the General Atomics Predator.

In 1997, General Atomics began the development of the International Gnat (I-Gnat), an enlarged and improved variant of the Gnat-750. A contemporary of

An Air Force MQ-1 Predator. The change in designation from "RQ-1" to "MQ-1" occurred in 2002 with the addition of the "armed reconnaissance role." At the time, operational squadrons were the 15th and 17th Reconnaissance Squadrons. (U.S. Air Force)

An armed MQ-1 Predator, its unit markings deleted, in flight over a desert landscape. (U.S. Air Force photo by Lieutenant Colonel Leslie Pratt)

first-generation Predators, the I-Gnat used the same aft fuselage as the RQ-1 Predator, but with a slimmer nose. A Rotax 912 or turbocharged Rotax 914 engine was used, and the payload capacity was increased. The I-Gnat later demonstrated an endurance of 48 hours and a ceiling of 30,500 feet.

The Predator program began as the DarkStar and Global Hawk had, as an Advanced Concept Technology Demonstration (ACTD) program. Like Global Hawk, however, this ACTD would evolve into an operational aircraft sooner than anticipated. Indeed, it was the first, hence its having been assigned the first "Q" designator, Q-1. Because it was to be a reconnaissance aircraft, it became the RQ-1. Preproduction aircraft were designated as RQ-1A, while production aircraft were designated as RQ-1Bs. Later, when Predators were armed, they became multi-mission aircraft and were redesignated as MQ-1s, or more specifically as MQ-1Bs.

The Predator is designed with inverted "V-tails" and a slender fuselage. This, wrote Lieutenant Colonel Lawrence Spinetta, who later commanded Predators for the 11th Reconnaissance Squadron, helps with its stability, although it remains pitch-sensitive. According to Spinetta, "Unquestionably, the best attribute of unmanned aircraft is high endurance. The Predator has many of the same flight characteristics as a glider; its 48.7-foot wingspan allows it to literally float on air . . . Aircrew do not have to be strapped to an ejection seat for missions that last 24 or more hours. The average Predator mission is well beyond the stamina—and the bladder limit—of aircrew flying tactical aircraft."

As Spinetta points out, the Predator's four-cylinder, four-stroke, 115-hp Rotax engine, "literally sips gas. It is exceedingly wimpy compared with other modern Air Force aircraft . . . it is the same type of engine commonly used on snowmobiles. But the Predator's primary

An MQ-1 Predator takes off for a training mission at Indian Springs Auxiliary Field (now Creech AFB) in Nevada. (U.S. Air Force photo/Senior Airman Larry Reid, Jr.)

mission, providing persistent surveillance, does not require a ton of thrust."

Reconnaissance payload options for the Predator included the Northrop Grumman TESAR synthetic aperture radar (SAR) with 1-foot resolution and all-weather reconnaissance capability. It can also fly with a laser designator and rangefinder, as well as electronic support and countermeasures gear and a moving target indicator (MTI). The Raytheon Multi-Spectral Targeting System (MTS) provides real-time imagery. The television system is equipped with a variable zoom and a telescopic spotter. These "eyes" of the surveillance gear are contained in a Versatron/Wescam electro-optical Skyball gimbal located in the "chin" of the aircraft. Because it contains the laser target designator, crews call this spherical turret a "laser ball."

Predators were provided with UHF and VHF radio relay links, a C-band line-of-sight data link, and Ku-band satellite data links.

As with other UAVs, Predators are acquired and delivered as multi-aircraft "systems." In the case of the RQ-1, the system includes four aircraft, a ground control station in a 30-foot trailer, and a Trojan Spirit data distribution terminal equipped with an 18-foot satellite dish for Ku-band transmissions.

The ACTD prototype of the Predator line made its debut flight in June 1994. These days, it usually takes years for an aircraft to become operational after its first flight. Not so in this case. Less than a year later, in April and May 1995, Predator aircraft were demonstrated at the Roving Sands 95 air defense exercise. They performed so well in this stateside demonstration that the decision was made to deploy them overseas to the Balkans in July 1995 as the centerpiece of the Air Force's first UAV squadron, the 11th Reconnaissance Squadron at Indian Springs Auxiliary Airfield (Creech AFB after 2005) in Nevada. The 11th was later joined by the 15th and 17th Reconnaissance Squadrons, all of which were under the umbrella of the 57th Operations Group at Nellis AFB.

The first operational deployment of the Predator overseas, Operation Nomad Vigil, occurred almost immediately. Between July and November in 1995, Predators operated out of Gjader in Albania, under the control of the United States European Command. The mission was to support the joint operation over Bosnia known as Provide Promise. During this deployment, Predators also flew in support of Operation Deliberate Force, the NATO air campaign against Serbian forces which had overrun the United Nations "safe zone" at Srebrenica in Bosnia, perpetrating what has been called the worst case of mass murder of civilians to occur in Europe since World War II.

Even as the U.S. Air Force was taking the Predator into combat in the Balkans, the CIA had already deployed its smaller sibling, the Gnat-750, to the Balkans in 1994. Flying out of a base in Albania, the Gnats conducted surveillance operations over the imploding Yugoslavia. Even after the arrival of the more capable Predator, improved Gnat-750s were redeployed to the Balkans by the CIA under the appropriate operational code name Lofty View.

During their first deployment, the 11th Reconnaissance Squadron birds flew 52 missions with two losses, one to Serbian ground fire and a second destroyed by its operators to keep it from falling into enemy hands.

The Nomad Vigil deployment was promptly followed by Nomad Endeavor in March 1996, during which the squadron supported NATO's Operation Joint Endeavor through December 1996, and Operation Joint Guard, which ended in June 1998. This time based at Taszar in Hungary, Predators flew an average six missions a week—weather permitting. Indeed, the bad weather of the Balkan Wintertime, led the 11th to retrofit its RQ-1s with deicing gear. In April 1997, when Pope John Paul II made his historic visit to war-torn Bosnia, a Predator from the 11th Reconnaissance Squadron flew two dedicated security surveillance missions totaling 22.5 hours. On the first day of the papal visit, the Predator was the only aircraft to provide real-time imagery.

A summer of fighting between ethnic Albanian separatists and the ethnic Serbian army of what was left of Yugoslavia in Kosovo was quieted by a United Nations Security Council Resolution in September 1998, which was monitored by NATO's Operation Eagle Eye to monitor this cease fire. Again, the Taszar-based Predators of the 11th Reconnaissance Squadron were back in action as some of the eyes of Eagle Eye.

When the Kosovo cease-fire collapsed in early 1999, NATO undertook Operation Allied Force, a three-month air offensive against Yugoslavia beginning on 24 March. By the time that Allied Force began, there were no longer Predators in the Balkan Theater, but the 11th Reconnaissance Squadron was rapidly redeployed, this time to the U.S. Army's Eagle Base, near Tuzla in Bosnia. The 11th remained in the theater for several months after the end of hostilities in June 1999, and made periodic redeployments to Tuzla in 2000 and early 2001. Meanwhile, the U.S. Navy had also committed shipboard-based RQ-2 Pioneer UAVs to the Allied Force action in 1999, but they were compelled to terminate operations because of bad weather.

The experience of American forces in the Balkans with the Predator was better than with the RQ-2s, but not by much, although the RQ-1 redeemed its earlier shortcomings during its 1999 reprise in Kosovo. As Richard Newman later wrote in *Air Force Magazine*, "Air planners were prepared to take advantage of Predator's real-time capabilities. Video feeds were downloaded via satellite links to the command center at Aviano AB, Italy. Planners there relayed data to airborne forward air controllers to help them find targets that, without spotters on the ground, were difficult to locate. The setup produced some dramatic moments. During a bomber raid in southern Kosovo, a Predator circled above Yugoslav troops even as they were being struck. This enabled staff officers at the operations center to see the effects of a B-52 strike for themselves—while it happened."

A big part of the Predator's downside in the Balkans had been the learning curve involved in an all-new type of aircraft. In a widely reported briefing in September 2001 by a senior defense department official who declined to be named, it was stated that, "A good number of them were lost [due to] operator error. It's hard to land this thing. The operator has the camera pointing out the front of the plane, but he really has lost a lot of situational awareness that a normal pilot would have of where the ground is and where the attitude of his aircraft is . . . so we have a lot of losses just from hitting the ground."

Of the 68 Predators that had been delivered to the U.S. Air Force, 19 were lost, but only four were confirmed to have been shot down in the Balkans. The rest were lost mainly due to operator error. This was not a good report card for an aircraft that was about to go into combat once again, this time in a war zone where it would finally have the opportunity to prove itself indispensable.

The Turn of the Century

As the twenty-first century approached, numerous UAV concepts were coming of age in various corners of the United States military establishment. The RQ-1 Predator and RQ-2 Pioneer—as well as the U.S. Army's RQ-5 Hunter—had demonstrated their capabilities in combat situations, while the RQ-3 DarkStar and RQ-4 Global Hawk were seen as the archetypes of the class of UAVs that might one day compete for the high profile reconnaissance mission of the U-2.

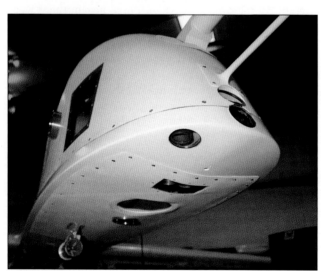

The caption writers at the NASA Dryden Flight Research Center described this view of the Altus UAV as "looking ever so much like an alien spacecraft." How would they have known? Seen here are some of the instruments and camera lenses mounted in its nose for a lightning study over Florida flown during the summer of 2002. (NASA photo by Tom Tschida)

In addition to U.S. Air Force programs, such as Global Hawk and Predator, other services had other programs ongoing then earmarked for reconnaissance operations. Of course, the first U.S. Air Force UCAV had been born a recon drone. The U.S. Navy found itself matching UAVs to a wide variety of missions. These ranged from close-in fire support for Marine amphibious operations to long-range maritime surveillance.

Despite the obvious tactical potential and amazing technology, most late-twentieth century UAVs were still seen as idiosyncratic experiments. Among tactical planners, there was a sense that these machines represented an important future weapon, but many had trouble envisioning exactly how this would evolve.

Looking back at the literature of the 1990s, it's evident that a big driving force in UAV development was cost. This was the post–Cold War era of optimism about the future of lessening world tensions, and a declining defense budget.

General Ronald Fogleman, the Air Force Chief of Staff, said that during the long-range planning process that led to the creation of the Air Force's "Global

At the same time that General Atomics developed the Predator UAV for the U.S. Air Force, it was creating the similar Altus aircraft for NASA. It had a slightly longer wingspan and was flown as a performance and propulsion test bed for future high-altitude science platform aircraft under NASA's Environmental Research Aircraft and Sensor Technology (ERAST) program at the Dryden Flight Research Center. In July 1999 an Altus flew at 55,000 feet for over four hours. (NASA/Sandia Labs photo by Dick Jones)

A General Atomics Altus aircraft on the runway at Rogers Dry Lake adjacent to NASA's Dryden Flight Research Center in May 1996. (NASA photo)

Engagement" doctrine, the Rand Corporation had produced a study asserting that the Air Force "can no longer . . . spend money the way we have been."

Fogleman went on to say that in order to cut costs, Air Force planners had to think "outside the box" and part of that mandate was to explore emerging technologies "such as UAVs."

Air Force Major General Kenneth Israel, who headed the Defense Airborne Reconnaissance Office (DARO), explained in an interview with John Tirpak of *Air Force Magazine* that was published in September 1997, "UAVs are going to be a big, high leverage, [high] payoff capability for us . . . UAVs not only save lives, but they also really are very inexpensive to operate."

Israel added that, in a force structure characterized by a "high-low mix" of aircraft, UAVs could have an important niche. "They make a difference in the way you fight, in the way you think," he asserted, noting that, in ground war games where UAVs play a role, "everybody . . . is watching the sky" for the snooping robotic airplanes." One comment that set the stage especially well for the story of the combat UAV in the twenty-first century came after UAVs played an unexpectedly prominent role in war games held in 1997 at the U.S. Army's National Training Center at Fort Irwin. Said Major General Paul Kern, commander of the 4th Infantry Division, to Army Chief of Staff General Dennis Reimer, "I will give up a tank battalion for a UAV company."

Going To War

The image of the armed UAV on a hunting trip deep inside enemy territory is one of the most vivid to have merged into popular culture as the United States responded to the attacks of 11 September 2001. However, while the armed UAV became an icon of

Marine Unmanned Aerial Vehicle Squadron-2 (VMU-2) crews practice a rocket-assisted launch of an RQ-2 Pioneer during weapons and tactics training at Laguna Army Air Field at Yuma Proving Ground in 2001. (U.S. Marine Corps photo by Corporal Kyle Davidson)

VMU-2's Staff Sergeant Brent Shaw (a Marine) takes his RQ-2 Pioneer through its basic control procedures before handing over control to an internal pilot during the unit's weapons and tactics training at Laguna Army Air Field at Yuma Proving Ground in October 2001. (U.S. Marine Corps photo by Corporal Kyle Davidson)

General Paul Kern, commander of the 4th Infantry Division, was impressed by UAV capability. After their unpredictably impressive performance in 1997 war games, he told Army Chief of Staff General Dennis Reimer, "I will give up a tank battalion for a UAV company." (U.S. Army photo)

An RQ-4A Global Hawk rests on a southwest Asia runway prior to a July 2002 mission over Afghanistan. (U.S. Air Force photo by Staff Sergeant Reynaldo Ramon)

"The whole nation is looking at us in uniform to do its business. Is there any higher calling than that?" U.S. Air Force Chief of Staff General John Jumper asked of a group of Air Staff officers and enlisted members gathered in the Pentagon auditorium on 21 September 2001. Secretary of the Air Force Dr. James G. Roche said "Down the road today's airmen are going to look back at this time with pride." He was referring to the attacks of 11 September. (U.S. Air Force photo by Tech Sergeant Jim Varhegyi)

This pair of views of the Taliban's Divisional Regiment Headquarters at Mazar-e-Sharif in Afghanistan were taken by U.S. Air Force Predator drones before and after it was attended to by American strike aircraft on or about 11 October 2001. (Department of Defense photo)

It is suggested by the angle of these photos of the Taliban's Charkhi motor vehicle and ordnance repair facility in Afghanistan that they were taken by an RQ-1 Predator flying relatively low. These images were officially released on 15 October 2001. (Department of Defense photo)

twenty-first century warfare, the concept was already on the drawing board at the Pentagon when American Airlines Flight 77 hit the building that morning.

During the 1990s, as reconnaissance UAVs were cropping up on the fringes of tactical doctrine, even more ambitious notions were beginning to percolate. Far out of the mainstream, Defense Department planners were asking "what if" and thinking about arming UAVs. In its formative stages in 2001, the Unmanned Combat Air Vehicle (UCAV) program (later J-UCAS) was already looking long term at an aircraft that would, at some point in the future, laser-designate targets, conduct Suppression of Enemy Air Defense (SEAD) missions, and attack heavily fortified, high-value targets.

In the summer of 2001, a few months before he became Chief of Staff of the U.S. Air Force, General John Jumper had told John Tirpak of *Air Force Magazine*, "I don't think there's any doubt that . . . UCAVs will come, and we will work the concept of operations to include them."

In 2001, even as the UCAV concept was still part of "tomorrow's" tactical theory, the U.S. Air Force was well on the way toward arming its existing RQ-1s.

Jumper had become Chief of Staff on 6 September 2001, less than a week before the United States found itself thrust into a war. He came to the post as a combat commander who'd had direct experience with UAVs in a combat theater. After serving in the dual role as commander of U.S. Air Forces in Europe (USAFE), and as commander of Allied Air Forces Central Europe (AFCENT) during Operation Allied Force/Noble Anvil in the Balkans, he served a year and a half as commander of Air Combat Command.

He had seen the Predator go to the Balkans as a surveillance aircraft that morphed into a targeting tool. The synthetic aperture radar could provide imagery of targets, but it couldn't do anything about taking them out. The Predator could only watch as enemy tanks lumbered toward friendly positions. The laser designator and rangefinder system on the RQ-1's chin—the "laser ball"—could "laze" the tank, or put a laser beam on it. An F-16 with laser-guided munitions, such as a GBU-24 Paveway III, could then find and destroy the "lazed" target.

As Jumper would later describe, this transition "a breakthrough." As he put it, the laser ball "turns the Predator from just a pure surveillance system into something that actually . . . directs weapons on the targets."

Not part of its originally specified equipment, Predators were equipped with a Raytheon AN/AAS-44(V) sensor turret, incorporating a laser designator in addition to a thermal image.

At this point in the story, it would seem logical to say that the Air Force moved quickly to exploit what they had discovered about its UAV, and to actually arm the Predators. However, when he returned to the United States to take over Air Combat Command, Jumper discovered that when the Predators had been shipped state-

General John Jumper was an enthusiastic promoter of UAV capabilities both as commander of Air Combat Command in the 1990s, and as Air Force Chief of Staff after the turn of the century. (U.S. Air Force photo by Tech Sergeant Jim Varhegyi)

side, the laser balls had been removed. The general ordered them re-installed. He also ordered that the Predators be taken to the next step. General Jumper ordered that the Air Force should look into arming Predators.

The immediate problem in arming the small drone was weight. The Predator was never designed to be armed. Its total payload capacity is less than 500 pounds, the weight of the lightest standard "dumb" bomb. Laser-guided GBU-24s weigh four times that. The solution was the laser-guided AGM-114 Hellfire, an air-to-surface, anti-armor missile that had been designed for use aboard Army and Marine Corps attack helicopters. They weigh about 100 pounds each.

Jumper saw the Hellfire as ideal for what he described as "fleeting, perishable targets that don't require a big warhead that we can just go ahead and take care of."

As reported by Jane's Information Group on 17 August 2001, the Air Force had begun test firing the AGM-114C Hellfire from a Predator six months before.

In these tests, conducted at Indian Springs Auxiliary Airfield in Nevada, the Predator fired 16 Hellfires, scoring a 75 percent direct hit rate, and putting all but one shot within about a 20-foot radius. The only wide miss was a missile malfunction. A second phase of testing had taken place at the Naval Air Warfare Center Weapons Division's China Lake facility in California, involving a successful high-altitude shot of the AGM-114 Hellfire from a range of five km.

As America went to war in 2001, the operational UAV fleet was small. The U.S. Navy had RQ-2 Pioneers, as the Air Force had the Predators and a few RQ-4 Global Hawks, although this type was still in flight test.

On 7 October, the United States launched Operation Enduring Freedom. The Taliban government of Afghanistan was hosting the personnel and infrastructure of the al-Qaeda terrorist gang that had planned and executed the 11 September attacks. Enduring Freedom was aimed at

As dawn breaks over the battlefield, a Predator is prepped for another mission. (U.S. Air Force photo by Staff Sergeant Jeremy Lock)

deposing the Taliban, destroying the al-Qaeda infrastructure, and killing or capturing as many al-Qaeda gangsters as possible—especially its top leadership, including Osama bin Laden, Ayman al-Zawahiri, and Khalid Sheikh Mohammad, who had masterminded the string of terrorist attacks that culminated with the 11 September calamity.

The operation relied heavily on special operations personnel—belonging to both the military and to the CIA—supported by U.S. Navy and U.S. Air Force attack aircraft.

As had been the case in the Balkans in the preceding decade, there were two separate contingents of American Predators in action over Afghanistan, one controlled by the U.S. Air Force, and another by the CIA. While press reports occasionally attribute a specific action to one agency or the other, it is not always clear whether the attribution is accurate, or merely a guess by the reporting journalist or his sources.

As David Fulghum reported four years later in the 27 February 2005 issue of *Aviation Week*, it was the CIA that first used armed Predators, although they were flown remotely by U.S. Air Force pilots, and they "were launched on combat missions from bases in Uzbekistan. Since both the Army and Air Force [in the 2001–2005 period] operate similar UAVs, the CIA's small fleet could be flown from the same bases in the theater or from small bases in remote areas."

As Fulghum pointed out, UAVs, including Predators, were also operating from bases in the United Arab Emirates and Djibouti to monitor insurgent operations in Somalia and "other African nations where failed or weak governments offer no interference with efforts to recruit, arm, and launch new groups into the terrorist pipeline."

When one considers how far the Predator concept came in the decade after its first hot zone deployment

in the Balkans in the 1990s, we are reminded how far the concept had come since Reginald Denny first conceived radio-controlled aircraft as other than toys. On the flip side, it is interesting how close modern unmanned aerial vehicles are to their roots in the RC hobby. Indeed, Lieutenant Colonel Spinetta of the 11th Reconnaissance Squadron would write in the June 2009 issue of *Fly RC* magazine, the Predator is "the ultimate RC aircraft . . . Predator aircrew have perfected remote-control warfare."

The Predator Becomes a Predator

Though it was named "Predator," the notion of actually arming the RQ-1 to kill prey had not originally been part of the plan. Though the concept emerged before Operation Enduring Freedom, it would take combat in Afghanistan to turn the Predator into a predator.

None of the operational RQ-1s were armed when the war started, but this quickly changed, and the Predator was high on the list of weapons that the United States Central Command (CENTCOM) would deploy in Operation Enduring Freedom. Like General Jumper of the Air Force, the CENTCOM commander, U.S. Army General Tommy Franks, saw and understood. Recognizing the Predator's unique capabilities, he included several Predator teams among the first troops he ordered to go overseas. At least one team each had gone to Pakistan and Uzbekistan in September.

As noted above, the Predators would be flown operationally by both U.S. Air Force and Central Intelligence Agency pilots.

Because the enemy, especially al-Qaeda, consisted of small bands of personnel that were either on foot or in light vehicles, the Predator would eventually prove itself as the right weapon for a new kind of battlefield. It was light, quiet, and simple to deploy and operate. It could identify and track targets four or five miles away without being seen. It was also now armed.

The Predator's first missions in Afghanistan were similar to its Kosovo operations, and would involve spotting targets for AC-130 gunships. An unnamed CENTCOM officer told Richard Newman, writing for *Air Force Magazine*, that the Predator allowed the gunships to start hitting the enemy immediately after they arrived in the target area, rather than having to orbit once or twice to get oriented. "The AC-130, when it's teamed with the Predator, pretty much hits what it's going after," he said.

There is a learning curve when a new weapon is first sent onto a battlefield, but the Predator was already battle tested in the Balkans. As an attack platform, however, it still needed some fine tuning.

So too did the Hellfire. The missile was designed to be used against tanks and armored vehicles. When it was first used against unarmored, "soft" targets, the missile sliced through them and penetrated the ground beneath them. The U.S. Army's Redstone Arsenal solved the problem by retrofitting the Hellfires with a metal sleeve that maximizes fragmentation.

The U.S. Air Force feared immediate stress damage to the Predator's fragile composite wing, but this issue did not materialize. Nor did carrying the Hellfires degrade

Senior Airman Joseph Gollhofer, a 46th Expeditionary Reconnaissance Squadron crew chief, cleans the small lens that the ground-bound pilots will use to fly this MQ-1 Predator on its next mission. Pilots describe the view as "like seeing through a straw." (U.S. Air Force photo by Technical Sergeant Dan Neely)

the endurance of the Predator. Typically, a Predator flies a 24-hour operational mission, but the extra weight and drag only reduced this by about two hours.

Meanwhile, the U.S. Air Force had also experimented with arming Predators with AIM-92 Stinger, air-to-air missiles, a cousin of the FIM-92 Stinger, a man-portable surface-to-air missile that had been in service for more than a dozen years. The AIM-92 weighed about a third of the Hellfire's 100 pounds, and were carried by some American and European helicopters. Predators that were thus equipped were used in Operation Southern Watch reconnaissance missions over Iraq.

Some of the biggest problems hamstringing Predator operations in the fall of 2001 were political. After a decade of involvement in conflicts with complex rules of engagement, Americans were unused to fighting a war against an enemy that had actually attacked the United States. On the first night of the operation, a convoy of vehicles fleeing the city of Kabul reportedly contained the personal SUV of Mullah Omar, the supreme leader of the Taliban. Using high-resolution imaging, an armed Predator is said to have confirmed Omar's presence by reading his license plate.

Rather than taking the shot, the CIA controller managing this Predator decided he lacked the authority to order a fire on such a high-value target. The request to open fire was transmitted to the duty officer at CENTCOM headquarters at MacDill AFB in Florida. It was referred to General Franks, who took the advice of his Judge Advocate General (JAG) to *not* attack Omar. When Secretary of Defense Donald Rumsfeld learned of this, he was furious and is said to have kicked in a door. He clarified the rules of engagement so as to allow such a thing never to happen again.

While the opportunity to take out the primary protector of Osama bin Laden had slipped away, a month later, an armed Predator had its baptism of fire against a high-value target.

Muhammad Atef, a.k.a. Abu Hafs al-Masri, was a top al-Qaeda military commander who had helped plot the simultaneous 1998 bombings of American embassies in Africa. A fugitive on the FBI's top 22 Most Wanted Terrorists, he appeared in a video—released in September 2006—that showed him with Osama bin Laden, planning the 11 September attack.

On 16 November 2001, he was in a house near Kabul, when it came into the sights of an RQ-1 whose operator had been informed of Atef's presence. Shortly after Enduring Freedom had begun, Atef had said, "The calculations of the crusade coalition were very mistaken when it thought it could wage a war on Afghanistan, achieving victory swiftly."

However, it was Atef whose miscalculations left his lifeless body amid a pile of broken masonry in Kabul. The Taliban itself confirmed his demise on 17 November.

As described by General Jumper, the RQ-1 was on its way to proving itself the ideal weapon to "take care of a range of targets that we called fleeting and perishable—ones that get away quickly."

Writing in the March 2002 issue of *Air Force Magazine*, Richard Newman called the Predator "an unlikely star [in Afghanistan] . . . an ungainly, slow-flying airplane."

He went on to assess exactly *how* and *why* the aircraft had made such a difference, noting that, "as

Staff Sergeant James Barr, a maintenance member of the 46th Expeditionary Reconnaissance Squadron, connects an aircraft starter cart to an RQ-1 Predator to start the engine. (U.S. Air Force photo by Technical Sergeant Dan Neely)

airpower analysts pore over the facts of the war, they seem convinced that Predator played a key role in one of the war's major breakthroughs: the sharp compression of the sensor-to-shooter cycle, the amount of time that elapses between the moment a target is identified and the moment it is attacked. Slashing that time from hours to minutes—or less—has long been a goal of the revolution in military affairs, a fundamental shift in warfare in which rapid processing of targeting data and other information would supposedly provide dramatic advantages on the battlefield. The Predator appears to have validated some of those beliefs."

As an unnamed general at CENTCOM told Newman, recalling the frustration experienced during the 1991 Gulf War, when it often took days for intelligence experts to complete their analysis and obtain the classification clearances necessary to get targeting information to aircrews. "In the past, we have always relied on something associated with a time delay. A third party was always involved in distribution. Now, there's no intel geek involved in the processing."

The sudden star status of the Predator was immediately apparent—even at the top of the chain of command. In a speech at the Citadel in Charleston, South Carolina, on 11 December George W. Bush said, "These past two months have shown that innovative doctrine and high-tech weaponry can shape and then dominate an

Senior Airman Jason Biselx, a 46th Expeditionary Reconnaissance Squadron crew chief, checks a brake assembly on one of his unit's MQ-1 Predators during a preflight inspection. (U.S. Air Force photo by Technical Sergeant Dan Neely)

Staff Sergeant Kevin Strickland, a maintenance crew chief with the 46th Expeditionary Reconnaissance Squadron, works on an RQ-1 Predator's Rotax 914 engine at a forward deployed location. (U.S. Air Force photo by Technical Sergeant Dan Neely)

unconventional conflict." Bush continued, "Our commanders are gaining a real-time picture of the entire battlefield, and are able to get targeting information from sensor to shooter almost instantly . . . Before the war, the Predator had skeptics because it did not fit the old ways. Now it is clear the military does not have *enough* unmanned vehicles."

Though it was still technically in flight testing, the RQ-4 Global Hawk also joined the action in the skies over Afghanistan in early November 2001. With its synthetic aperture radar, the Global Hawk offered an all-weather surveillance capability that was much needed because of the winter storms and constant cloud cover. It also offered the unprecedented ability to remain over a battlefield for more than 24 hours, providing a continuous stream of data.

The huge aircraft's operational debut had come much sooner than expected. As had been the case with the E-8 Joint Surveillance Target Attack Radar System (J-STARS) aircraft in 1991 during Gulf War I, the RQ-4 was still being tested, but commanders in the field needed its capabilities—so it went to war. The Global Hawk would be assigned to the 12th Expeditionary Reconnaissance Squadron (a component of the 9th Reconnaissance Wing at Beale AFB) that was based at an undisclosed forward operating location in Southwest Asia close to Afghanistan.

Beginning in January 2002, the RQ-4 Global Hawks were assigned to the 380th Air Expeditionary Wing, based at al-Dafra AB in the United Arab Emirates. It was from here that the big aircraft would fly their missions across Southwest Asia in the coming years, missions that took them across both Afghanistan and Iraq.

During the operations in Afghanistan in the winter of 2001–2002, the Predator had been only one of a larger team of players, often vectoring AC-130 gunships to targets and providing valuable real-time data to the gunners before they arrived on the scene. However, a year after these operations began, the Predator finally proved its potential as a lone attack platform, firmly staking out its place in the history of warfare.

On 4 November 2002, a sport utility vehicle was travelling through the monotonous grey gravel hills of the Marib region, about 100 miles east of Sanaa, the capital of Yemen. Among the six men inside were Qaed Senyan al-Harthi and Kamal Derwish, a pair of Yemenis who were members of Osama bin Laden's al-Qaeda terrorist gang. Al-Harthi, who also went by the street name "Abu Ali," was bin Laden's overseer for Yemen. He was also one of the schemers who had planned the suicide attack that had damaged the USS *Cole* in Yemen 25 months earlier, killing 17 Americans. Derwish was a Yemeni who'd assumed the pseudonym "Ahmed Hijazi," immigrated to the United States, and became a citizen. In turn, he had headed an al-Qaeda "sleeper cell" in Lackawanna, New York.

High above the SUV, traveling scarcely faster, was a gangly, soap-colored airplane. Through a television link in this unmanned craft, an American sitting in a control center about 350 miles away in Djibouti had been watching the SUV for about an hour.

Airmen from the 64th Expeditionary Reconnaissance Squadron position a Predator for flight. The "pilot" was 7,000 miles away. (U.S. Air Force photo by Master Sergeant Deb Smith)

The Predator fired a Hellfire, and suddenly the six terrorists were instantly engulfed in a furiously burning ball of unleaded gasoline. They didn't have even a moment to think about the irony of all those civilians who'd burned to death in those other high-octane balls of fire in the buildings that al-Qaeda had targeted on 11 September 2001.

Muhammad Atef had been taken out by a coordinated effort of several assets of which the Predator was just one. November 2002 marked the first time—of many to come—that a lone Predator had destroyed a high-value target. It was a small, but important, turning point in military history.

Another remarkable milestone came just six weeks after the Yemen take-down. On 23 December a Predator was involved in its first air-to-air dogfight. Flying an Operation Southern Watch mission over Iraq, a Stinger-armed Predator was challenged by an Iraqi MiG-25 Foxbat. One of the world's fastest military aircraft was mixing it up with one of the world's slowest. The Predator was the first to fire, but the Stinger went wide. The Foxbat pilot returned fire. Though the Predator went down in flames that day, it was one of those great "what might have been" moments of aerial combat.

U.S. Air Force General Richard Myers, the chairman of the Joint Chiefs of Staff, noted Iraq had been trying to shoot down coalition aircraft for several years, and called it "a lucky shot." He added that this had not been the first time that Iraqi gunners had shot down a Predator. A Defense Department spokesman confirmed that as many as three Predators had been shot down by anti-aircraft fire during 2001 in the no-fly zones in northern and southern Iraq. To put this incident into the context of this book, the losses of the Predators are a clear indication of operations in dangerous areas where the loss of a human pilot would not have been risked. The little robots had given their lives to get the pictures.

It was in 2002, as the Predator had emerged as a poster child for the effectiveness of *armed* UAVs, that the RQ-1 reconnaissance drone designation was superseded by the designation MQ-1, identifying the Predator as a "multi-mission" platform.

The accomplishments of the armed Predators over Southwest Asia resulted in an unanticipated shift in strategic thinking about air power. From the periphery of such planning, UAVs moved to center stage. Nick Cook, aerospace consultant for the London-based *Jane's Defense Weekly*, best summarized the abruptly changing paradigm when he pointed out in January 2003 that the "development of the Unmanned Combat Air Vehicle (UCAV), as revolutionary as its technology is, is a mirror-image of the early evolution of the aircraft as a fighting machine. Just as modern combat aircraft owe their niche in today's military inventories to a time when pilots of scout aircraft started dropping grenades out of open cockpits, so the first operationally blooded UCAV, an AGM-114 Hellfire-equipped variant of the General

Atomics RQ-1 Predator, happens to be an evolution of a platform designed originally for surveillance purposes."

As William B. Scott wrote in the 8 July 2002 issue of *Aviation Week & Space Technology*, unmanned aerial vehicles had become "the darlings of senators, representatives and generals . . . The Pentagon established a joint-service UAV Planning Task Force to coordinate the development and use of future UAV systems . . . and money started flowing to the UAV community."

Thomas Cassidy, the president and CEO of General Atomics Aeronautical Systems, told David Fulghum of *Aviation Week* in an interview published on 1 March 2003, that "before 9/11 we were building two Predators a month, and the Air Force was talking about ramping down. Now the questions are, 'What can the company do? How can it ramp up?' What we've done is add additional people and facilities, including a new 40,000-square-foot hangar at our Grey Butte airport . . . We're now ramped up to about four airplanes a month."

By 2003, General Atomics had grown from a handful of people in the early 1990s to a work force of 850, of whom 350 had been hired after the turn of the century. The United States had taken delivery of more than 80 RQ-1s, which had accumulated 65,000 flight hours in the hands of Air Force and CIA pilots, about half of these hours in combat, while as Cassidy pointed out, maintaining a 96 percent operational readiness rate "in some really lousy locations." Another customer for General Atomics, the Italian Aeronautica Militaire, was in the process of equipping its 28th Group at Amendola AB with Predators.

Elsewhere in Europe, there was the Crecerelle, a tactical UAV that melded the British Banshee aerial vehicle with a French ground control system developed by System de Drones Tactiques Intermediaires (SDTI) program, a version of which had also been sold to Denmark, the Netherlands, and Sweden. As reported in *Aviation Week*, Sagem and Dassault Aviation in France formed a joint venture called MCMM (Multi-Charges Multi-Mission) "to explore hunter-killer UAVs capable of carrying various types of guided submunitions such as the BONUS, STRIX and 2.75-inch rockets."

Germany continued to develop the Brevel tactical UAV, which had originated as a Franco-German project. Germany was also looking at the Global Hawk for its maritime reconnaissance requirements over the North Sea—a mission for which the aircraft would ultimately be acquired.

Among the strong UAV advocates who emerged during this period was retired U.S. Air Force Colonel John Warden, a former fighter pilot and an architect of the 1991 Gulf War air campaign. He pointed out that the ability of a UAV to loiter over a target was "a big plus . . . especially when it's accompanied by the ability to shoot." He went on to say that an enemy operating from a fixed facility on the ground "is doomed (even if deeply buried). Surface movement—which previously provided some possibility of survival—becomes less feasible when you have to [worry] about a silent machine overhead that could shoot you at any time. [Armed UAVs] have the capability to create a mini-revolution in air warfare."

Warden suggested that by 2020, nine out of ten air breathing American combat aircraft would be unmanned. "They are rapidly approaching the point where they will be able to do most things a man can do," he said. "Other than untangle complicated shoot/no-shoot decisions on the spot."

As would have been expected, there were also those who seized on the exceptions. General Howell Estes, a retired fighter pilot who had commanded the first operational F-117 unit, provided a reminder of the "reality" of air combat when he pointed out that "a man's brain is far better than any UAV's computer, which [today] has about the same capability as a cat's brain, when it comes to reasoning or the thought process."

Writing in *Aviation Week* in February 2003, Steven Zaloga of the Teal Group, an independent aerospace and defense industry market analysis firm, pointed out further technical drawbacks to the tactical UAV concept. "The employment of the Global Hawk and Predator

Senior Airman Ray Campbell helps guide an MQ-1 Predator under a sun shade. (U.S. Air Force photo by Second Lieutenant Gerardo Gonzalez)

over the past year highlights two of the most significant obstacles to UAV proliferation," he said. "Their high attrition rate and the need for additional satellite uplink bandwidth to accommodate the enormous flow of data inherent in any proliferation of UAVs in the future. Because of their importance, both issues are receiving attention from the UAV community."

Not surprisingly, one of the biggest proponents of the Predator as a warplane was the man whose company makes it. "Their beauty is dwell time—persistence and endurance," said Thomas Cassidy. "You sit out there and wait. Nobody knows you're there. If anybody moves, you catch them. That's why Predator has been successful. The United States has had Predators airborne nearly continuously, 24 hours a day, for over a year. They have been shot at a lot; now they're shooting back. We have revolutionized air warfare."

Both cheerleaders and skeptics agreed, however, that the future of combat air operations would see unmanned aircraft in the mix with manned aircraft—even if they did not agree on the respective proportions.

By 2002–2003, there was little doubt that the Predator had assured a place for the armed UAV in tactical operations. There was no way of knowing where the concept was headed, but there was little doubt that the turning point had been rounded.

"I want to see a Predator coming back with MiG kills painted on its side," said Cassidy, as he proudly reflected on the December 2002 dogfight with the Iraqi MiG-25, and on the future of weapons-toting drones.

Food for thought, and a good candidate for the "final word" file came in 2002 from Burt Rutan, the president of Scaled Composites and the legendary designer of many ingenious aircraft. "If war is fought by robots, there will be no heroes," said he, "because nobody's life is at risk. Societies need heroes, and I don't see UAV pilots becoming war heroes."

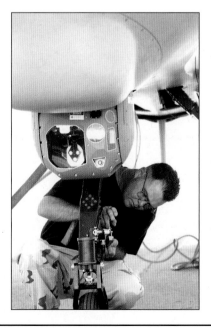

Technical Sergeant Thomas McGuire inspects the nose landing gear of an MQ-1 Predator after a mission. (U.S. Air Force photo by Second Lieutenant Gerardo Gonzalez)

Senior Airman Brady Martindale (left) and First Lieutenant Andrew Hackleman inspect the main landing gear of an MQ-1 Predator. Martindale was an avionics specialist, and Hackleman a maintenance officer with the 332nd Air Expeditionary Wing. (U.S. Air Force photo by Second Lieutenant Gerardo Gonzalez)

CHAPTER THREE

PLANNING UNMANNED WARPLANES OUTSIDE THE BOX

An artist's conception of a Northrop Grumman X-47B J-UCAS launching from an aircraft carrier, and another one in the distance comes in to land. Above to the left, a Lockheed Martin F-35 Lightning II approaches. (Northrop Grumman)

A few years before a Predator first opened fire on a bad guy who had been tracked and acquired by a pilot thousands of miles away, DARPA and the U.S. Air Force were seriously studying unmanned aerial vehicles that would have the word "combat" inserted at the moment of conception. In the 1990s, both military tacticians and aerospace industry technicians were starting to think "outside the box" in which their predecessors had operated.

DARPA and the armed services were beginning to think conceptually of an unmanned aircraft that would, at some point in the future, not only laser-designate targets as Predators had in Kosovo, but conduct Suppression of Enemy Air Defense (SEAD) missions on their own, and attack heavily fortified, high-value targets.

This new generation of aircraft would be designed from the ground up as unmanned *combat* aerial vehicles. At first, both the U.S. Air Force and U.S. Navy identified such UAVs as Unmanned Combat Aircraft Vehicles (UCAV), although in April 2003, the two services merged their UCAV programs under a single *joint* management office known as Joint Unmanned Air Combat Systems (J-UCAS). We refer to the early aircraft by the UCAV acronym because that was how they were known at the time, and because UCAV implies a vehicle, while UCAS implies a broader "system of systems."

It was also around this time that Unmanned Aerial Vehicles (UAV) started being referred to in the halls of the Pentagon as Unmanned Aerial *Systems* (UAS).

The ambitious concept linked unmanned aircraft with a whole spectrum of attack missions, including missions that were once flown only by aircraft with an intelligent pilot aboard—and especially missions where those intelligent, human pilots would be in extraordinary danger of being killed. The United States military doesn't like to lose aircraft, but really hates to lose pilots.

Back in 1997, Air Force Colonel Mike Francis, the director of architecture and integration at the Defense Airborne Reconnaissance Office, told David Fulghum of *Aviation Week* that his agency was taking an enthusiastic interest, not just in arming drones, but in developing aircraft that could fly the full mission profile of an armed reconnaissance or a strike aircraft.

"We know where manned aircraft are going," explained Francis, obviously keen on the broad potential of the concept. "For example, if everybody is flying the same [manned] aircraft, the imbalance offered by the introduction of an [unmanned] aircraft that can turn at 20g, could give the advantage to the latter.

"Why put the pilot in a volume and weight constrained space, if you don't have to?" Francis then asked rhetorically. He went so far as to say that in the twenty-first century, UCAVs "could redefine the aircraft carrier as an aircraft that carries other aircraft." Indeed naval aircraft carriers had once been an out-of-the-box concept. When it comes to aircraft carriers, one might think that armed drones might not have so easily leaped to the mind of a Navy man, the Chief of Naval Operations had also commissioned a study of armed unmanned aerial vehicles in 1997. Again, their future use was embraced. In a prelude to what has since become a keystone of UCAV doctrine, this report observed that such aircraft "provide a chance to destroy critical targets before local air superiority has been achieved and the air defenses beat down."

At the Air Force's Air Combat Command, Major Rob Vanderberry explained that this would also make the decision to launch high-risk attacks easier to make. These aircraft will allow Air Force leaders to breathe easier when making a combat decision," he said. "What UCAV lets us do is attack a target without the concern of losing a pilot, or having someone become a prisoner of war."

Of course, in the 1990s, another consideration in planning for future air combat was the dwindling budget. Taking the pilot and life support systems out of the aircraft not only saved weight, but it saved on complexity, and reduced cost. Unmanned aerial vehicles don't put lives at risk, and that had led to the common misconception that they are cheap. They are generally less expensive than manned aircraft, but they are not cheap enough to be disposable. The costs of the larger UAVs in service around the turn of the century ranged from around a half million dollars to nearly the equivalent of manned aircraft prices. The payloads, sensors, airframes and the control and communication networks that are combined to provide the necessary capability are not inexpensive.

The UCAVs, like the UAVs, would not be designed to be expendable. The armed services didn't *intend* to lose them, but they would be, in Defense Department parlance, "attritable." This meant that a commander could *afford* to lose one, especially when the alternative is the loss of a manned aircraft and an aircrew.

The century, military, and industry planners often categorized the missions most suitable for unmanned, rather than manned combat aircraft, as those which were "the dull, the dirty, and the dangerous." These included long, dull, repetitive reconnaissance missions; missions into a battlefield environment made dirty by chemical or biological weapons; or missions against targets that are very dangerous for human pilots.

The SEAD missions would be among the latter. As had been the experience of the U.S. Air Force in Operation Desert Storm in 1991, SEAD mission attack aircraft are exposed to high volumes of fire from antiaircraft artillery (AAA) and surface-to-air missiles (SAMs), in which human crews risk their lives. In the UCAV future, only the airplanes would be at risk in SEAD missions.

Airframe designers had already moved beyond the notion of simply hanging weapons on reconnaissance drones. Even before the parent company merged with Boeing in 1997, the McDonnell Douglas Phantom Works was already working on the project that would evolve into the X-45 program.

The X-45 UCAV Demonstrator

The first time that the word "combat" was inserted in the UAV acronym of a specific project that would become a real aircraft was on 9 March 1998 when DARPA issued its document MDA972-98-R-0003, the Phase I request for proposals for an Unmanned Combat Air Vehicle Advanced Technology Demonstrator (UCAV ATD). The aircraft would be designated with an X-for-experimental prefix, as X-45.

In their initial request for proposals, DARPA and the U.S. Air Force envisioned an aircraft that would

The Boeing X-45A UCAV during engine tests in the spring of 2001. (DARPA)

Fabrication of the upper composite skin of the first Boeing X-45A. (DARPA)

A close-up of fuselage fabrication for the first Boeing X-45A UCAV in April 2000. (DARPA)

demonstrate the technical feasibility of a UCAV system that could "effectively and affordably prosecute twenty-first century SEAD/Strike missions within the emerging global command and control architecture."

DARPA envisioned nothing short of a weapons system that expanded tactical mission options for "revolutionary new air power."

The Air Force envisioned the X-45 as a weapon system that could potentially engage multiple targets in a single mission with minimal human supervision. DARPA envisioned something that would require minimal maintenance, and that could be stored for extended periods of time, unpacked, and used almost immediately in "small-scale contingencies" and major theater wars. Both agencies asked the industry to create a versatile system that could operate from an ordinary runway, conducting its missions alone, in groups or in cooperation with manned tactical aircraft.

This groundbreaking request for proposals envisioned an aircraft that would be able to perform combat missions of a type that did not yet exist, such as high-risk

The fuselage jig assembly for the Boeing X-45A UCAV aircraft as seen in December 1999. (DARPA)

tasks where the danger to human pilots was extreme, or missions where the UCAV is more cost effective than current platforms. For instance, the initial operational role for the UCAV was seen as being that of a "first day of the war force enabler" tasked with performing the SEAD mission. The experimental X-45 was seen as the proof-of-concept demonstrator of such an enabler.

The SEAD missions would call for operational UCAVs to knock out the enemy air defenses before the manned bombers entered hostile air space. After accomplishing the SEAD mission, UCAVs would be used on other high-value and/or time critical targets. Strategically, this would present an enemy with a "no win" tactical situation in which its defenses would be ineffective.

DARPA also noted, "advances in small smart munitions would allow these smaller vehicles to attack multiple targets during a single mission and to reduce the cost per target killed [and] improvements in sensor technology would allow significant advances in surveillance and reconnaissance over high threat areas."

Recalling recent experience with the RQ-3 DarkStar and RQ-4 Global Hawk, DARPA also asked for "intelligent function allocation" to allow the UCAV to operate *autonomously*, while stressing the idea that the human controller would be expected to provide executive level mission management to "remain in the decision process."

On 16 April 1998, DARPA and the Air Force made the Phase I contract awards, picking four contractors to enter the preliminary design phase. These four were Lockheed Martin Tactical Aircraft Systems, Northrop Grumman Military Aircraft Systems, Raytheon Systems, and the Boeing Company. Over the course of the preceding two years, Boeing had acquired both McDonnell Douglas and the North American Aviation component of Rockwell International. Based in St. Louis, McDonnell Douglas had previously developed the Sky Owl and Sparrow Hawk tactical UAV demonstrators.

Attaching the wings of the first Boeing X-45A. The second ship, Air Vehicle 2, is in the background. (DARPA)

Structural Mode Interaction (SMI) testing of the first Boeing X-45A UCAV demonstrator during the spring of 2001. (DARPA)

The Boeing X-45A Air Vehicle 1 in formation flight with a NASA F/A-18 Hornet over Edwards AFB. (NASA photo by Jim Ross)

The underside of the X-45A UCAV with its weapons bay door open during tests on 1 February 2003. (NASA photo by Lori Losey)

Dropping a JDAM during weapons tests involving the first Boeing X-45A UCAV demonstrator. (NASA photo by Jim Ross)

The X-45A Flight Operations Control Center (FOCC) during May 2002 flight testing. (DARPA)

The second Boeing X-45A UCAV demonstrator on its takeoff roll at Edwards AFB for its first flight on 25 November 2002. (NASA photo by Jim Ross)

Larry Birckelbaw, DARPA's UCAV program manager, explained that Phase I "Challenged the industry teams to truly 'think out of the box' and to let the mission requirements drive them to an overall, optimized system solution . . . Overcoming the technical challenges to conduct these demanding and dangerous missions with an unmanned system will provide the warfighter with a revolutionary capability that saves lives."

It was on 24 March 1999 that DARPA and the Air Force selected Boeing—specifically the Phantom Works component, created by McDonnell Douglas before its merger with Boeing. The contract called for Phantom Works to proceed with the 42-month second phase, the development, fabrication, and flight testing of two X-45A demonstrator air vehicles and a reconfigurable mobile mission control station.

Lieutenant Colonel Michael Leahy, PhD, the Air Force's UCAV program manager, said that the industry teams had "Pushed this concept to the limits possible in a paper study. We're very excited to take the next step."

Leahy summarized the importance of the concept by observing that it would "exploit real-time on-board and off-board sensors for quick detection, identification, and location of fixed, relocatable, and mobile targets. The system's secure communications and advanced cognitive decision aids will provide ground-based, human operators with situational awareness and positive air vehicle control necessary to authorize munitions release."

Dave Swain, the executive vice president of Phantom Works, promised that his organization would draw upon "the extensive experience and resources Boeing has to offer in the areas of manned strike aircraft; weapon systems technology; unmanned air vehicles; and command, control, communications, computer, intelligence, surveillance, and reconnaissance technology."

Rich Alldredge, who was then the UCAV program manager at Phantom Works, added, "Removing the pilot

Boeing X-45A Air Vehicle 1 touches down at Edwards AFB on 1 August, 2004, as the F/A-18 chase plane cruises overhead. (DARPA)

Both Boeing X-45A UCAV demonstrators on the ramp at the Dryden Flight Research Center on 11 July 2002, with the UCAV program's T-33 chase plane posed in the background. Air Vehicle 1 is color-coded in blue, its sister ship in red. (Author photo)

The Flight Operations Control Center (FOCC) for the X-45A was similar to those used for operations of other unmanned aerial vehicles before and since. From the outside, the mobile FOCC looked very much like a motor home. (Author photo)

eliminates the need for pilot systems and interfaces, and allows for a smaller, simpler aircraft. No sorties are required for pilot training, and UCAVs can be placed in flight-ready storage for years, eliminating consumables, maintenance, and personnel requirements."

The X-45A airframe took shape at the former McDonnell facility at Lambert Field near St. Louis, while the mission control system was developed by Boeing in Seattle, and other Boeing facilities in southern California and Arizona also contributed to the project.

Roll-out of the first X-45A airframe came at a ceremony in St. Louis on 27 September 2000, with a large audience of customers, suppliers, and employees on hand. The futuristic airframe was about 26 feet long, with a wingspan of nearly 34 feet. With no vertical tail surfaces, "height" is a misnomer in listing specifications. The fuselage is 3 feet 7 inches thick at its thickest. The X-45A weighed approximately 8,000 pounds empty, and had the ability to carry a 3,000-pound payload in two weapons bays.

For flight-test purposes, one bay would be fitted with an instrumentation pallet so that crews can have easy access to evaluate test results between flights. The other would eventually be tested as an active weapons bay.

The plan called for the X-45A—like existing UAVs and intended future UCAVs—to be designed so that it could be broken down and packed in a shipping crate. This delivery-truck-sized container was designed so that a half dozen of them would fit into the cargo hold of an Air Force C-17 Globemaster. It was said that operational UCAVs could be stored in ready-to-ship containers for years until they were needed. At that point, they could be deployed in their containers along with their mobile Mission Control Station (MCS). When the need arose, the container-packed UCAVs would be flown to a forward location within an 800-mile radius of the intended target. Crews would then unpack and assemble them, a task which is intended to take just a few hours for each. Meanwhile, the MCS would be made ready and the strike mission would be launched.

The X-45A Air Vehicle 1 was airlifted from St. Louis to the NASA Dryden Flight Research Center at Edwards AFB in California on 9 November 2000. The second X-45A would follow on 15 May 2001.

Even as American forces were conducting the first missions of Operation Enduring Freedom in Afghanistan, the Air Force was preparing for the flight testing the X-45A. At Dryden, low speed taxi tests would begin on 26 September 2001, followed by the first high speed test on 21 March 2002. The long-anticipated first flight of Air Vehicle 1 came two months later on 22 May successfully demonstrating flight characteristics and basic operations, especially the command and control link between the X-45A and its controller on the ground. During this 14-minute debut, the aircraft reached an airspeed of 225 mph and an altitude of 7,500 feet.

Air Vehicle 2 made entered the program with a first flight exactly six months later on 22 November. Color coded in red and white to distinguish it from the blue and white Air Vehicle 1, it flew for a half hour, matching the speed and altitude of its sister ship's first flight.

The two birds started flying coordinated flight tests, as the joint demonstration program began on 28 April 2003. These flights of both X-45As were seen by DARPA as the technical heart of the program and "the key to unlocking the transformational potential of the weapon system."

All the flights were controlled from the prototype X-45A mobile MCS, a "trailer" about the size of an average travel trailer, that was similar to control stations then in use for operational reconnaissance UAVs.

24 March 2004 marked the first day that an Unmanned Aerial Vehicle designed specifically for strike missions actually delivered ordnance. An X-45A dropped an inert 250-pound bomb released over the Precision Impact Range Area in the Southern California desert near Edwards AFB. The unguided weapon was released from the aircraft's internal weapons bay at 35,000 feet while the X-45A was flying at approximately 442 mph.

"What an historic day for aviation!" effused George Muellner, the former Air Force general who was now the general manager of Boeing Air Force Systems. "Our team has shown the world that an autonomous unmanned combat aircraft can respond to human direction and successfully release a weapon from an internal bay. It also demonstrated the combat capability of the X-45 J-UCAS and how it will become a revolutionary force enabler capable of conducting attacks in high-threat environments."

Nearly a year later, on 14 February 2005, the two X-45As marked the program's 50th flight with their first simulated combat mission, an exercise called Peacekeeper (not to be confused with the ICBM of the same name). The two X-45As departed Edwards AFB, climbing to altitudes of 24,500 and 25,500 feet, while separated by approximately 25 miles. Flying at Mach .65, the mission was a combat air patrol simulating a SEAD mission.

On the ground, two simulated "pop-up ground threats" would be the targets. When the first one "popped up," the X-45As autonomously determined which of them held the "optimum position, weapons, and fuel load to properly attack the target." Having done so, the X-45As changed course, and the pilot-operator on the ground "allowed it" to attack the simulated target. A second target soon popped up and was hit.

The Peacekeeper software that permitted this successful operation had undergone, according to Boeing, 2,800 hours of testing in "a high fidelity System Integration Laboratory," as well as flight testing in the T-33 "X-45A surrogate" aircraft.

"With nearly three years of X-45A test experience completed, our next challenge was to show that our unmanned systems can handle the pop-up threats that are common in warfare," exclaimed Darryl Davis, Boeing's X-45A program manager. "We've begun demonstrating that with this mission."

A pair of X-45Cs as they might have appeared during a deep penetration mission. (DARPA)

Boeing X-45C

Even before the Peacekeeper exercise, Boeing and the Air Force were taking the next step toward transforming the X-45A concept into an operational weapons system. The plan had been for the two X-45A Advanced Technology Demonstrators to be followed by a full-scale X-45B test aircraft, and finally an operational UCAV. In 2002, as this author discovered during a series of briefings he attended at Edwards AFB, the operational aircraft was already being tentatively discussed under the unofficial designation A-45.

In the meantime, the X-45B was to have looked like a scaled up variation on the X-45A. It would have been larger than the X-45A—about 32 feet long and 4 feet thick, with a wingspan of 47 feet. According to the plan, the operational UCAV was seen as having the same dimensions as the X-45B.

However, a few months later, in early 2003, DARPA and the U.S. Air Force began to rethink this scheme. Acknowledging the growing problems of access to distant landlocked theaters, such as Afghanistan, where U.S. forces were then in combat, UCAV planners reconsidered. They revised the operational goals of the UCAV program for increased payload, range, and endurance.

As a result of this rethinking, the X-45B was canceled and replaced by the X-45C concept. It was different from the X-45A in appearance, but it was about the same size as the X-45B would have been. Built to include two full weapons bays, the X-45C air vehicle prototype was intended to have provisions for a synthetic aperture radar (SAR), electronic support measures (ESM), MILSTAR satellite interface, and aerial refueling. The avionics pallet of the X-45A would be replaced in the X-45C with a fully integrated avionics suite.

Like the X-45A, the X-45C was intended to incorporate low-observable "stealth" technology. As with the X-45A, there would be no vertical tail on the X-45C. Although the X-45A aircraft both had nose probes for testing purposes, the X-45C and notional "A-45" would be "clean." As David Lanman, deputy chief of UCAV advanced technology demonstration at AFRL put it: "UCAV systems [must be] as low-observable as possible, to achieve their intended missions . . . If you had a radar antenna or refueling boom projecting into the air from the surface of a UCAV, that would significantly cut down on its mandated stealthiness."

In 2003, as the concept was taking shape, the X-45C aircraft were being thought of as rugged prototypes that *could* be used in operational situations. This was in contrast to the X-45As, which had been built solely as technology demonstrators. As the X-45C was being planned, the Air Force envisioned that it could be deployed with gravity bombs, as well as GBU-31 and GBU-32 Joint Direct Attack Munitions (JDAMs) as well as other guided air-to-surface weapons.

Two notional Boeing X-45Cs race a storm as they fly a hypothetical mission deep into enemy territory. (DARPA)

The naval version of the Boeing X-45C J-UCAS as it might have appeared during a carrier landing. (DARPA)

A front view of the Northrop Grumman X-47A Pegasus at its rollout on 30 July 2001. (DARPA)

Northrop Grumman X-47A Pegasus

In the first years of the century, the U.S. Navy's UCAV-N program was on a development track slightly behind that of the X-45A, which was being run by DARPA as a U.S. Air Force program. The requirement of the initial UCAV-N study was to demonstrate the technical feasibility for a stealthy UCAV system to accomplish generally the same tasks that were planned for the Air Force UCAV, including surveillance, strike, and Suppression of Enemy Air Defenses (SEAD)—but to do them while operating from an aircraft carrier.

Both Boeing's Phantom Works and Northrop Grumman's Integrated Systems Sector (ISS) were working to develop this naval UCAV, with the experimental designations X-46A and X-47A assigned to the Boeing and Northrop Grumman aircraft respectively in June 2001. Boeing's UCAV-N, which would have been similar to the X-45C, never made it off the drawing board, but Northrop Grumman went to the other extreme. Corporate management made the decision to use company funds to build an actual flying aircraft as a demonstration of their proposal for the UCAV-N.

Named Pegasus, this prototype was first revealed in its preliminary design configuration in February 2001 by Northrop Grumman's new Advanced Systems Development Center in El Segundo, California. While the demonstrator carried the designation X-47A, a refined UCAV-N prototype, built under the U.S. Navy/DARPA UCAV-N program would be designated as X-47B.

In the design process, Northrop Grumman drew on its considerable recent high-technology tactical aircraft experience, including the design and development of the B-2 Spirit—the original stealth bomber—and the RQ-4 Global Hawk, which was the largest tactical reconnaissance UAV yet deployed. The company also had a substantial background in systems integration with its E-8 Joint Surveillance Target Attack Radar System (J-STARS) aircraft, the E-2C Hawkeye airborne early warning command and control aircraft, and its significant role in the McDonnell Douglas (now Boeing) F/A-18 Hornet and Super Hornet strike fighter aircraft.

Though conceived and designed at Northrop Grumman ISS in El Segundo, California, the actual Pegasus airframe was built mostly of non-metal composite materials at Scaled Composites in Mojave, California. Scaled Composites itself has an impressive pedigree, being owned and operated by the legendary Burt Rutan, the creator of numerous extraordinary aircraft from NASA's Proteus high-altitude research aircraft to

Voyager, the first—and to date, only—aircraft to circumnavigate the earth nonstop.

Pegasus rolled out at the Scaled Composites facility in Mojave on 30 July 2001, ten months after the debut of the X-45A. The kite-shaped aircraft was 27 feet 11 inches long with a nearly equal wingspan of just under 27 feet 10 inches. With no vertical tail surfaces, the X-47A stood just 6 feet above the tarmac. At the roll-out, Scott Seymour, the vice president for Northrop Grumman's Air Combat Systems, commented, "UAVs represent a transformational capability that can cost-effectively augment manned systems. We are working closely with our customers to leverage the synergy of manned and unmanned aircraft to accomplish current and future mission requirements."

When the phrase "future mission requirements" left his lips, little could Seymour have predicted the dramatic shift in the concept of military application of UAVs that would abruptly occur as a result of events that would

An "under the chin" look at the Northrop Grumman X-47A Pegasus on 30 July 2001. Note the company's Pegasus product logo, featuring the mythological flying horse of the same name. (DARPA)

take place just six weeks later on 11 September.

After a series of engine run tests between December 2001 and March 2002, and a successful autonomous start and shutdown of the aircraft's Pratt & Whitney JT15D-5C turbofan engine in April, the Pegasus began taxi tests in July, one year after roll-out. The first flight of the X-47A came on 23 February 2003 at China Lake, nine months after the maiden flight of the Boeing X-45A. As fully configured for flight operations, the Pegasus weighed 3,835 pounds dry, with a total fuel capacity of 1,580 pounds. The JT15D-5C provided 3,200 pounds of thrust.

Having successfully lifted off at 7:56 am, the Pegasus touched down 12 minutes later near a pre-designated point to simulate the tailhook capture point on an aircraft carrier flight deck, and thus to demonstrate the landing accuracy of the X-47A's "shipboard-relative" global positioning satellite system. Gary Ervin of Northrop Grumman's Air Combat Systems observed later that morning, "Regular unmanned flight operations aboard a flight deck at sea have never been attempted, and Pegasus addressed some of those key concerns today."

The X-47A, like the X-45A, was intended as a demonstrator aircraft that would evolve into a later tactical configuration that would look somewhat different than the "A" model. Just as the X-45A was intended to have evolved into the X-45B and later the X-45C, Northrop Grumman refined the look of its X-47A into an X-47B. This configuration was formally unveiled on 15 April 2003.

The design of the X-47B included the kite-shaped aerodynamics of the X-47A Pegasus, but added short wings shaped like the outer wing sections of the Northrop B-2. As such, the kite shape was blended into a flying wing shape that increased the overall wingspan by about a third. As the company explained it, the kite design enabled "efficient integration of propulsion and weapons, while the wing extensions provide aerodynamic efficiency."

The new design was also aimed at affording the tactical variant longer endurance, as well as "high survivability

The Northrop Grumman X-47A Pegasus takes off on its first flight from NAS China Lake on 23 February 2003. (DARPA)

and the low-speed, aerodynamic flying qualities for precision landing and autonomous launch and recovery [aircraft carrier] operations."

DARPA formally approved the X-47B configuration two weeks later on 1 May 2003, awarding Northrop Grumman a contract worth up to $160 million to produce and demonstrate full-scale X-47B UCAV aircraft. This formal approval of the X-47B coincided with DARPA's decision to merge the X-45 UCAV program and the X-47 UCAV-N program into the single joint project under its new Joint Unmanned Combat Air Systems (J-UCAS) Office.

Three Years as a Joint Program

Having entered the official lexicon five years earlier, the term Unmanned Combat Air Vehicle (UCAV) was superseded in April 2003 by the term Joint Unmanned Combat Air Systems (J-UCAS). Located with DARPA's other offices in Arlington, Virginia, the new J-UCAS office was opened in October, staffed by representatives from DARPA, as well as both the Air Force and the Navy. DARPA would remain as the lead agency until November 2005, at which time, they would step away and J-UCAS would exist briefly as a true *joint* Navy-Air Force program.

Administratively, the idea was to bring both the X-45, which was primarily a U.S. Air Force program, and the X-47, mainly a U.S. Navy project, under the same umbrella. Both programs had a great deal in common. Previously, the two separate programs had been specifically targeted toward their service-specific needs, but the Defense Department now recognized the potential for "significant synergy" by combining them. Though destined for separate military services, both aircraft were generally in the same size and weight class, and both were designed to be autonomous, unmanned, stealth attack aircraft.

In addition, J-UCAS specifically sought to reduce administrative and acquisition costs, as well as operation and support costs. At the time, DARPA noted the various features that the two programs had in common, but which were distinct from other combat aircraft. "Removing the pilot from the vehicle eliminates man-rating requirements, pilot systems, and interfaces." DARPA reported, "New design philosophies can be used to optimize the design for aerodynamics, signature, reduced maintenance, and low cost manufacturing processes."

Between the lines, the press release added that merging two parallel columns of bureaucracy and redundancy would also reduce cost.

Whether they were acronymed as UCAV or UCAS, in 2003, the Pentagon was very committed to the idea of unmanned *combat* aircraft, just as it was to reconnaissance UAVs. Released in March of that year, the Department of Defense report that was entitled *Unmanned Aerial Vehicles Roadmap*, articulated an integrated policy for unmanned aerial vehicles that outlined the development of such aircraft for the quarter century

ending in 2027. The executive summary of the document noted that, "The overarching goal of this roadmap, in concert with the Defense Planning Guidance (DPG), is to define clear direction to the Services and Departments for a logical, systematic migration of mission capabilities to a new class of military tools. The goal is to address the most urgent mission needs that are supported both technologically and operationally by various UAV systems."

The report noted that, "Some missions can be supported by the current state of the art in unmanned technology," but that there were "Other mission areas . . . in desperate need of additional capability and present high risk to aircraft crews. These mission areas, highlighted in this roadmap, will receive significant near-term effort by the Department."

As often happens inside the Pentagon, roadmaps have a shelf life far shorter than a quarter century, and this roadmap was succeeded by another that was signed off upon in August 2005, intending to chart the course to 2030. The mission areas in both UAV roadmaps included *offensive* combat operations, and need to allocate resources to meet the twenty-first century need for a program like J-UCAS.

As had been the case under the earlier, separate UCAV programs, the *Joint*-UCAS program would continue to be conducted in a confusing series of "multiple overlapping spirals" of increasing capability that moved toward the system of objectives.

The first such spiral was designated "Spiral Zero," though it was not to be confused with the earlier "Spiral Zero" evaluation that the X-45A had previously undergone. The new Spiral Zero would involve the two existing X-45A and a single X-47A demonstrator aircraft, along with all their associated simulation, mission control, and support systems.

The succeeding Spiral One would involve evaluation of the stealthy X-45C and X-47B full-scale demonstrators.

When envisioned back in 2003, these were seen as spiralling into aircraft that were the same size and configuration as the ultimate tactical aircraft, which were then being referred to informally—and over optimistically—as "A-45" and "A-47."

Boeing began assembly of the first X-45C in early June 2004, and unveiled a full-scale mock-up of the aircraft at the Farnborough International Air Show in the United Kingdom on 19 July 2004. The mock-up, 39 feet long with a 49-foot wingspan, continued to make the rounds. Its June 2005 appearance at the 2005 Naval Unmanned Aerial Vehicle Air Demo held at the Webster Field Annex of NAS Patuxent River underscored the notion that Boeing was promoting their "jointness" of their X-45C vehicle as a potential future competitor for the Pegasus as a possible naval UCAS.

In October 2004, Boeing announced that DARPA awarded the company $767 million in funding, "to continue the X-45C portion of the Joint Unmanned Combat Air Systems (J-UCAS) demonstration program over the

Preferred parking. Placed on display, this mock-up of the Northrop Grumman X-47B J-UCAS crowds the handicapped parking spaces of an empty parking lot. The "B model" is based on the "A model," but incorporates short, swept wings. (Northrop Grumman)

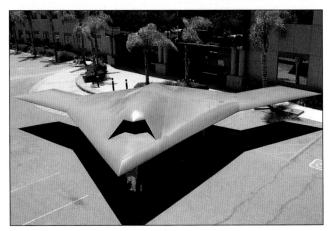

next five years . . . to design, develop, and demonstrate three full-scale, flight-worthy air vehicles and two mission control elements." This was, according to Jane's Information Group, in addition to the $291 million then under contract. In July 2005, the company announced an additional $175 million in X-45C funding, that was, in part to include a "full demonstration of a new Autonomous Aerial Refueling technology . . . [that would] culminate in

This photo of the Northrop Grumman X-47B J-UCAS with other carrier aircraft Photoshopped into the background shows the aircraft's folding wing feature, a must for carrier operations. (Northrop Grumman)

In this artist's conception, an X-47B J-UCAS, possibly inbound from a carrier, makes landfall over a cratered coastline. (DARPA)

An operational X-47B of VAR-95 shares deck space with an F/A-18 Hornet on the flight deck of the USS Ronald Reagan *in this artist's conception.* (DARPA)

an in-flight X-45C refueling by a KC-135 tanker in 2010."

Having passed the Mid-Term Design Review with the X-45C in 2004, Boeing confidently planned a first flight in 2006. Indeed, the X-45 program was the winner of a 2005 Flight International Aerospace Industry Award. However, by late 2005 it was planned that the X-45C's first flight would not occur until the spring of 2007.

Then came the Pentagon's February 2006 Quadrennial Defense Review, and a decision to cancel the J-UCAS program, or at least the "jointness" of it, and to terminate the X-45C entirely. The program changed to a Navy-only program, preserving the X-47, and the acronym changed to UCAS-N. The U.S. Air Force, meanwhile, was seen to have traded the X-45C for a new strategic bomber program, called Next Generation Long Range Strike (NGLRS) and then referred to informally as "B-3."

Ironically, this announcement came just three months after DARPA had handed J-UCAS over to the services, and only a week before Boeing was ready to roll out the first X-45C aircraft.

As Tim McLaughlin wrote in the 2 March 2006 issue of the *St. Louis Post-Dispatch*, "Boeing's first St. Louis-made X-45C, an unmanned robotic plane designed for the Air Force, is shiny and new, and ready to roll. But there's a problem. It has no place to go. The Pentagon doesn't want the X-45C. The Joint Unmanned Combat Air Systems program, which included nearly $800 million to build three X-45C planes, officially has been scrapped. Boeing confirmed Tuesday that it had canceled a VIP ceremony scheduled this month to mark the delivery of the first X-45C to the Air Force."

Jim Albaugh, the chief executive of Boeing's St. Louis defense operations, mused, "programs come and go, but if you have the right capabilities, you're going to be OK over the long haul . . . These programs have been restructured and canceled and resurrected a half dozen times over the last couple of years . . . and I think we'll be in good shape as these programs get reconfigured."

Albaugh went on to say that Boeing would go after the same Navy contract for which Northrop Grumman had the inside track with the X-47. As McLaughlin reported, "Boeing said it believes the X-45C's technology can be crafted to meet the Navy's concept for using robotic planes to gather intelligence and conduct long-range surveillance and reconnaissance missions from aircraft carriers."

David Fulghum had written in *Aviation Week* in 2003, quoting an unnamed Air Force official, that Boeing already had a separate and classified UAV that served as "a testbed for designing and testing new stealth capabilities . . . [and] a modular design that allows company researchers to fly it in various shapes and configurations. For example, different wings, tails, and noses have been tested on the aircraft."

In April 2006, Jane's Information Group published its Executive Overview on unmanned aerial vehicles. The groups' UAV Editor Kenneth Munson, headlined the piece with the phrase "All roads lead to . . . where?"

Referring to the 2005 UAV Roadmap, Munson observed that it had "bounced around the Pentagon for nearly six months beyond its expected issue date [only to have] already undergone its first major change of direction, barely a further six months into the 25-year period for which it was designed."

He went on to report that the budget was reduced for the Northrop Grumman X-47B, with the elimination of a planned third prototype.

Several months later, in October 2006, after 64 flights, the two X-45A UCAVs were formally retired and turned out to pasture as museum pieces. One went to the National Museum of the U.S. Air Force at Wright-Patterson AFB in Ohio, and the other to the Smithsonian's National Air and Space Museum in Washington, D.C.

The first chapter in the story of the dedicated Unmanned Air Combat Vehicle had begun with a flurry of promise and enthusiasm, only to sputter to a whimpering halt. But that, as they say, was just the end of the beginning.

Polecat

Outside the confines of J-UCAS, the Lockheed Martin Skunk Works had also been developing a similar aircraft on its own during the early years of the century. Designated by the company as Unmanned System P-175, the aircraft was name Polecat, a term which is synonymous with "Skunk" in American slang.

According to comments that Frank Mauro, Lockheed Martin's director of unmanned systems, made to *Aviation Week*'s Amy Butler, the company undertook the project against the backdrop of a perception within the industry that it had abandoned unmanned aerial vehicle technology after DarkStar.

"We've taken some hard shots in the past three or four years that [we were] not in the UAS game, and there is a perception that our future is at risk. We are putting our money where our mouth is."

The money totalled $27 million over a period of 18 months. Mauro added that the cost of the Polecat's development was a "significant" share of the company's research aircraft budget during this period. However, it is also significant that the Polecat was developed in a year and a half, a very short time to bring an aircraft that involves innovative technology from initial concept to first flight. In the case of the Polecat, the first flight took place in complete secrecy during 2004, at the same time that the well-known X-45 program was in test flight.

Built 98 percent of composite materials, the Polecat had a wingspan of 90 feet, compared to 33 feet 10 inches in the X-45A, and 19.5 feet for the X-47A. An innovative "twisting strut" inside the Polecat's wings had, according to Lockheed, been designed to "flex in air and improve the laminar flow over its swept wings, propelling the UAV to high altitudes."

Lockheed Martin also pioneered a low-temperature curing process for composites used in the aircraft. In this case, the composites were cured at only 150 degreesF, rather than the 350 degrees of a conventional autoclave. The idea was cost savings.

The intended operational altitude of the Polecat was specified at 60,000 feet, much greater than that of the X-45A or X-47A. Frank Cappuccio, executive vice president and general manager of Advanced Development Programs and Strategic Planning at Lockheed Martin, later said, "No one has ever developed in this configuration a high lift-to-drag ratio, and we are going to do it

The Lockheed Martin P-175 Polecat is seen here during an early flight test. This photograph was released at the Farnborough Air Show in June 2006, six months before the aircraft was lost in a crash. (Lockheed Martin)

higher than anyone has done it . . . [the Polecat] was specifically designed to verify three things: new, cost effective rapid prototyping and manufacturing techniques of composite materials; projected aerodynamic performance required for sustained high altitude operations; and flight autonomy attributes. In addition, the company investment and the resulting successful flights are proof positive of our commitment to developing the next inflection point in unmanned systems."

The Polecat had a gross weight of 9,000 pounds, and was powered by two FJ44-3E Williams International engines. Polecat was designed with a payload bay between the wings that could accommodate a half ton of sensors, recon gear, or weapons.

It was not until the occasion of the Farnborough International Air Show in England in July 2006 that Lockheed Martin chose to reveal the existence of the unmanned aerial demonstrator to the public. In so doing, Frank Cappuccio called the Polecat "an effort to better understand the flight dynamics of a tailless unmanned air system in support of our ongoing research and development work for the U.S. Air Force's future Long Range Strike Program as well as to field the next generation of structural composite concepts."

It is important to point out an important design feature shared by the X-45, the X-47 *and* the Polecat. None of these aircraft were designed with vertical tail surfaces. The Northrop B-2 Spirit "all wing" stealth bomber, which first flew in 1989 was such an aircraft, but this design feature was still considered very leading edge technology. This was despite the fact that this technology had been pioneered near a half century earlier in Germany by the brothers Walter and Reimer Horten. (The Horten IX, designated as Go.229, had made its first

powered flight in February 1945 at Oranienburg after a year of unpowered glide tests.)

It was in the *Aviation Week* report of the Polecat unveiling that Amy Butler specifically described the configuration as a "tailless 'Horton' [sic] wing design."

While Cappuccio mentioned that the Polecat was being considered as an Air Force long-range bomber, there was also some media speculation that the Polecat might be offered for consideration under the U.S. Navy's Broad Area Maritime Surveillance program.

Cappuccio also alluded to the stealthiness of the Polecat, noting that the engine intakes were masked to deflect radar, and explaining that without vertical structures and a tail, the aircraft was "inherently low-observable" though it had not been "coated" with radar-reflecting material because "it is not expected to fly operationally."

Though the aircraft was not to be flown operationally, Lockheed had big plans in mind to use the Polecat in an ambitious series of high altitude test flights—and hoping to induce some orders from the tight-fisted government that had pulled the plug on the J-UCAS program earlier in the year. However, it was not to be.

On 18 December 2006, over the Nevada Test Range north of Nellis AFB, the sole Polecat prototype suffered what Lockheed Martin characterized as an "irreversible unintentional failure in the flight termination ground equipment, which caused the aircraft's automatic fail-safe flight termination mode to activate."

The aircraft was lost in the ensuing crash.

In March 2007, *Flight International* reported that the notion of "building a replacement" for the Polecat was under consideration. Indeed a company statement affirmed that "it is certainly being discussed."

CHAPTER FOUR

DEPLOYING WARPLANES
INSIDE THE SANDBOX

MQ-1 Predators from the 46th Expeditionary Strike and Reconnaissance Squadron, ready at Joint Base Balad in Iraq, before a mission launch in July 2006. (U.S. Air Force photo by Master Sergeant Jonathan Doti)

As the first chapter in the story of unmanned aircraft being built from the ground up as warplanes closed with the J-UCAS cancellation in 2006, there were two real wars raging, and unmanned aerial vehicles were routinely flying real combat missions. As the UCAV and UCAS programs flew on for years without firing a shot, UAVs born as passive drones were both taking fire and shooting back. The spindly little RQ-1 had done more to perpetuate the combat cred of UAVs than either the UCAV or UCAS.

After 17 months of Operation Enduring Freedom operations in Afghanistan, the United States, the United Kingdom, and other Coalition partners launched Operation Iraqi Freedom on 19 March 2003. Though Saddam Hussein's regime was toppled and his army defeated in six weeks, the war in Iraq would devolve into a deadly, low-intensity war of attrition that would drag on for years.

In those first six weeks, however, the defeat of Iraqi conventional forces was a decisive one, in which Coalition superiority in weapons and technology shone brightly.

Among those which shone brightest were the Predator and other UAVs. In a 26 March briefing, Dyke Weatherington, then deputy of the Defense Department's UAV planning task force, noted the many types of UAVs that were then serving in Iraqi skies. In discussing the "broad range of capabilities" that they were bringing to their support of the troops, he listed the U.S. Army's RQ-5 Hunter, FQM-151 Pointer, and RQ-7 Shadow; the Marine Corps' RQ-2 Pioneer and tiny RQ-14 Dragon Eye; as well as the RQ-4 Global Hawk and RQ-1 Predator.

The Air Force had Predators in the vicinity of Baghdad from the beginning of the war, and Global Hawks over Baghdad, operating in a continuous orbit running as far north as Kirkuk and Urbil.

Several Predators were sent in low over Baghdad early in the war. Having had their sensor systems pulled out, they were intended as decoys to entice Iraqi surface-to-air missile sites to lock on with their radar, so that the sites could be identified and attacked by manned aircraft fielding radar-guided munitions.

Much to the surprise of Air Force commanders, most Predators survived this decoy mission. One, however, went down in the Tigris River in the heart of Baghdad. Iraqi television crews were dispatched to film a frantic search for the pilot of the downed aircraft. Dozens of uniformed and civilian men took part in the search, but the pilot was never found. He was hundreds of miles away in his control station.

Meanwhile, the Global Hawks provided much of the theater-wide strategic reconnaissance upon which the senior planners at CENTCOM based their day-to-day war plans. Indeed, when offensive operations practically ground to a halt during the sandstorms that raged from 24 to 27 March, Global Hawks casually observed enemy troop movements using their synthetic aperture radar to look through the swirling sand as though it was not

Deputy for the Unmanned Aerial Vehicles Planning Task Force, Office of the Secretary of Defense, Dyke Weatherington briefs reporters on the UAV Roadmap report during a Pentagon press conference on 18 March 2003. The UAV Roadmap outlines development of unmanned aircraft for the next 25 years. On 25 February 2008 he was reassigned as deputy director, unmanned warfare, Office of the Under Secretary of Defense. (Acquisition, Technology and Logistics), Washington, D.C. (Defence Department photo by Helene Stikkel)

there. A Global Hawk working in cooperation with an E-8 Joint Surveillance Target Attack Radar System (J-STARS) aircraft is credited with providing tactical commanders with the data that resulted in the virtual obliteration of the Iraqi Medina Armored Division.

The RQ-4s operated with much the same payload package as the manned U-2s, but, while the U-2 pilots had to land in order to sleep, RQ-4 pilots simply turned the controls over to another pilot while the aircraft itself remained aloft on its 24- to 40-hour mission. When the big aircraft landed at bases, such as in Qatar, the turnaround time for the next mission was relatively short. According to Tim Beard of Northrop Grumman, this turnaround time was as little as eight hours.

There were other recon drones in action during those operations. In its 6 July 2003 issue, Aviation Week magazine reported, "a classified Lockheed Martin unmanned reconnaissance aircraft" was also used during the Iraq operations—nearly a year ahead of the Polecat's debut. As David Fulghum wrote in the magazine, "the aircraft is described by a U.S. Air Force official as a derivative of the DarkStar program that was canceled after the demonstration aircraft was test flown and then declared operationally unsuitable . . . The classified UAVs operation caused consternation among U.S. Air Force U-2 pilots who noticed high-flying aircraft operating within several miles of their routes over Iraq, a distance they considered too close for comfort. The mysterious aircraft's flights were not coordinated with those of the other manned and unmanned surveillance aircraft."

Said the same unnamed official, "It's the same concept as DarkStar, it's stealthy, and it uses the same apertures and data links. The numbers are limited. There are a couple of airframes, a ground station, and spare parts."

A second "Air Force official" who once had oversight of UAV and UCAV programs told Fulghum that the mystery Lockheed Martin UAV was a "DarkStar-like thing."

Even not counting this "Son of DarkStar," the opening six weeks of Operation Iraqi Freedom had been a watershed moment in the history of warfare. Only three UAV types, Global Hawk, Pointer, and Predator, had seen service over Afghanistan, and only the Pioneer had been used the last time the West went to war against Saddam Hussein in 1991.

By 2003, it seemed that UAVs were so important that a modern army dare not go to war without them.

Predators At War

For the first time in history, armed unmanned aerial vehicles were an accepted part of the routine weapons mix well before the opening moments of a conflict. In

An MQ-1 Predator with the 46th Expeditionary Reconnaissance and Attack Squadron prepares to land at Joint Base Balad in Iraq, after a mission on 8 November. Predators provide armed intelligence, surveillance and reconnaissance capabilities for ground force commanders. (U.S. Air Force photo by Tech Sergeant Erik Gudmundson)

Lieutenant Colonel Geoffrey Barnes performs a preflight inspection of an MQ-1 Predator unmanned aircraft system at Ali (formerly Tallil) Air Base in Iraq. Barnes commanded the 46th Expeditionary Reconnaissance and Attack Squadron Detachment 1, deployed from Creech AFB, Nevada. (U.S. Air Force photo by Airman 1st Class Christopher Griffin)

turn, commanders on the ground came to expect, and to rely heavily on the utility of the Predators as the ground war extended across Iraq and met with more concentrated enemy resistance.

Lieutenant General Walter Buchanan, commander of U.S. Air Force's Ninth Air Force and U.S. Central Command Air Forces (CENTAF), has spoken of how the perception of the tactical value of UAVs—especially the Predator—had evolved. Looking back at the Southern Watch operations that preceded Iraqi Freedom, Buchanan recalled that in the mission briefings, the commander would "get up and say, 'OK, we're going to have the F-15Cs fly here, the F-16s are going to fly there, the A-6s are going to fly here, tankers are going to be here today. Then he would say, 'And, oh by the way, way over here is going to be the Predator.' We don't go over there, and he's not going to come over here and bother us . . . It was almost like nobody wanted to talk to [Predator operators] . . . It wasn't too long before . . . people were incorporating the Predator into the mission plan."

As the generals took notice and scrambled to put the once overlooked tool to work to their advantage, it was the soldiers and Marines in harm's way who reaped the advantages in real time.

Staff Sergeant Theodore Muto, an MQ-1 Predator crew chief with the 432nd Aircraft Maintenance Squadron, evaluates data from an MQ-1 engine run at Creech AFB, on 22 April 2009. MQ-1 crew chiefs were required to attend an engine-running class to maintain their certifications. (U.S. Air Force photo by Senior Airman Nadine Barclay)

"Not only does the Predator function as the eyes of the generals who are directing the air war, but it also serves as the eyes of young soldiers on the ground," wrote Lieutenant Colonel Lawrence Spinetta, who later commanded Predators for the 11th Reconnaissance Squadron. "It is very comforting when you are in harm's way to know that you have a technologically advanced aircraft circling over your position 24/7. The infantry solider may be asleep, but the Predator never is!"

The Predator's first *offensive* combat mission occurred three days into the war. On 22 March a USAF MQ-1 Predator remotely piloted by Major Mark Lilly found an Iraqi ZSU-23 mobile, radar-guided anti-aircraft artillery gun outside the town of al-Amarah—and took out not just the radar antenna, but the entire anti-aircraft complex with a single Hellfire missile.

An MQ-9 Reaper taxis into Creech AFB on 13 February 2007, marking the first operational airframe of its kind to land here. This Reaper was the first of many soon to be assigned to the 42nd Attack Squadron. (U.S. Air Force photo by Senior Airman Larry Reid, Jr.)

Flying missions averaging about 20 hours, Predators were operated remotely by a pilot and sensor operator working from a satellite-linked ground control station. Continuous real-time surveillance of the battlefield was passed along to the theater air component commander. The Predator teams also included crew chiefs and specialists in avionics, ground equipment, communications, satellite communications, munitions, and supply.

Initially, the principal operating base for Predators and other tactical UAVs was Ali al-Salem Air Base, just west of Kuwait City. Predators also operated from bases in Jordan, but as the war progressed, UAV operations were relocated to forward operating bases inside Iraq. Though "owned and operated" by the 11th Reconnaissance Squadron in Nevada, the Predators went into the theater assigned to the 386th Air Expeditionary Wing's 46th Expeditionary Reconnaissance Squadron, which was based at Tallil AB inside Iraq, when the base was secured.

During the March 2003 ground offensive, Predators provided ground commanders with real-time information about enemy forces that lay ahead, as the U.S. Army's 3rd Infantry Division headed north toward Baghdad. Said Air Force Captain Traz Trzaskoma, a Predator pilot, in an interview with Air Force Print News, "We've been watching for where the bad guys hide, move, or want to hide, and if we're carrying Hellfire missiles, we can take care of a target ourselves."

Using low light television (LLTV) and their real-time video stream, Predators were also an invaluable resource for special operations forces teams working behind enemy lines. "A special forces team was going into an area, and at the last minute we [told them] their landing zone wasn't the best," Trzaskoma said. "We helped change the mission at the last second. Then we helped them find a better place to land."

In May 2008, an MQ-1 Predator like this one crashed near Ali Base in Iraq. According to the Air Combat Command Accident Investigation Board report, the intermittent failure of the ignition module caused loss of power resulting in loss of thrust. The pilot was unable to recover thrust control. The ignition module assembly ultimately controls the spark to the engine cylinders to run the engine. (U.S. Air Force photo by Staff Sergeant Suzanne Jenkins)

Staff Sergeant Stephanie Hughes reviews loading procedures during weapons load training on 22 April 2009 at Creech AFB. MQ-9 Reaper load-crew members were conducting monthly training to maintain their qualifications on the airframe. Sergeant Hughes was a Reaper load-crew team chief assigned to the 432nd Aircraft Maintenance Squadron. (U.S. Air Force photo by Senior Airman Larry Reid, Jr.)

"The Predator gives 'ground-pounders' the opportunity to sneak a peek over the next hill, beyond the horizon, or down a side street along their travel route in a crowded city," Colonel Spinetta writes. "Amazingly, aircrew can set up the Predator to broadcast their images directly to a laptop computer that troops on the ground can carry into battle. The system's official name is "remote optical video enhanced receiver," but soldiers almost unanimously refer to it by its acronym, 'ROVER.'"

California Air National Guard MQ-1 Predator pilots meet in their hangar at March Air Reserve Base in November 2006 following the activation ceremony for the 196th Reconnaissance Squadron. (U.S. Air Force photo by Master Sergeant Mike Smith)

An MQ-1 Predator assigned to the Arizona Air National Guard's 214th Reconnaissance Group was parked in a hangar at Davis-Monthan AFB, Arizona, following the unit's activation in August 2007. (U.S. Air Force photo by Senior Airman Christina Kinsey)

A MQ-1B Predator from the 361st Expeditionary Reconnaissance Squadron takes off from Ali Base on 9 July 2008. (U.S. Air Force photo by Tech Sergeant Sabrina Johnson).

ROVER was used by the Joint Tactical Air Controllers (JTACs), the people on the ground responsible for approving close air support strikes. JTACs could see exactly what the Predator is looking at, "so all it takes is a quick glance at the screen to verify that the appropriate target is about to be hit so they can expeditiously give clearance to fire.

"Move the crosshairs an inch to the left!" Spinetta said, quoting the words uttered by a JTAC only moments before a Hellfire slammed into an enemy sniper position.

Of course, one of the remarkable aspects of UAVs over Iraq was that in many cases, they were operated by people who were nowhere near Iraq. As Richard Newman wrote in *Air Force Magazine*, "Hollywood has long portrayed the American military as all-knowing and capable of spellbinding technological feats. As the troops know, reality is often far less impressive. However, more than ever before, the front-line troops in Iraq relied on high-tech virtual warriors operating nowhere near the war zone. Hundreds of troops who typically would have

deployed to the theater stayed at their home bases in the United States and elsewhere, contributing to the success of the armed action through satellite and computer links, all without adding to the U.S. footprint in the region."

The U.S. Air Force had an entire 1,700-person intelligence group in a distributed ground station (DGS) at Langley AFB in Virginia, working 12-hour shifts to provide real-time intelligence support to Central Command (CENTCOM), directing U-2s and remote-controlling Predators. At one point during the first week of the war, Captain Bob Lyons got word that a Marine reconnaissance team near Basra reported it was surrounded by enemy troops and needing reinforcements. Lyons and his team used UAVs to assess the terrain and look for Iraqi activity near the potential helicopter landing zones. Real-time video showed the choppers with the reinforcements where to go and where not to go.

The DGS also conveyed Predator pictures of time sensitive targets such as convoys of enemy troops or mobile surface-to-air missiles to CENTCOM strike

Shilo Thompson and Brandon Walker load a Hellfire missile on an MQ-1B Predator in July 2008 at Ali Base in Iraq. The two aircraft mechanics were with the 361st Expeditionary Reconnaissance Squadron. (U.S. Air Force photo by Tech Sergeant Sabrina Johnson)

Three contract maintainers walk an RQ-1 Predator unmanned aerial vehicle into a shelter. They were assigned to the 46th Expeditionary Aircraft Maintenance Unit at Joint Base Balad in Iraq. The 46th Expeditionary Aircraft Maintenance Unit, responsible for maintaining the RQ-1s, was about half airmen and half contractors. Most of the contractors were prior military and about half were former airmen. (U.S. Air Force photo by Airman 1st Class Jason Ridder)

An MQ-1 Predator sits on the parking ramp in front of a bullet-pocked Saddam-era hangar at Joint Base Balad in Iraq. (U.S. Air Force photos by Staff Sergeant Tony Tolley)

Robert Attard works on an engine from an RQ-1 Predator. He was a contract maintainer assigned to the 46th Expeditionary Aircraft Maintenance Unit at Balad. (U.S. Air Force photo by Airman 1st Class Jason Ridder)

Senior Airman Jason Atwell operates a bomb lift while Staff Sergeant Stephanie Hughes and Senior Airman Gale Passe prepare to load an AGM-114 Hellfire II air-to-ground missile onto the MQ-9 Reaper. (U.S. Air Force photo by Senior Airman Nadine Barclay)

Captain Trevor Laribee checks the propeller during his pre-flight inspection on an MQ-1 Predator prior to takeoff from Ali Base in Iraq. He was assigned to the 361st Expeditionary Reconnaissance Squadron and was deployed from Creech AFB. (U.S. Air Force photo by Airman 1st Class Jonathan Snyder)

planners so that strike aircraft knew where to go and where not to go.

A Predator flown by Major John Breeden was provided surveillance for U.S. Marines and British commandos as they captured the oil fields near the al-Faw Peninsula in southern Iraq. Breed spotted a force of approximately 200 enemy troops preparing an ambush and was able to call in a U.S. Air Force AC-130 Specter gunship to hose down the Iraqi position with high caliber automatic weapons fire.

As troops on the battlefield quickly learned, one of the key advantages of the Predator is its unobtrusiveness. It is as stealthy to the human senses as an aircraft like an F-117 was to radar. "The Predator's engine is whisper-quiet," Colonel Spinetta said. "When it's operated at higher altitudes, folks on the ground can neither see nor hear the bird of prey above. The opposite, however, is not true."

As Colonel Spinetta points out, the Predator's Multi-spectral Targeting System (MTS), with its electro-optical and infrared cameras, and its laser designator and a laser illuminator, can track and target

Staff Sergeant Lance Nettrouer of the 361st Expeditionary Reconnaissance operates the sensors of an MQ-1 Predator during a mission over Iraq in December 2007. (U.S. Air Force photo by Airman 1st Class Jonathan Snyder)

An MQ-1 Predator unmanned aerial vehicle from the 361st Expeditionary Reconnaissance Squadron takes off from Ali Base for a mission over Iraq in December 2007. (U.S. Air Force photo by Airman 1st Class Jonathan Snyder)

"intimate details of its quarry below . . . You can, for example, clearly see and identify the loads of trash that litter the streets of Sadr City in Baghdad."

As might have been predicted, there was a exceptionally high operational demand for the services of a relatively small fleet of RQ-1 aircraft, and Predators were in service continuously. "With the enormous amount of hours we fly, our down time is almost nonexistent," said Sergeant Jeffery Duckett, a Predator maintenance superintendent. "What that means is that everyone has to perform top-notch maintenance every day to sustain our wartime taskings. Take away any one of these components, and our mission effectiveness degrades significantly."

Airman Jason Biselx, a Predator crew chief told *Air Force News*, "The main challenge of 24-hour ops with long-endurance missions is the amount of periodic and phased maintenance needed. Time-change items come up faster, phases arrive quicker, and major engine overhauls start to really stack up. During a one-week period early in Operation Iraqi Freedom, we had major engine overhauls every night. Another key challenge is fine tuning a small, dual-carbureted engine for high-altitude, long-endurance flight."

In October 2004, after three years of combat in Southwest Asia, the Predator force had logged 100,000 hours—with the Air Force alone—and was averaging 2,000 hours a month over Iraq and Afghanistan. That same month, Dyke Weatherington of the Pentagon's UAV Planning Task Force, told the Precision Strike Technology Symposium held in Laurel, Maryland, that such an accomplishment was "pretty remarkable when you realize that the system has not, at least officially, reached IOC [initial operational capability] yet."

He went on to summarize that, through October 2004, Predators had fired 115 Hellfires and laser-designated 525 targets for strikes by manned aircraft in Afghanistan, while in Iraq, the numbers were 62 and 146 respectively.

Nor were Predator operations in Southwest Asia limited to Afghanistan and Iraq. On 27 February 2005 David Fulghum reported in *Aviation Week* that the Predators operated by the CIA were flying missions over *Iran* from "airstrips in Kurdish-controlled areas of Iraq near the Iranian border" to monitor progress on the Iranian nuclear program.

As Fulghum pointed out, Iranian newspapers and even China's Xinhua News Agency in Tehran, had been publishing stories for months about "unidentified aircraft intruding into eastern and southwestern Iran. Local reports identified the intrusions as originating in Afghanistan and Iraq."

"The aircraft being flown over Iran belong to the CIA, not the Defense Department," a senior Air Force official told Fulghum. "They are using the I-Gnats and Predators [such as those that had been] used early in the Afghanistan war. They are not wide-area collectors like the Global Hawk. They focus on small areas, and that's what they need to find those dispersed [nuclear weapons

Airman 1st Class Justin Cole communicates with the pilot of an MQ-1 Predator in preparation for a night mission from Ali Base in Iraq in November 2007. (U.S. Air Force photo by Airman 1st Class Jonathan Snyder)

At Ali Base in Iraq, Airman 1st Class Justin Cole cleans the front sensor of an MQ-1 Predator. By November 2007, when this photo was taken, Predators were fully operational and flying 24-hour operations. (U.S. Air Force photo by Airman 1st Class Jonathan Snyder)

Conducting a pre-flight inspection on an MQ-1 Predator are Airman 1st Class Justin Cole, Tech Sergeant Marcus Cottengim, and Chief Master Sergeant Roy Cupper. (U.S. Air Force photo by Airman 1st Class Jonathan Snyder)

development] sites. The data are sent back to Beale [AFB in California, the Global Hawk home base] just like the Global Hawk imagery. The information is then separated by its code word [prefix] and sent to the proper agency."

Back in Iraq, the Predator was getting high marks, especially as a real-time "eyes in the sky" platform, from ground troops from both the U.S. Army and Marines. Commenting on Predator actions during Operation Spear in June 2007 in Anbar Province, Lieutenant Colonel Scott Wedemeyer of the 2nd Marine Aircraft Wing, said that the Predator "allows us to see threats that may be around a corner, behind, or maybe even on top, of a building . . . We were able to see what appeared to be the point of origin for the mortar attack. The [Predator] allowed us to investigate the site, confirm the enemy position, and attack it without putting our forces at any unnecessary risk . . . Tools like these allow us to shorten the engagement cycle."

By the summer of 2007, the 46th Expeditionary Squadron was averaging around 3,300 flying hours out of Balad Air Base each month.

"The sorties and hours are increasing as a result of increased demand," Major Jon Dagley explained in an August news release. "As [troops] continue to recognize how the Predator works, what it brings to the fight, and what it can do for them, its demand will only continue to skyrocket . . . The Predator is coming into its own as a no-kidding weapon versus a reconnaissance-only platform."

Indeed, a year later, Air Force Predators and Reapers were averaging more than 13,600 hours monthly worldwide, according to Lieutenant Colonel Michael Paoli.

Staff Sergeant Cole Moreland, an unmanned aircraft systems weather forecaster assigned to the 432nd Operation Support Squadron Weather Flight, produces mission execution forecasts and observing radars for flying RQ-9 Reaper missions. (U.S. Air Force photo by Senior Airman Larry Reid, Jr.)

Avionics mechanic Russell Gordy works on a cooling fan on an MQ-1 Predator after a perimeter surveillance mission over Joint Base Balad in Iraq. (Air Force photo by Airman 1st Class Jonathan Steffen)

An MQ-1B Predator aircraft taxies into a hangar here after a mission in August 2008. As reported by the Air Force at the time, a one-dollar headset modification made by Staff Sergeant Ray Stetler allows Predator pilots to use Voice Over Secure Internet Protocol communications through their headsets. Sergeant Stetler was the NCO in charge of base information and infrastructure for the 407th Expeditionary Communications Squadron at Ali Base in Iraq. (U.S. Air Force photo by Airman 1st Class Christopher Griffin)

Airman 1st Class Jesse Morse of the 46th Expeditionary Reconnaissance and Attack Squadron operates the onboard sensor of an MQ-1 Predator before take-off. Airmen at Creech AFB control Predators during much of their missions, but pilots and sensor operators in Iraq operated the aircraft during takeoff and landing. (U.S. Air Force photo by Staff Sergeant Don Branum)

Senior Airmen Gale Passe (left) and Jason Atwell prepare to load an AGM-114 Hellfire II air-to-ground missile onto a MQ-9. Load-crew members were also required to wear their gas mask to simulate loading in a hostile environment. Airmen Passe and Atwell were Reaper weapon loaders assigned to the 432nd Aircraft Maintenance Squadron. (U.S. Air Force photo by Senior Airman Larry Reid, Jr.)

A U.S. Air Force MQ-1B Predator, assigned to Detachment 1 of the 46th Expeditionary Reconnaissance Squadron, rolls down the taxiway at Ali Air Base in Iraq for an October 2008 mission. (U.S. Air Force photo by Senior Airman Christopher Griffin)

A U.S. Marine Corps AV-8B Harrier assigned to Marine Attack Squadron 513 out of Marine Corps Air Station Yuma, waits as an MQ-1 Predator passes by at Creech AFB. In November 2008, airmen of the 11th Reconnaissance Squadron teamed with Marines for a joint training exercise at the base. (U.S. Air Force photo by Senior Airman Larry Reid, Jr.)

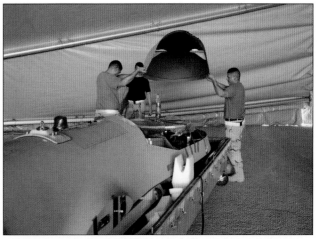

Air Force airmen from the 432nd Aircraft Maintenance Squadron at Creech AFB remove the canopy from a new MQ-1 Predator at Ali Air Base in Iraq in October 2007. (U.S. Air Force photo by Airman 1st Class Jonathan Snyder)

Senior Airman Jason Atwell of the 432nd Aircraft Maintenance Squadron secures the fins onto a GBU-12 Paveway II laser-guided bomb. (U.S. Air Force photo by Senior Airman Larry Reid, Jr.)

Ben Roserug and Jim Dooley unload an AGM-114 Hellfire missile from an MQ-1 Predator after flying a mission from Joint Base Balad in Iraq. (U.S. Air Force photo by Airman 1st Class Jonathan Steffen)

Seen here fastening wires onto a GBU-12 Paveway II laser-guided bomb is Senior Airman Jason Atwell, a weapons loader assigned to the 432nd Aircraft Maintenance Squadron. (U.S. Air Force photo by Senior Airman Larry Reid, Jr.)

Airman 1st Class Gale Passe of the 332nd Expeditionary Aircraft Maintenance Squadron disarms a GBU-12 laser-guided munition attached to an MQ-9 Reaper at Joint Base Balad in Iraq in November 2008. (U.S. Air Force photo by Tech Sergeant Erik Gudmundson)

An MQ-9 Reaper lands at Joint Base Balad in Iraq on 10 November 2008. This Reaper was deployed to the 46th Expeditionary Reconnaissance and Attack Squadron from Creech AFB. (U.S. Air Force photo by Tech Sergeant Erik Gudmundson)

In comments issued as a public affairs release in August 2007, Colonel Marilyn Kott, deputy commander of the 332nd Expeditionary Operations Group, said, "the air battle staff asks for the Predator constantly because it provides such a fine (intelligence, surveillance, and reconnaissance) platform, and it's always airborne . . . The crews flying the Predator report possible enemy activity and give the joint terminal attack controller and the ground and air commanders [who] can agree that the activity needs to be stopped right away and [we] can target the perpetrators."

Colonel Kott added that over the preceding years of Operation Iraqi Freedom, the 332nd and the Predator operators in the United States had increased Predator capability, "developing logistics and technologies to make the system more successful in a deployed environment."

As the Predators hunted bad guys for the Army and Marines, they also did the same for their own. This included hitting the insurgents that occasionally tried to lob mortar rounds into the Predator force's own base. Flying out of Balad AB, the MQ-1s typically flew 20-hour combat air patrols under the control of operators back at Creech AFB before returning to base, where 46th Expeditionary Reconnaissance Squadron crews would recover the UAVs. By 2007, the mission plan included loading in some extra fuel for the Predators to end their patrol with a once-around of the Balad perimeter.

As Captain Richard Koll of the 46th told Nathan Hodge for an article published on 8 November 2007 by Jane's Information Group, the local Joint Tactical Air Controller would authorize the Predators to "fly around the line, scanning certain areas that are possibly known for mortar attacks. Basically, we scan known indirect fire hotspots."

By 2008, to reflect the evolving mission of its Predators, the squadron was renamed as the 46th Expeditionary Reconnaissance *and Attack* Squadron (our italics).

Unmanned aerial vehicles had become essential. Indeed, Defense Secretary Robert Gates would later describe the appetite by ground commanders for the unique capabilities of both armed and unarmed UAVs as "insatiable."

Enter the Reaper

As the Predator fleet approached its 100,000-hour milepost in 2004, General Atomics was making progress on a larger aircraft that was then being called "Predator B," which would later be officially named "Reaper."

Several years earlier, even before Operation Enduring Freedom, General Atomics had been working on the idea of a multi-mission "hunter-killer" UAV, and the first prototype of the concept made its debut flight in February 2001. Designated by General Atomics as the Predator B-001, it was powered by a Garrett AiResearch TPE-331-10T turboprop engine. This UAV was like the

An MQ-9 in pre-operational camouflage, still bearing the name "Predator B." In September 2006, Air Force Chief of Staff General Michael Moseley announced that "Reaper" had been chosen as the name for the MQ-9 unmanned aerial vehicle. He made the final decision after an extensive nomination and review process, coordinated with the other services. "The name Reaper was one of the suggestions that came from our airmen in the field. It's fitting as it captures the lethal nature of this new weapon system," General Moseley said. (NASA photo)

Equipped with a pod-mounted infrared imaging sensor, the Altair UAS aided fire-mapping efforts over wildfires in central and southern California in October. General Atomics developed the Altair version of its Reaper under NASA's Environmental Research Aircraft and Sensor Technology (ERAST) project. (NASA photo)

RQ-1/MQ-1 Predator, but with wings extended from 48 feet to 66 feet.

In turn, the company built a Predator B-002 that was the same size as the B-001, but powered by a Williams FJ44-2A turbofan engine. It was capable of flying at 60,000 feet, but it had an endurance of 12 hours, compared to 30 hours for the B-001. The U.S. Air Force ordered a pair for evaluation.

A third aircraft, the Predator B-003, had an all-new airframe with a wingspan of 84 feet. Powered by a

TP-331-10T turboprop, it offered an endurance of 36 hours. To distinguish it from the earlier Predator B, the company dubbed it Altair. This variant earned production contracts from both NASA and the Air Force. The NASA ships were intended for high altitude scientific research, while the Air Force saw the aircraft as the next step in deploying an armed UCAV.

One of the practical applications of the NASA Altair was a joint NASA and U.S. Forest Service fire mapping research project. In one of the first applications of this activity, NASA responded to a request from the California Office of Emergency Services for aid in tracking the Esperanza Fire in October 2006.

While NASA retained the name Altair, the Air Force continued using the term Predator B for several years before changing in 2006 to the more sinister appellation "Reaper," to avoid confusion with the MQ-1B variant of the original Predator. According to Air Force Chief of

Lieutenant Colonel Geoffrey Barnes and Senior Airman Claudio Vela, Jr., prepare to land an MQ-1 Predator from a nearby control room on 3 September 2008 at Ali Base in Iraq. Colonel Barnes and Airman Vela were deployed from Creech AFB, and were assigned to the 46th Expeditionary Reconnaissance and Attack Squadron. (U.S. Air Force photo by Airman 1st Class Christopher Griffin)

An MQ-9 Reaper prepares to taxi out of a hangar at Joint Base Balad in Iraq. A Reaper employed a 500-pound GBU-12 laser-guided bomb against anti-Iraqi forces 16 August 2008, marking the Reaper's first weapons engagement since it began flying combat sorties over Iraq in July. (U.S. Air Force photo by Tech Sergeant Erik Gudmundson)

An MQ-1 Predator taxies on the flightline at Ali Base in Iraq after a mission. The unmanned aircraft system was assigned to the 46th Expeditionary Reconnaissance and Attack Squadron. (U.S. Air Force photo by Airman 1st Class Christopher Griffin)

Staff General Michael Moseley, "the name Reaper is one of the suggestions that came from our airmen in the field. It's fitting as it captures the lethal nature of this new weapon system."

Lethal indeed. Designated as MQ-9, the new aircraft could have justifiably been designated as an "AQ-9" attack aircraft. "The Reaper represents a significant

Lieutenant Colonel Geoffrey Barnes performs a preflight inspection of a 46th Expeditionary Reconnaissance and Attack Squadron MQ-1 Predator at Ali Base in Iraq. (U.S. Air Force photo by Airman 1st Class Christopher Griffin)

evolution in UAV technology and employment," Moseley said. "We've moved from using UAVs primarily in intelligence, surveillance, and reconnaissance roles before Operation Iraqi Freedom, to a true hunter-killer role with the Reaper."

Like the Predator, the Reaper is constructed mainly from carbon fiber composite material, principally with carbon fiber sheets bonded to a core of Nomex honeycomb or Rohacell foam.

According to the U.S. Air Force, the MQ-9 carries 15 times the payload of the Predator. While the MQ-1 is typically armed with the AGM-114 Hellfire missile, the MQ-9 can also carry the AGM-65 Maverick, a much more potent air-to-ground weapon designed for such heavy-duty tasks as busting tanks. Ironically, it had been an early version of the Maverick that was test fired from a Firebee UAV three decades before Operation Enduring Freedom. Other weapons that can be carried by the MQ-9 include 500-pound bombs. The inboard pylons can accommodate 1,500 pounds of ordnance, those at mid-wing 600 pounds, and those at the outer wing another 200 pounds each.

Fully loaded, the MQ-9 has an endurance of 14 hours, but if two 1,000-pound external fuel tanks are strapped on, the aircraft can carry 1,000 pounds of ordnance on missions up to 42 hours.

Airman 1st Class Hugo Garnica communicates with an MQ-9 Reaper pilot using a land mobile radio at Joint Base Balad in Iraq. He was performing a preflight check to ensure the unmanned aircraft vehicle was operational. (U.S. Air Force photos by Airman 1st Class Jason Epley)

Raytheon dual-mode GBU-49 Enhanced Paveway II precision-guided weapons on the pylons of an MQ-9 Reaper. The first Global Positioning System guided release of the GBU-49 from a Reaper took place on 13 May 2008 at the Naval Air Warfare Center Weapons Division at China Lake, California. Six successful GBU-49 weapon releases were made that day. The first two drops were inert weapons to ensure the GBU-49's GPS guidance was working properly. The final release employed four weapons at one time, also known as a ripple, with three weapons on GPS guidance and the fourth weapon guided by laser. The three GPS weapons "shacked" (a successful, direct hit on a ground target) their targets and the laser-guided weapon came very close. (U.S. Air Force photo)

Schuyler Dunn replaces a part of the Multispectral Targeting System Ball on an MQ-1B Predator at Ali Base in Iraq. Mr. Dunn was an aircraft technician with the 361st Expeditionary Reconnaissance Squadron. (U.S. Air Force photo by Tech Sergeant Sabrina Johnson)

An MQ-9 Reaper arrives at Creech AFB, having flown in from California after a 250-mile, 2-hour flight in 2007. The aircraft was piloted by Lieutenant Colonel Jon Greene, 42nd Attack Squadron commander. Along side him was his sensor operator Senior Airman Aaron Aguilar, also of the 42nd. (U.S. Air Force photo)

Paul Rudolph and Schuyler Dunn replace a Multispectral Targeting System Ball on an MQ-1B Predator on 9 July 2008 at Ali Base in Iraq. The two aircraft technicians were assigned to the 361st Expeditionary Reconnaissance Squadron. (U.S. Air Force photos by Tech Sergeant Sabrina Johnson)

An MQ-9 Reaper remotely piloted aircraft takes off on 17 July 2008 from Joint Base Balad in Iraq. The Reaper flew its first combat mission over Iraq the next day. (U.S. Air Force photo by Tech Sergeant Richard Lisum)

Avionics mechanics Jonathan Hagy and Russell Gordy work on an MQ-1 Predator at Joint Base Balad in Iraq. (U.S. Air Force photo by Airman 1st Class Jonathan Steffen)

The MQ-9 patch naturally includes the images of both the aircraft and the "Grim Reaper," seen here wearing a fighter pilot's helmet. (U.S. Air Force)

Major Morgan Andrews inspects an MQ-1 Predator before its flight from Joint Base Balad in February 2009. Major Andrews was the 46th Reconnaissance and Attack Squadron director of operations. "It was great anytime you get a new airplane, just like getting a brand new car was nice," Major Andrews said. "Being part of Operation Iraqi Freedom has been a good deployment for me to be over here and be involved on this side with a new Predator." (U.S. Air Force photo by Senior Airman Tiffany Trojca)

Senior Airman Charles Cui assists in the flight of an MQ-1 Predator at Joint Base Balad on 13 February 2009. Airman Cui was a 46th Expeditionary Reconnaissance and Attack Squadron sensor operator. "It was a lifetime opportunity; you were responsible for a lot of people on the ground helping them as their eye in the sky," said Airman Cui. "I have a great chance to help people down below the plane, especially security forces. Overall, it's a pretty cool mission." (U.S. Air Force photo by Senior Airman Tiffany Trojca)

Real Value, Real Issues

The Predator turned heads during the Operation Iraqi Freedom invasion in 2003. It got everyone's attention and asserted itself—or rather its operators asserted it—as a weapon whose time and place had come. However, as combat in Iraq continued longer than expected, and as battlefield conditions and requirements changed, the Predator went from the star of a lightning war to an indispensable necessity in ongoing operations.

A case in point was Operation Phantom Fury, the November–December 2004 American operation to subdue insurgent street gangs in the Iraqi city of Fallujah. Having eyes in the sky loitering overhead was indispensable. Having eyes in the sky did not mean that there were no issues. In past wars, not knowing what was over the next hill presented problems. Lack of communication presented problems. In Fallujah, the problems came from too much information and from communications that were *too* seamless.

When two people are looking at the same thing at the same time from different angles, there are always discrepancies. As General Walter Buchanan pointed out in remarks to journalists in October 2005, "when you're dealing with an urban environment . . . it was very, very hard to quickly get the pilot's eyes *exactly* on the target that the JTAC and the ground commander were talking about . . . If you took an overhead picture of Fallujah and looked down, it's a town full of flat brown roofs . . . There's one instance in Fallujah where from the ground I looked up and saw three different buildings. From the air, the roofs were all connected."

When asked what the Predator meant to him, Buchanan replied, "It gives me the ability to put a persistent stare overhead. That's where I talk about the target development piece. Other airframes don't have the loiter time to be able to quietly stay, to hang, overhead for hours at a time if necessary, and develop a target. Quite honestly in this insurgent environment, that's been one of the real values of a long loiter UAV, especially with the reachback that the Predator provides."

As the dual conflicts in Afghanistan and Iraq continued, the value of the Predators increased and their tasking grew exponentially. The U.S. Air Force noted a 520 percent increase in MQ-1 Combat Air Patrols from 2004 through 2008. In the year from July 2005 to June 2006 alone, U.S. Air Force Predators flew 2,073 sorties and participated in more than 242 separate attacks.

In his remarks in 2005, Buchanan also cited problems that came simply from the fact that the United States had so many air assets over the Iraqi theater, "We have over 1,000 UAVs on the ground, in the [area of responsibility], with the majority of those flying below 3,000 feet. That is a very thick environment. We have in fact had occasions where they have run into helicopters. Fortunately, to my knowledge, we have not hurt anybody [in collisions] yet. We have damaged airplanes and knocked them down, but we've not injured anybody . . . Above 3,000 feet, we

A newly arrived Predator takes off on a mission from Joint Base Balad. The 332nd Air Expeditionary Wing received a new MQ-1 and immediately put it to action. After arriving disassembled and packed in a crate, the remotely piloted plane was reassembled within two days and up and flying its perfect first trip into blue Iraqi skies on "Friday the Thirteenth." Twenty minutes before sundown, the MQ-1 aircraft launched from the desert base without a hitch, rising high into the light blue sky to help provide overwatch and security for U.S. and coalition forces. In the control booth, Lieutenant Colonel Debra Lee and sensor operator Senior Airman Charlie Cui operated the aircraft. "While we flew this first mission completely local as we ran patrol around the base," Lee explained. "On other missions we will hand the aircraft back home through our satellite system and let our other crews back in the States control it." (U.S. Air Force photo by Senior Airman Tiffany Trojca)

Captain Richard Koll (left) and Airman 1st Class Mike Eulo, both of the 46th Expeditionary Reconnaissance Squadron, perform function checks after launching an MQ-1 Predator in August 2007 at Joint Base Balad in Iraq. Captain Koll, the pilot, and Airman Eulo, the sensor operator, handled the Predator in a radius of approximately 25 miles around the base before handing it off to personnel stationed in the United States to continue its mission. (U.S. Air Force photo by Master Sergeant Steve Horton)

An MQ-1B Predator prepares to land at Joint Base Balad in Iraq, after a combat mission in support of Operation Iraqi Freedom. When an MQ-1B Predator aircraft crashed in January, it caused $1,436,765 in damages. Engine failure caused the crash of an MQ-1B Predator remotely piloted aircraft 17 January 2007 at a forward location in Southwest Asia, according to an Accident Investigation Board report released by Air Combat Command today. According to the investigation, there was clear and convincing evidence the mishap was caused by a crack in the crankshaft that ultimately caused the failure of a connecting rod in the aircraft's engine. When the rod failed, it wedged itself in the opposing engine cylinder causing the crankshaft to stop and the engine to seize. The aircraft crashed in an unpopulated location. The remains of the aircraft and all classified equipment and weapons were recovered. (U.S. Air Force photo by Senior Airman Olufemi Owolabi)

Showing hardware in time of war: Staff Sergeant Angelo Munoz (left), Captain Chad Miner, and Staff Sergeant Patrick Perry of the 432nd Aircraft Maintenance Squadron from Creech AFB answer questions about the MQ-1 Predator on 20 June 2007 at the 47th International Paris Air Show at Le Bourget Airport in France. The Predator was one of seven Department of Defense aircraft on display that year. "We put warheads on foreheads" said Sergeant Munoz. (U.S. Air Force photo by Airman 1st Class Marc Lane)

Major John Chesser (left) and Lieutenant Colonel Micah Morgan inspect the arming devices on a munition affixed to an MQ-9 Reaper at Joint Base Balad in Iraq. The Reaper can carry up to 3,750 pounds of munitions, including GBU-12 laser-guided bombs and Hellfire missiles. Colonel Morgan was the 46th Expeditionary Reconnaissance and Attack Squadron commander, and Major Chesser was a Reaper pilot with the 46th ERAS. Both officers were deployed from Creech AFB. (U.S. Air Force photo by Tech Sergeant Richard Lisum)

A nighttime view of MQ-1 Predators at Joint Base Balad in Iraq. (U.S. Air Force photo by Senior Airman Kerry Solan-Johnson)

deconflict via altitude. I deconflict via space. I deconflict via time. . . . But folks have got to play by those rules, and I will tell you not everybody who's flying UAVs in the Area of Responsibility is a rated pilot that understands that and that deconfliction piece."

While one can detect a trace of hesitance in Buchanan's perspective on UAVs, there was nothing of the sort in comments made by Captain Fred Atwater, commanding the 46th Expeditionary Reconnaissance Squadron at Balad AB.

"[They're] the largest game in town and an integral part of just about every large joint operation in Iraq," he said in remarks reported by *Air Force Magazine* in June 2006. "The most rewarding missions are the ones where you escort a group of soldiers on a foot patrol. You weave them through hostile terrain and get them home safely."

It's probable that the foot patrols shared Atwater's enthusiasm, just as helicopter pilots shared Buchanan's concerns.

In addition to the crowded airspace issue that troubled General Buchanan, the crowded *electronic* space hampered Predator operations over Iraq. As David Fulghum reported in the 14 January 2007 issue of *Aviation Week*, American technology interfered with *other* American technology in an "electronically polluted" environment.

In one example Fulgham cited, a smart system that jammed improvised explosive devices locked onto another smart system and also jammed surveillance and communication systems. Data links on Predators flying out of Balad AB "were degraded to a range of 35 miles while the same aircraft operating in Afghanistan had a data link range of 120 miles. The problem is so pervasive that antennas have been put on 110-foot-high poles to get them out of the worst interference."

Another concern that arose with regard to Predator operations over Iraq was that of misuse. The reputation of the aircraft as a jack of many trades led often to requests from ground commanders for Predator sorties in situations that were seen by some as not the best use of its time. One such instance interpreted as misuse was the hunt for improvised explosive devices (IEDs).

"It's a waste," said General Ronald Keys, commander of the U.S. Air Force Air Combat Command, in remarks to a Transformation Warfare conference that were reported by Michael Fabey of *Aerospace Daily & Defense Report* on 21 June 2007. "People come to me and tell me they want a Predator . . . I ask, 'What are you looking for?' Unfortunately, the military is basing some of its decisions on anecdotes instead of real metrics . . . Indeed, the only metric being used is whether the Air Force is meeting certain tasking orders, instead of making sure those assets and flights are effective and the best use of time and aircraft . . . We ought to be attacking the system [the process before the IED is emplaced, the network], not the thing that's buried out there."

Calling the ground environment in Iraq "a junkyard," Keys went on to say that using a Predator's sensors to look for IEDs in that clutter yielded too many false positives. He said that Air Combat Command had developed a "concept of deployment" for the Predators that put the emphasis on hitting shooters and bomb-makers rather than bombs.

Washington Drone Wars

As the American armed forces were structuring the doctrine for tactical unmanned aerial vehicle operations in the skies over Iraq and Afghanistan, these vehicles and operations were the subject of another conflict on a different front—Washington, D.C.

In a controversial 5 March 2007 memo, Air Force chief General Michael Moseley, proposed that his service take over management of *all* Pentagon UAV/UAS programs and be made the executive agent for all medium-altitude (over 3,500 feet) and high-altitude UAVs. His idea was for the Air Force to exercise operational control even of Army and other special operations tactical unmanned aerial vehicles. The Air Force had made the same proposal in 2005 in the wake of the midair collisions between UAVs and manned aircraft referenced earlier in this book in the quotes from General Walter Buchanan.

In 2005, the idea had been rejected by the Joint Chiefs of Staff, but the Pentagon did establish Joint Unmanned Aircraft Center of Excellence at Creech AFB, where the U.S. Air Force Predator fleet was based.

"All UAVs operating above the designated coordinating altitude must have common, interoperable systems to facilitate . . . safe and seamless operations," the Air Force asserted in an official fact sheet after Moseley's 2007 memo was issued. "As [executive agent for medium- and high-altitude] UAVs, the Air Force would be postured to integrate these requirements into the UAV programming and acquisition process at the outset."

The aircraft in question included the MQ-1 Predator, the RQ-4 Global Hawk, and the MQ-9 Reaper, which were all Air Force UAVs, as well as the U.S. Navy's Broad Area Maritime Surveillance (BAMS) system. Parenthetically there were still a number of airframes under consideration for the BAMS program in 2007, but the Navy would officially select the Global Hawk in April 2008.

Smaller, low altitude UAVs were not necessarily among those that Moseley had in mind. The U.S. Army had achieved success in Iraq with such tactical aircraft as the BQM-147 Dragon Drone and the RQ-11 Raven (a successor to the older FQM-151 Pointer) which have wingspans of just eight feet and four feet respectively. However, some aircraft, such as the Army's RQ-7 Shadow (which has a 14-foot wingspan), have service ceilings in excess of 3,500 feet. This was seen by some as infringing upon the Air Force's claim on high performance aircraft of all types.

"Designating the Air Force as the [executive agent] for medium- and high-altitude UAVs is the step we can take now to increase combat effectiveness," General Moseley said at a press conference in April 2007. "If I sound emotional about this, it's because I believe there is a way to fight a joint and coalition fight much more effectively, much more efficiently, and afford these systems."

As had been the case when the Air Force proposed itself as Department of Defense UAV executive manager back in 2005, the U.S. Army and U.S. Navy took exception to the idea, touching off an intense inter-service debate. Michael Fabey reported in *Aerospace Daily & Defense Report* on 27 March that the Air Force countered that increased coordination and "operational deconfliction" was necessary. The Army responded that its commanders on the ground in Iraq and Afghanistan had to retain direct operational command over Army unmanned aerial vehicles in those respective theaters.

"It makes absolute good sense to me that things flying above 3,500 feet should be part of an ATO, air tasking order, so that there's deconfliction of the airspace," Marine General Peter Pace, the Joint Chiefs of Staff Chairman—who had opposed the similar Air Force proposal in 2005—told reporters in April. "[But] we need to be careful not to override the needs of the troops on the ground by some kind of a generic package [carried by individual UAVs] . . . It's not a bad idea to take a look at all UAV operations to see who ought to be on the control stick, so to speak, for those operations. And if that's a place where the Air Force could free up Army troops to do other things, it's worth a discussion."

While the chairman was walking the line on Moseley's statement, other members of the Joint Staff were not as politically neutral. Admiral Michael Mullen, Chief of Naval Operations and Pace's later successor as JCS Chairman, said on 29 March, "I've seen the memorandum . . . As I read it, I'm not supportive."

The Army was as far from supportive as it could be.

"We absolutely disagree, and every other service does, too, and the Joint Staff does as well," said U.S. Army Aviation Director Brigadier General Stephen Mundt in an interview with *Defense Daily*. "Someone explain to me when a line in the sky became a . . . core competency. My helicopters fly above 3,500 feet. That does not mean they belong to the Air Force."

Using the example of the RQ-7, which has a service ceiling of 16,000 feet, Mundt sought to illustrate the operational difficulties of having the Air Force control battlefield UAVs.

"Under their plan," Mundt suggested sarcastically, "I give them the Shadow, [and now] I have to put my request in and compete to get that same capability back, which is ludicrous."

Still looming large in the institutional memory of the U.S. Army is Operation Anaconda in March 2002, when its troops encountered tough going in a fight with al-Qaeda in the mountains of Afghanistan. It has been theorized that had the Army "owned" Predators, or other such armed UAVs, things might have gone better.

"If we had had more UAVs [able to carry out attacks] on landing zones prior to us going in there, we would not have had this problem," Lieutenant General Robert Noonan told *Defense Daily*. "We don't have enough organic UAVs. We feel very strongly that all of our brigades have got to have UAVs."

Air Force Brigadier General Jan-Marc Jouas, commander of the Air Intelligence Agency replied on 28 March 2007 that "Mundt's caustic comments, reminiscent of an era prior to the maturation of jointness and service interdependence, would have been better aimed at reducing competing UAV programs and mission redundancies."

"Some [Army pilots] are flying the UAVs when we're flying fixed-wing aircraft," said General Ronald Keys, commander of U.S. Air Force Air Combat Command. "In some cases we're actually competing against each other."

In its official fact sheet release, the Air Force stated, "It is reasonable to expect that the present [medium- and high-altitude] UAV investment budget could be reduced perhaps by up to 10 percent . . . DOD cannot afford the inefficiencies that result from individual service UAV stovepipes."

"The word 'stovepipe,' a pejorative term, refers to an artificial walling-off of an activity so as to prevent the involvement of others outside of the organization," explained Rebecca Grant in the July 2007 issue of *Air Force Magazine*.

She went on to say that "of specific interest to the Air Force is a potential merger of the closely related Air Force Predator and Army Warrior programs, and a similar consolidation of the Air Force Global Hawk and its Naval sibling, the BAMS Global Hawk. [The] U.S. Air Force's plan would transfer procurement authority for all of these systems to the Air Force to save on costs, eliminate duplication, and direct investment to areas where it would be most useful."

As she pointed out, the Army's disagreement was rooted in an assumption that Army systems need to be generated by ground force personnel or they might not be appropriate to ground force requirements. In other words, ground commanders were perceived as being more likely to get support from Army UAVs than from Air Force UAV operators.

Air Force Lieutenant General David Deptula, the Deputy Chief of Staff for Intelligence, Surveillance, and Reconnaissance (ISR), countered the arguments made by Mundt and other members of the other services by pointing out that, while the Air Force may "own" UAVs like the Predator, it places them at the disposal of a *joint* command.

"Every operational Predator that the Air Force has is currently assigned to Central Command," Deptula said, as quoted in Rebecca Grant's article. "[The CENTCOM commander] divvies those up between . . . major areas of operation, principally Afghanistan and Iraq . . . The system we have allocates medium- and high-altitude UAVs to combatant commanders to execute, and it works very, very well . . . [for example] GPS [the Global Positioning System] is 100 percent owned and operated by the Air

U.S. Air Force Lieutenant General David Deptula, deputy chief of staff for intelligence, surveillance, and reconnaissance, was both a proponent of UAVs operationally, and a key figure in advocating the U.S. Air Force as the executive agent for most American military drones. (Defense Department photo by U.S. Air Force Master Sergeant Jerry Morrison)

Force, yet its effect has become so ubiquitous that it's depended upon by all the services without any concern. We can do that with medium- and high-altitude UAVs."

But it was not to be. On 13 September 2007, Deputy Secretary of Defense Gordon England officially ruled against the idea of the U.S. Air Force as executive agent for all high flying UAVs (or UASs).

As Amy Butler reported four days later in *Aerospace Daily & Defense Report*, "in lieu of forming an executive agency in the Air Force, England directs that an interagency task force will address how to promote interoperability and efficient operations of UASs. This decision also relieves the Navy of concerns that the Air Force could subsume oversight of its high-dollar UAS contracts."

Enter the Warrior

Against the backdrop of the conflicted skies over Iraq and the conflicted turf of Washington, the U.S. Army retained the institutional memory of how Operation Anaconda might have been different had it

been able to deploy armed UAVs of its own. After Anaconda, and as the war in Iraq unfolded, the Army came to feel that it was not getting the service it needed from Air Force Predators in a timely way.

It cannot be argued that the Army had a point. Predators were being controlled from Combined Air Operations Center (CAOC) that was far away from the action. It was natural that Army commanders would want a serious UAV attack capability that was controlled, as were Army recon drones, at the brigade level or lower.

Army officers complained that they often had to reserve Predator coverage several days before a planned operation, and that often the support was unavailable when needed.

The Air Force response was that while it was generally possible for them to support multiple ground commanders during a single 20-hour Predator flight, one ground commander or another might ask for an extension of his allotted time if the tactical situation on the ground changed. This would obviously ruin the schedule for the remainder of the day, and impact the ground commanders that were farther down the list.

Major Robert Kadavy at the aviation directorate at U.S. Army headquarters, could understand this rationale. As he pointed out, the enemy rarely follows a predetermined agenda, adding that ground commanders desire "the ability to make changes, because they know a plan three days out is never going to be exactly on that timeline."

Nevertheless, for ground commanders, excuses were excuses, and air support was needed when it was needed. Colonel Jeffrey Kappenman, the UAS manager for the U.S. Army Training and Doctrine Command (TRADOC) wrote in the 2nd Quarter 2008 issue of *Joint Force Quarterly*, "It is imperative that units in physical contact with the enemy have the continuous sensor coverage needed to dominate and win the engagement. Army commanders at all tactical levels (division and below) have identified a requirement for organic UAS to support their operations. The single largest gap in UAS support to tactical maneuver forces today resides at the division level."

Kappenman stated emphatically that in combat operations, "the risk to platoons is often measured in seconds or minutes, with complex terrain compounding that risk . . . Troops in contact with the enemy cannot afford to wait for a UAS request to move through the division staff, the corps staff, and the [joint forces] staff, then await reallocation decision-matrixing by the [joint forces] leadership, and then, if approved, wait for the asset to travel en route to the ground forces."

As later summarized in a 2009 U.S. Army Posture Statement, "Maneuver forces must be able to detect, identify, locate, and track targets in near-real-time to warn friendly forces, develop the situation prior to contact, and take advantage of fleeting opportunities."

The way to achieve this was to hasten the development of a robust armed drone of their own. The U.S. Army had already taken steps toward taking matters into their own hands, having launched the Extended-Range Multi-Purpose (ERMP or ER/MP) UAV competition in 2002.

Even as the Drone Wars had been raging in Washington, the Army was moving toward getting that armed UAV they craved. Initially, they had entertained a proposal from IAI and TRW for an upgraded RQ-5 Hunter. Even though the Army did experiment with light armament for the RQ-5, both it and its successor, the RQ-7 Shadow, were small aircraft with a range of just a couple dozen miles, so they were unlikely candidates to carry serious offensive armament on serious ground support missions.

Meanwhile, General Atomics proposed a Predator variant, and this matched the criteria of what the Army felt was necessary.

The U.S. Army wanted its General Atomics Warrior to be designated as MQ-12, but DOD considered them to be variants of the MQ-1B Predator, and they were designated as MQ-1C. (Defense Department photo)

Private First Class Logan Ford, a member of the U.S. Army's Task Force Odin from Fort Hood, Texas, paints his unit's crest on a wall at a remote base in Iraq in November 2007. Soldiers from Task Force Odin were part of the Combat Aviation Brigade, 1st Infantry Division from Fort Riley, Kansas, supporting Task Force Iron, 1st Armored Division in northern Iraq. (U.S. Army photo by Major Enrique Vasquez)

The Task Force ODIN acronym stands for Observe, Detect, Identify, and Neutralize, but the insignia pictures Odin, the chief god of Norse mythology, who is typically pictured with his pair of wolves. The Task Force is an Army aviation battalion created to conduct reconnaissance, surveillance, targeting, and acquisition (RSTA) at attack operations against insurgents using improvised explosive devices in Iraq. (U.S. Army)

The General Atomics proposal was selected in August 2005, and a $214 million contract for system development and demonstration was issued. The plan evolved to acquire 132 aircraft and 55 ground stations grouped into 11 ERMP "systems," for around a billion dollars.

The ERMP aircraft, initially called Sky Warrior by the company, was officially named "Warrior" to avoid confusion of the Douglas A3D (later A-3) Skywarrior, a manned bomber that had served with the U.S. Navy 50 years earlier.

As a designation, the Army hoped for the Warrior to be given the next available "Q" designator. Both the Reaper and Warrior had evolved from the Predator, and the Reaper had received the all-new MQ-9 designation, so this seemed reasonable. However, instead of designating the Warrior as MQ-12, the Defense Department decided that it was officially a Predator *variant*, so the new aircraft became the MQ-1C.

Deputy Secretary of Defense Gordon England who had earlier ruled out the idea of the U.S. Air Force being the Department of Defense executive agent for high flying unmanned aerial vehicles, also came out in support of the idea of merging the acquisition programs for the Predator and Warrior. It was a move that lessened the Army's autonomy with regard to the program, but it was also a move that Congress had embraced because of a potential budget savings estimated at 10 percent.

Writing in the April 2009 *Armed Forces Journal*, Air Force Lieutenant General David Deptula and retired Brigadier General Harold "Buck" Adams, later addressed the issue of UAV hardware acquisition. As they pointed out, unmanned aerial systems "need to be acquired in the context of a joint concept of operations to ensure that the separate services are not duplicating effort, but at the same time are available to joint force commanders to meet their needs at every conflict level—tactical, operational, and strategic."

The MQ-1C has a length of 28 feet, a foot longer than the MQ-1B, and a wingspan of 56 feet, nearly 8 feet greater than the MQ-1B. The appearance of the "C model" is similar to that of the Predator, but the Warrior has a larger nose fairing to accommodate a Synthetic Aperture Radar/Ground Moving Target Indicator (SAR-GMTI) system, and it carries an AN/AAS-52 Multi-spectral Targeting System (MTS) beneath its nose. It was capable of carrying four AGM-114 Hellfire missiles, or GBU-44 Viper Strike guided bombs. The endurance of the MQ-1C aircraft is rated at 36 hours, less than the Reaper but about the same as the MQ-1B Predator.

As the new Warrior ERMP entered development in 2005, General Atomics created an interim aircraft, which the U.S. Army could deploy operationally to war zones ahead of time to battle test Warrior systems. This aircraft was based on the earlier General Atomics I-Gnat, which was a contemporary of early Predators dating back to 1998.

The Extended Range (ER) variant of the I-Gnat, the I-Gnat ER, became the "Warrior-Alpha," of which a reported 16 were sent overseas. Nine were deployed to Iraq, three to Afghanistan, and four to other unspecified foreign locations. As reported in the *Defense News C4ISR Journal* on 3 November 2007, the Warrior-Alpha "had flown more than 6,000 hours and had contributed to the killing of 3,000 insurgents in Iraq."

However, it was actually an armed RQ-5 Hunter that became the first U.S. Army unmanned aerial vehicle known to have actually destroyed an enemy target. On 1 September 2007 two insurgents were taken out with a GBU-44 Viper Strike glide bomb. The kill was described by Colonel Don Hazelwood, project manager for Army Unmanned Aircraft Systems at Redstone Arsenal, as "the first confirmed use of an Army weaponized UAV."

The fact that he chose the phrase "first confirmed" indicated that there may have been others before that

U.S. Army Colonel Michael Cavalier (right) Task Force Charger, 82nd Combat Aviation Brigade, presents Army Major General David Rodriguez, 82nd Airborne Division commander, a framed display photo of the MQ-1C Warrior. (U.S. Army photo by Specialist Aubree Rundle)

Vice Chairman of the Joint Chiefs of Staff Navy Admiral Edmund Giambastiani talks with U.S. Army Second Lieutenant Kirmanie Stuart, executive officer, about the Warrior Alpha unmanned aerial vehicle at Camp Speicher in Iraq on 20 June 2007. (U.S. Air Force photo by Tech Sergeant Adam Stump)

date. Warrior-Alpha, meanwhile, was then being flown with AGM-114 Hellfire missiles.

Between April and November 2007, the number of video terminals capable of displaying live imagery beamed from U.S. Army UAVs increased five-fold to around 1,000. As Kim Henry of Redstone Arsenal public affairs wrote in a news release, such terminals were being installed inside M1126 Stryker armored vehicles on their way to Iraq, as well as in the cockpits of AH-64 Apache attack helicopters.

The Warrior is controlled through the One System Ground Control Station (OSGCS), which was originally developed by AAI as part of the RQ-7 Shadow system package. Used by both the U.S. Army and Marine Corps, One System is used to operate multiple unmanned aircraft types over a battlefield, merging and disseminating the intelligence video that is collected from them. Indeed, the Army operates all of its unmanned aerial vehicles using the One System. As was demonstrated in October 2008 using a Warrior, it is possible for an unmanned aerial vehicle to take off and land autonomously using the One System.

Another issue on which the two services disagree is that of UAV pilot rank. While the Air Force uses only officers as pilots for all aircraft types, the Army and Marines prefer enlisted personnel as pilots for unmanned aerial vehicles.

As Colonel Kappenman explains the rationale for this, "a significant advantage of employing enlisted Soldiers to operate Army UASs, in lieu of commissioned officer pilots who serve brief tours as UAS operators, is that the former spend their entire military career as UAS operators. This allows them to hone their skills with years of experience and become highly proficient at their craft, reducing both accident rates and training costs."

While Kappenman speaks convincingly for those within the Army who are insistent on not having their UAV attack capability at the mercy of a controller in a distant Combined Air Operations Center, there is an alternate perspective.

As Rebecca Grant wrote in *Air Force Magazine*, the MQ-1C "gives the Army an organic capability . . . The problem is that the Army Warriors are available for tasking through the land component only. If this approach were taken to its logical conclusion, every division might own its medium-altitude UAVs for [intelligence-surveillance-reconnaissance] and strike operations, but it would make none available to any other division. Warrior UAVs would deploy as part of a division's equipment set, just like Stryker vehicles, and then rotate home with the rest of the force."

In fact, the Army chose to create a dedicated aviation battalion to operate the Warrior-Alpha, and eventually the whole MQ-1C fleet.

The Army's Secret Air Force

Created on orders from General Richard Cody, the U.S. Army's vice chief of staff, the new dedicated MQ-1C aviation battalion was called Task Force ODIN. The name is an acronym for Observe, Detect, Identify, and Neutralize, but the name "Odin" was also that of the thundering principal god of Nordic mythology. The task force insignia features a depiction of a spear-wielding Odin.

Formed at Fort Hood, Texas, ODIN was first deployed overseas in October 2006 to Camp Speicher in the north-central Iraq city of Tikrit. Even before the debut of the MQ-1C, the task force had already received a Meritorious Unit Commendation for Warrior-Alpha operations in conjunction with the 25th Infantry Division.

Marking the first flight of the MQ-1C Warrior on 15 April 2008, Thomas Cassidy, head of the General Atomics Aircraft Systems Group, Aeronautical Systems, observed in a prepared statement that "Army tactical commanders at the division level and below are now one step closer to having the RSTA information they need to offer increased protection to their troops on the ground."

Little was said about Task Force ODIN and Warrior-Alpha during 2007. As the turf war raged in Washington, the U.S. Army quietly pursued its own initiative of integrating the Warrior concept into its battlefield operations in Iraq. After the attempt by the Air Force to be named the executive agency for unmanned aerial vehicles, the Warrior was a key to Army independence.

The Army's plans for UAVs went beyond just the Iraq theater. Quoting Tim Owings, deputy project manager for Army unmanned aerial systems, Kris Osborn wrote in the 12 December 2008 issue of *Army Times* that the Army planned to deploy its UAVs to "new counterinsurgency and counterterrorism efforts in Africa and South America and stepped-up initiatives in Afghanistan."

"I think you are going to see a variety of new capabilities exploited. You can link manned sensors and manned attack sensors up with unmanned platforms. With that construct comes the ability for interoperability," Owings said. "We will increasingly be able to take software models from a Shadow band and reuse those capabilities [with Army Black Hawk and Kiowa helicopters]."

If little was said about Warrior-Alpha, less was said about the first MQ-1Cs to reach the war zone. Though General Atomics didn't officially turn the first Block 1 MQ-1Cs over to the Army until March 2009, two "Block 0" prototypes had already been in Iraq for a number of months serving with Task Force ODIN. As Tim Owings explained, "Block 0 was inserted after Block 1 was conceived to allow the service to have more hands-on experience with the more robust MQ-1C airframe and the Thielert heavy-fuel engine."

Gradually it occurred to the media that the creation of Task Force ODIN essentially meant that the U.S. Army was building an "air force." Though the service had attack helicopters and small fixed-wing utility aircraft, the Warriors provided the Army with a contingent of fixed-wing combat aircraft. StrategyWorld.com reported on 8 March 2009 the U.S. Army was now "using missile firing, fixed wing combat aircraft, some-

An MQ-1 Predator of the 432nd Wing takes off from Creech AFB as another waits its turn. (U.S. Air Force photo by Master Sergeant Rob Valenca)

Sergeant Dustin Scott, an unmanned aerial system maintainer, prepares an RQ-7 Shadow for launch at Forward Operating Base Kalsu in Iskandariya, Iraq, 20 miles south of Baghdad. Task Force 49's UAS unit, Quicksilver Troop, 4th Squadron, 3rd Armored Cavalry Regiment, maintained a fleet of 12 Shadow aircraft. (Defense Department photo by Master Sergeant Eric Reinhardt)

thing it has not been able to do for many decades (since the U.S. Air Force was created out of the old U.S. Army Air Forces [in 1947]). The air force has accepted, for the moment, that unmanned aircraft are not the sole preserve of the air force, and the army is taking that and building a new air force for itself."

The New York Times also discovered Task Force ODIN, interpreting it as the Army's way of seizing control of its air power from an indifferent Air Force, and stating that the unit "represents a new move by the service toward self-sufficiency, and away from joint operations."

Eventually, the Army could envision the Warrior armada outgrowing Task Force ODIN. At the end of 2008, Colonel Randy Rotte, deputy director of Army aviation said that the Army planned to equip each of its 11 combat aviation brigades with a dozen MQ-1Cs.

As Thom Shanker wrote for *The New York Times* in the 22 June 2008 issue, "Ever since the Army lost its warplanes to a newly independent Air Force after World War II, soldiers have depended on the sister service for help from the sky, from bombing and strafing to transport and surveillance. But the wars in Iraq and Afghanistan have frayed the relationship, with Army officers making increasingly vocal complaints that the Air Force is not pulling its weight . . . In Iraq, Army officers say the Air Force has often been out of touch, fulfilling only half of their requests for the sophisticated surveillance aircraft that ground commanders say are needed to find roadside bombs and track down insurgents."

According to a 2009 U.S. Army Posture Statement, Warriors were a key element in the hunt for roadside bombs, or the "Persistent Air and Ground Surveillance to Counter Improvised Explosive Devices." In this statement, the Army noted, "Task Force (TF) Odin was created in Iraq to observe, detect, identify, neutralize, and attack IED networks and currently fields 26 manned and unmanned air platforms dedicated to counter IED surveillance. The TF's success led to the decision to create a similar organization for Afghanistan; the manpower and equipment are now forming for that element."

Shanker also mentioned a classified video clip from a UAV camera that was then circulating in the Pentagon. It showed an insurgent using palm fronds to smooth dirt over a bomb he had buried late at night along a major convoy route. Moments later, "he disappeared in 30-millimeter fire from an Apache that was alerted by the remotely piloted Army surveillance craft overhead."

As discussed in Shanker's article, Secretary of Defense Robert Gates showed "keen interest in the Army initiative—much to the frustration of embattled Air Force leaders—as a potential way to improve battlefield surveillance."

Said Geoff Morrell, a Pentagon press secretary, Gates wanted to "make sure that we are looking at not just top-down solutions, but ground-up solutions. We need to pay attention to anything that works."

Enter the Fire Scout

As it was deploying its Warrior, the U.S. Army was also following a sister service into the world of unmanned tactical rotorcraft. First flown in 2002 and developed by Northrop Grumman for the U.S. Navy, the RQ-8 Fire Scout was born as a reconnaissance aircraft, but was destined to be the first American unmanned aircraft to be deployed as an armed helicopter.

Even as the armed Predator was staking out the turf on which it would achieve future notoriety, the idea of an unmanned rotary wing aerial vehicle was gaining momentum. Just as manned helicopters helped to revolutionize battlefield tactics in Korea and Vietnam, *unmanned* and *autonomous* helicopters have the potential of changing the way air operations are conducted in the twenty-first century. Among the earliest aircraft to pioneer this concept were the Boeing X-50A Dragonfly, and the Northrop Grumman RQ-8A Fire Scout.

The Dragonfly dated back to May 1998, when Boeing and DARPA agreed to share the cost of developing the rotary wing aircraft initially known as the Canard Rotor/Wing (CRW) after the Boeing-patented design concept on which it is based. The idea was to combine the hover efficiency and low speed flight characteristics of a helicopter with the high-subsonic cruising speed of a fixed-wing aircraft. Powered by a conventional turbofan

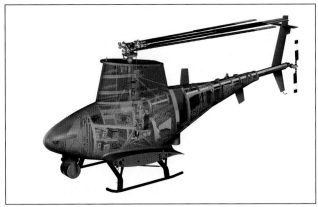

A cutaway illustration of an MQ-8B Fire Scout UAV rotorcraft. (Northrop Grumman)

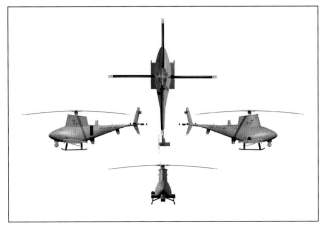

A four-view illustration of the MQ-8B Fire Scout. (Northrop Grumman)

engine in both rotary-wing and fixed-wing flight, an X-50A was intended to take off and land within confined areas—such as the deck of a small ship—yet to transition quickly to and from a fixed-wing mode.

Designed by Boeing's Phantom Works component, the Dragonfly was built at Boeing's helicopter development and manufacturing facility in Mesa, Arizona, that was once Hughes Helicopters, and which builds the AH-64 Apache series of attack helicopters.

The first of two X-50A aircraft rolled out in 2001, and made its debut flight on the morning of 4 December 2003 at the U.S. Army Proving Ground near Yuma, Arizona. The flight-test program experienced a serious setback four months later, when the first of X-50A was damaged in a mishap at Yuma on 23 March 2004. The second X-50A subsequently completed six flights before being lost in a crash at Yuma on 12 April 2006. Because neither prototype ever successfully transitioned to full forward flight mode, DARPA pulled the plug on the Dragonfly program in September 2006.

Meanwhile, the U.S. Navy had been evaluating various proposals under its Vertical Takeoff and Landing Tactical Unmanned Aerial Vehicle (VTUAV) program, looking at the aircraft as a platform for reconnaissance

An MQ-8B Fire Scout unmanned aerial rotorcraft hovers over the flight deck of the guided-missile frigate USS McInerney (FFG-8) on 8 May 2009 as the ship's crew prepares for flight operations over the Atlantic Ocean. The ship went on to deploy on an anti-drug trafficking mission to Latin America. (U.S. Navy photo by Mass Communication Specialist 2nd Class Alan Gragg)

and targeting support for Marine Corps forces ashore. Three contractors, Teledyne Ryan, Bell, and Sikorsky, submitted proposals. In February 2000, the Fire Scout proposal from Teledyne Ryan, now part of Northrop Grumman, was picked. The aerial vehicle itself was based on the Schweizer Aircraft Corporation Model 300 series manned turbine helicopter, which had previously been proven by over 20 million flight hours.

Chief of Naval Operations Admiral Gary Roughead (center) foreground, tours the Northrop Grumman MQ-8B Fire Scout facility in Pascagoula, Mississippi, on 31 March 2009, during a visit to the Gulf Coast region. (U.S. Navy photo by Mass Communication Specialist 1st Class Tiffini Jones)

Originally, the Navy planned to use the new rotorcraft to replace the RQ-2 Pioneer reconnaissance UAV as a shipboard unmanned aerial vehicle. However, the Fire Scout seems to have exceeded expectations. As Northrop Grumman put it, "The small footprint of the VTUAV would reduce the impact on flight deck operations compared to the Pioneer, resulting in a major paradigm shift on tactical UAV operations."

Northrop Grumman was awarded a $93 million cost-plus-incentive contract for the engineering and manufacturing development phase of the VTUAV project in February 2000. For its money, the Navy would receive one "system" of three vehicles, as well as technical manuals, operations security, operational and maintenance training, and technical support prior to the Fire Scout vehicle becoming operational. The aircraft was mandated to have continuous surveillance capability exceeding six hours, and an operational radius of 100 miles.

Aboard the Fire Scout, the sensor package would include electro-optical/infrared systems, as well as a laser target designator. The designator would be a "force multiplier" for ships equipped with Extended Range Guided Munitions (ERGMs), firing five-inch guns or land attack missiles. The VTUAV should also be able to conduct real-time battle damage assessment.

An illustration of a U.S. Army MQ-8B Fire Scout over a battlefield with AH-64D Apache attack helicopters in the background. (Northrop Grumman)

Navy planners also spoke of additional "mission areas for future growth payloads" that included mine countermeasures, battle management, chemical and biological weapons reconnaissance, signals intelligence, electronic warfare, combat search and rescue, communications and data relay, information warfare, ship missile defense, and anti-submarine warfare.

Delivered in the summer of 2001, the first unmanned Fire Scout VTUAV, officially designated as RQ-8A, made its debut flight at the Naval Air Systems Command Western Test Range Complex at China Lake in California on 19 May 2002. Flight tests proceeded without the setbacks that befell the Dragonfly program, and the first shipboard flights were conducted during the latter part of 2003 aboard the USS *Denver*. Much later, the aircraft became the first unmanned helicopter to land on a moving U.S. Navy vessel without a pilot controlling it. In January 2006, an RQ-8A touched down on the USS *Nashville* (LPD-13), an Austin-class amphibious transport dock, off the coast of Maryland near the Patuxent River.

In 2004, meanwhile, the U.S. Army chose to acquire the aircraft as a Future Combat System (FCS) program. They awarded Northrop Grumman a $115 million contract to develop a Fire Scout variant as the "Class IV unmanned aerial system (UAS)" under the designation RQ-8B. The Army described the vehicle as a key element of "tactical intelligence, surveillance, reconnaissance and targeting at the brigade level."

The U.S. Navy guided-missile frigate USS McInerney (FFG-8) brings an MQ-8B Fire Scout aboard on 10 December 2008 in Mayport, Florida. (U.S. Navy photo by Mass Communication Specialist 1st Class Holly Boynton)

The RQ-8B vehicles were similar to the RQ-8A Fire Scouts produced for the Navy, but would have a four-blade, rather than three-blade, rotor. This system used an improved airfoil rotor blade to enhance performance and increase payload capacity to 600 pounds, and fuel capacity to 60 gallons. The RQ-8B also had an uprated transmission system designed to take advantage of all of the engine's available horsepower.

An illustration of a U.S. Army MQ-8B Fire Scout in flight over rugged terrain. (Northrop Grumman)

Beginning in 2004, the United Kingdom Ministry of Defence also evaluated the Fire Scout for its Watchkeeper UAV battlefield imagery and intelligence program. Watchkeeper was intended to develop the ultimate replacement for the British-built Phoenix fixed wing UAV. For the Watchkeeper trials, Northrop Grumman incorporated a General Atomics Lynx all-weather, high-resolution, tactical synthetic aperture radar and moving target indicator (SAR/MTI) on the company's production-configured Fire Scout demonstrator.

In 2005, however, the British decided to "buy European." They contracted with the UK division of France-based Thales (formerly Thompson-CSF) aerospace firm to develop a variant of the Israeli Elbit Hermes 450 fixed wing unmanned aerial vehicle to meet the Watchkeeper requirement.

In the United States, the Fire Scout was quickly evolving past the point of its being merely a reconnaissance platform, and the new "B model" variant was redesignated as a multi-mission MQ-8B. Both the Army and Navy pursued an interest in this new variant, which was engineered for installation of two four-packs of 2.75-inch rocket launchers designed to fire the Advanced Precision-Kill Weapon System (APKWS) laser-guided rockets. Tests of this system were carried out in 2005 by Northrop Grumman at the Yuma Proving Grounds.

"We proved we could hit Arizona," Doug Fronius, the Northrop Fire Scout program manager joked to Richard Burgess of *SeaPower* magazine. "But the real purpose of that test was to demonstrate the ability to carry that class of weapon. That test proved to be extremely successful. The data was very good. And that, in itself, allowed the Navy to have the confidence that the technology level was such that they moved forward with weapons on their roadmap."

U.S. Air Force General Douglas Fraser, commander of the U.S. Southern Command, looks at an MQ-8B Fire Scout with Navy Captain Tim Dunigan, program manager of PMA-266, Multi-Mission Tactical Unmanned Aerial Strike Systems, in Mayport, Florida, in July 2009. (U.S. Navy photo by Mass Communication Specialist 1st Class Holly Boynton)

Sean McCann of the Canadian company Mist Mobility Integrated Systems Technology (MMIST) speaks with Marines about the company's CQ-10 SnowGoose rotary-wing UAV at NAS Patuxent River in Maryland in July 2003. By that time, the U.S. Special Operations Command had already bought five of the aircraft, which can provide pinpoint delivery of small cargo. (Defense Department photo by Jim Garamone)

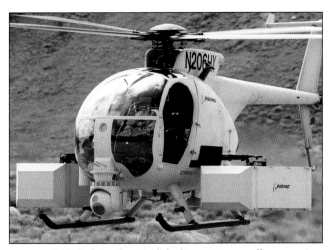

An unmanned Little Bird helicopter, smaller version than a manned A/MH-6M Little Bird helicopter, was tested and evaluated by personnel from the U.S. Marine Corps' Warfighting Laboratory in Bridgeport, California, during Javelin Thrust-09. (U.S. Marine Corps photo by Chief Warrant Officer Keith Stevenson)

Looking farther ahead, the Navy announced plans to equip its MQ-8Bs with the Coastal Battlefield Reconnaissance and Analysis (COBRA) system, designed to detect mines in shallow water. Armament options that were considered by the Navy included the APKWS, the GBU-41 Viper Strike laser-guided smart bomb, the Low-Cost Guided-Image Rocket, and the Common Very Lightweight Torpedo. As of 2009, the Navy was planning to purchase 168 MQ-8B aircraft.

The U.S. Navy had intended to deploy Fire Scouts aboard the new Freedom Class of small Littoral Combat Ships (LCS) in the first decade of the twenty-first century. However, the first vessel, USS *Freedom* (LCS-1), was not launched until 2006, and would not be commissioned for two years. By this time, the Navy made the decision to shift the initial deployment to frigates, and the Fire Scout's operational evaluation in May 2009 took place aboard a guided-missile frigate, the USS *McInerney* (FFG-8).

As explained by Fronius and reported by Burgess in *SeaPower* magazine, the frigate's smaller flight deck required the addition of a grid platform mounted on the ship's starboard recovery system, so that both MQ-8Bs and SH-60 Seahawk helicopters could be accommodated. Meanwhile, the Ground Control Station for the Fire Hawk was installed in the area that previously housed the control used for RIM-67 Standard Missile operations.

It was also aboard the USS *McInerney* that the MQ-8B made its first operational deployment in September 2009. Assigned to the Fourth Fleet, in support of the United States Southern Command, the two Fire Scouts aboard the frigate would operate as part of the aerial flotilla monitoring drug runners in speedboats. The Sandbox analog for the Fire Scout would be the warm waters off the cocaine coast of Central America, rather than the deserts of Southwest Asia.

Enter the Other Rotorcraft

When discussing the unmanned rotary wing aircraft being developed for the United States armed forces during the first decade of the twenty-first century, the Fire Scout certainly emerges as the most prominent. However, while the Fire Scout fits the definition of an armed drone, which is the subject of this book, our discussion of rotary winged UAVs is incomplete without mentioning a couple of important unarmed drones—and adding both that the potential for arming virtually any drone is always an option, and that this option seems often to be exercised.

The CQ-10A SnowGoose, first flown in April 2001, was developed initially to drop leaflets over hostile territory, but was later embraced by the U.S. Special Operations Command as a means of delivering small quantities of highly critical cargo to troops in hostile situations. This was a derivation of MMIST's Sherpa autonomous GPS-guided parafoil delivery system intended for pin-point delivery of small cargo items. Total capacity was 600 pounds.

Clark Butner, a UAV specialist with Naval Air Systems Command, once told Jim Garamone of American Forces Press Service that "Mogadishu [during the 1993 operation recorded in the book *Black Hawk Down*] would have been a perfect place for this type of capability. The [U.S. Army] Rangers didn't bring their [night optical devices] when they went on the mission. This aircraft could have dropped NODs to them, delivered plasma to them, and dropped ammo."

Developed by the Canadian firm, MIST Mobility Integrated Systems Technology (MMIST), the CQ-10A flies a mission profile that is programmed in the field on a small laptop computer.

Other rotary wing UAVs developed for delivery of small, high-value military cargo included remotely powered variants of the OH-6 Little Bird military helicopter and the Kaman K-Max civilian helicopter, as well as the A160 Hummingbird.

The Hummingbird was originally developed by San Diego-based Frontier Systems, a firm acquired by Boeing in May 2004. Based on a modified lightweight Robinson R-22 helicopter, the Hummingbird was first flown in January 2002. The A160 was extensively evaluated by DARPA and the U.S. Army, as well as by the U.S. Navy's Air Warfare Center Aircraft Division "to assess the military utility and affordability of a long-range VTOL UAV employing a wide variety of adaptable payloads."

At first, the aircraft was flown with a series of gasoline-powered piston engine types, but a follow-up version, designated as A160T, was debuted with a Pratt & Whitney turbine engine in June 2007. In May 2008, at the U.S. Army's Yuma Proving Ground in Arizona, the A160T demonstrated its ability to hover—out of ground effect—at 20,000 feet altitude, and to make an 18.7 hour flight, landing with over 90 minutes of fuel still on board.

For this, the aircraft received the Fédération Aéronautique Internationale's official endurance record for the longest unrefueled flight of a rotorcraft.

In May 2009, the United States Special Operations Command (SOCOM) announced the planned acquisition of 20 A160T Hummingbirds under the designation YMQ-18A. These aircraft would fly with the DARPA-developed Forester foliage penetration radar. As Major Scott Beall told Stephen Trimble of *Flight Global*, the command had found the Hummingbird "uniquely qualified for SOCOM's requirement for a long-endurance UAV," adding that he also expected the production MQ-18A to "compete against the Northrop

The A160 Hummingbird unmanned rotorcraft during 2008 flight test with the 21.5-foot-long FOPEN (FOliage PENatration) Reconnaissance, Surveillance, Tracking and Engagement Radar (FORESTER) antenna. FORESTER is a technology development program sponsored jointly by DARPA and the U.S. Army intended to produce an advanced airborne UHF radar system to track personnel and vehicles on the ground when they are hidden by foliage. (DARPA)

The Broad-area Unmanned Responsive Resupply Operations (BURRO) helicopter was used for resupplying ships at sea, and in conjunction with the Slice Multi-Task Boat for providing over-the-horizon sea-based logistics. The BURRO was an unmanned version of the Kaman K-1200 K-Max helicopter. (U.S. Marine Corps photo by Lance Corporal Christopher Vallee)

Grumman MQ-8B Fire Scout for the army's Class IV unmanned aircraft system."

Beall said that the aircraft would also be a candidate for a U.S. Marine Corps requirement to deploy an "immediate cargo UAS" to Iraq or Afghanistan. For the Special Operations Command, though, the Hummingbird would serve as a strike *and* surveillance aircraft.

Move over Fire Hawk.

Sharing the Crowded Skies

Though the Warrior gave the U.S. Army the brigade level UAV strike capability that it had sought, the skies over Iraq remained conflicted, and the UAV command and control environment grew ever more complicated. In 2008, as General George Casey moved up as Army chief of staff, Air Force and Army leaders began early to seriously discuss the issue of finding common ground to resolve these issues and the festering Washington Drone Wars.

At the end of June 2008, General John D. W. Corley, Air Combat Command (ACC) commander, representing the Air Force, and General William Wallace, commanding general of the U.S. Army Training and Doctrine Command (TRADOC), and Lieutenant General Michael Vane, director of the Army Capabilities and Integration Center, sat down across the same table at Langley AFB. The object was to attempt to formalize a new Concept of Operations (CONOPS) for Unmanned Aircraft Systems. Basically, it was a quest for mutual interest interoperability.

The two services were finally ready to develop a single comprehensive CONOPS for operations at the theater levels. In the meeting, they jointly considered such issues as airspace control, apportionment of available UAS assets, command and control, direct support of ground units involved in irregular warfare, and the relationship between air support and those supported.

"The environment we are operating in today, and what we expect to see tomorrow, has changed dramatically over the past few years," Wallace said, thinking about how the Warrior and Reaper had changed the battlefield equation with their increased capabilities. "Taking a joint approach on UAS issues will allow us to rapidly develop force capabilities . . . by identifying, linking, and synchronizing all of our activities, so we can give the best capability to joint warfighters who are fighting a very elusive, thinking, and adaptive adversary."

"As opposed to finding independent solutions, we are trying to find joint, collaborative solutions that best support the joint warfighter in any spectrum of war," Corley interjected. "If we can't share data, then we can't share information. If we can't share information, we can't command and control."

"We want to identify areas or opportunities for increasing interoperability in order to optimize support to the joint warfighter," Wallace said. "It's all about working together to get a capability to our troops quickly and effectively."

Working together was a bottom line issue, but the ultimate issue was accomplishing the mission. Putting it into perspective, Major Matt Martin, ACC's Predator and Reaper Operations Branch chief, said, "We need to have the ability to support full levels of joint operations from air-only major campaigns all the way down to counter-insurgency operations."

A follow-up meeting in September achieved what Kris Osborn and Michael Hoffman of *Defense News* described as a "breakthrough," as work began on formally drafting a joint CONOPS. "We have a joint agreement on unmanned aerial system CONOPS and we're moving in the right direction," said Lieutenant General James Thurman, the Army deputy chief of staff for operations.

Among the issues addressed by the CONOPS was that the two services would work harder to "deconflict" the increasingly crowded Iraqi airspace. As Osborn and Hoffman wrote, "At the beginning of the war in Iraq, the Army had only a handful of UAVs; now it has hundreds . . . Both sides will work to address a common concern: finding space in the sky to fly their burgeoning fleets of unmanned planes, which must share space with manned aircraft and artillery shells."

Under the CONOPS, the Air Force agreed to provide more UAS direct support missions to Army units on the ground, and the Army agreed to better communicate its specific needs. The Air Force also promised to locate airmen with ground units on the front lines, moving them out of the Combined Air Operations Center (CAOC).

Addressing the reality of the Warrior operations, the Army also conceded that as more MQ-1Cs were deployed, there would be fewer requests for armed Predator sorties from the Air Force.

Grace V. Jean wrote in the December 2008 issue of *National Defense,* "Under the plan, both services will be able to pool all Predators, Reapers and Sky Warriors in support of air and ground commanders."

Meanwhile, Major Matt Martin went so far as to say that the goal of the CONOPS was for Air Force Predators and Army Warriors to be "interchangeable for a variety of missions . . . Under the new procedures, the services would have the connectivity, communications, tactics and procedures in place to hand off one of those targets to another drone. The [Warrior] could track one,

Senior Airman Quantral Fletcher, an 887th Expeditionary Security Forces Squadron ScanEagle maintainer, prepares to launch a ScanEagle unmanned aerial system from a catapult at Burge Field at Camp Bucca in Iraq. As seen here, the aircraft does not need a runway to take off or land. It is launched into the air by a pneumatic catapult. (U.S. Air Force photo by Staff Sergeant Thomas Doscher)

Senior Airman Quantral Fletcher recovers a ScanEagle after a flight on 25 February 2009. The ScanEagle does not land like a traditional aircraft. Intstead, a piece of equipment called a SkyHook extends a bungee cord into the air, the cord slides across the edge of the wing until it's caught by a hook at the end of the wing. The ScanEagle is then lowered to the ground and recovered. (U.S. Air Force photo by Staff Sergeant Thomas Doscher)

the Predator could continue tracking the other, and all of the commander's requirements would be met."

Martin went on to say that the Army was working to convey target information gathered by unmanned aerial vehicles such as the little RQ-7 or RQ-11 to the Warrior. He added that the Air Force had even expressed an interest in being able to achieve "connectivity" to such a data loop, so that such information could be relayed to its manned attack aircraft as well as its UAVs.

General Wallace agreed, saying, "Regardless of who's flying it, everyone ought to have access to the data."

ScanEagle

Another player among the remotely piloted birds soaring in Iraq's crowded skies is the ScanEagle, a small tactical recon drone first deployed to the Sandbox with the U.S. Marine Corps in 2004. With a wingspan of just over 10 feet, it is in the same size range as the RQ-7 Shadow, but its endurance, rated at 24 hours plus, is much greater than other unmanned aerial vehicles of its size.

The aircraft originated with the Insitu Group of Bingen, Washington, a company that developed miniature robotic aircraft for both commercial and military use, including the first UAV to cross the Atlantic Ocean. Insitu had also developed the SeaScan UAV, which was used by the commercial fishing industry for fish spotting. The SeaScan evolved from a UAV that was created by the Australian company Aerosonde Ltd.

The ScanEagle project, initiated in February 2002, brought Insitu together with aerospace giant Boeing. With Insitu responsible for the airframe, Boeing provided the communications and payload components, as well as systems integration. In 2008, Boeing acquired Insitu outright, folding the company into its Integrated Defense Systems business unit.

As an aircraft-building subsidiary, Insitu quickly rose to the top among Boeing subsidiaries. Indeed, as Bill Sweetman wrote in *Aviation Week* in August 2009, "It's official: Boeing's Insitu subsidiary has outstripped Boeing Commercial Airplanes in delivery rates for air vehicles. The production rate of the ScanEagle UAV, which was 35 vehicles a month at the beginning of the year, has reached 54 a month to meet operational needs worldwide. Considering that Insitu delivered its 1,000th vehicle only a couple of months ago, the program is clearly growing at a rapid rate."

The ScanEagle's ability to operate autonomously for long periods of time makes it an attractive tactical asset. The first autonomous flight occurred in June 2002 at Boeing's remote test facility near Boardman in eastern Oregon. In this flight, lasting 45 minutes, the ScanEagle flew a pre-programmed course with a maximum altitude of 1,500 feet using the Global Positioning System. Eight months later, in February 2003, the little aircraft was transported to the Bahamas to participate in the U.S. Navy's Giant Shadow exercise. In a scenario worthy of Hollywood, the exercise was designed to examine the tactical integration of special operations forces and a stealthy attack submarine with the ScanEagle and an unmanned *underwater* vehicle. During Giant Shadow, the ScanEagle illustrated its capability to relay real-time data and video.

The ScanEagle's baptism of fire in Iraq came in the 2004 battle of Fallujah. As quoted by Jim Garamone of the American Forces Press Service in January 2005, a 1st Marine Expeditionary Force spokesman said that the newly-deployed aircraft, the ScanEagle system, developed by Boeing and the Insitu Group of Bingen, Washington, had its baptism of fire "performed flawlessly . . . during some of the heaviest urban combat Marines have been involved in since Hue City in Vietnam in 1968."

Marine Major General Martin Post (left) deputy commanding general, Multi National Force West is briefed about a ScanEagle by Marines with UAV Squadron 2, 3rd Marine Air Wing, at the Combat Outpost of Mudaysis in Iraq, on 3 October 2008. The Marines were engaged in operations to deter insurgent activity. (US Marine Corps photo by Corporal Seth Maggard)

A Dragon drone unmanned aerial vehicle at the Military Operations in Urban Terrain (MOUT) facility during LOE 1 (Limited Objective Experiment 1) at the Marine Corps Warfighting Laboratory. (Marine Corps photo by Sergeant Jason Bortz)

Since that time, the ScanEagle has taken part in numerous operations, fielded by units including Marine Unmanned Aerial Squadron 2, (VMU-2) as part of 2nd Marine Aircraft Wing. In *Marine Corps News* in November 2007, Lieutenant Devin Scully, the ScanEagle officer in charge and mission commander for VMU-2 Detachment B, described the ScanEagle mission in Iraq.

"The basic mission here is to provide intelligence, surveillance, and reconnaissance support via the ScanEagle UAV for supporting units such as (1st Battalion, 4th Marine Regiment) or (1st Light Armored Reconnaissance Battalion)," Lieutenant Scully said. "It is a number of different things depending on what the units need from us. We do anything from area scans, group scans, target development, battle damage assessment, whatever is needed. Our capabilities afford them so many things, in terms of providing overwatch, various types of missions, like helping to mark for air strikes and artillery strikes. We are basically their eyes 24/7. We go into areas that are either too hostile or if they don't want to send in ground units right away they send us in and we can fly at altitudes where (the enemy) can't see or hear us."

As Scully points out, Insitu personnel actually operate the ScanEagles. "The contractors fly the aircraft and work the camera, and the intelligence Marines sit next to them disseminating all the intelligence out. They direct that operator on the target and where to go. The contractors and Marines work very close together in order to accomplish the mission . . . There is great coordination between that ground unit and our ability to work that makes us extremely successful. The Marines have been flexible, every time that we need to support a new mission or operation, they have been flexible to provide that."

The U.S. Navy also acquired the ScanEagle for shipboard operations. The first ScanEagles were deployed aboard the LHAs and LHDs (amphibious assault ships), LPDs (amphibious transport dock ships), LSDs (amphibious dock landing ships). Late in 2007, the aircraft was deployed aboard a destroyer for the first time, this being the USS *Oscar Austin* (DDG 79), which conducted tests of the aircraft even as it was en route to the Central Command area of operations.

Also in 2007, the U.S. Air Force issued a contract to link the ScanEagle with the ShotSpotter acoustic gunfire detection system (GDS) for protection of its war zone bases. The idea was to develop a system able to detect an enemy sniper, and televise his location with the help of the ScanEagle's electro-optical camera system.

Meanwhile, Boeing Australia Ltd. had received contracts to provide ScanEagle aircraft and services to the Australian Army in both Iraq and Afghanistan. Canadian Forces also acquired the ScanEagle, and in March 2008 activated Small Unmanned Aerial Vehicle (SUAV) Troop Task Force Afghanistan to operate it. The primary mission was for "persistent UAV surveillance to counter the current improvised explosive device threat."

The mission that truly put the ScanEagle on the front page came in April 2009. The cargo ship *Maersk Alabama* was taken by pirates—a first for an American-flagged vessel off the coast of Somalia—and the ship's master, Captain Richard Phillips, was taken hostage. When the USS *Bainbridge* (DDG-96) intervened, a ScanEagle operating off the USS *Bainbridge* were the U.S. Navy's eyes in the sky, continuously monitoring the lifeboat where the pirates were holding their hostage. Using ScanEagle data, SEALs operating off the destroyer captured one pirate and killed three others as Phillips was rescued on 12 April.

"Holy cow. It was unbelievable; it felt like we were in a movie," Operations Specialist Carissa Riedman, a tactical information coordinator, told the *Navy Times*. "I never thought that in any aspect of my life that I'd be doing that in real life."

"We got to see [ScanEagle's] capabilities can work for the Navy," Commander Frank Castellano added. As noted in an Insitu media release "more than 1,000 ScanEagle UASs have logged over 200,000 operational hours [150,000 in Iraq and Afghanistan] with the global defense community," in the first five years of deployment, from Fallujah to Somalia.

While the ScanEagle was not yet known to have been flown with an offensive weapons capability, one remembers that the Predator was first deployed in the 1990s solely as a reconnaissance platform, and with underwing hardpoints designed only for surveillance payloads.

The quiet success of Insitu, which became the largest airframe builder within Boeing, is indicative of the growing importance of unmanned aerial vehicles among the world's military aircraft. Holy cow, indeed.

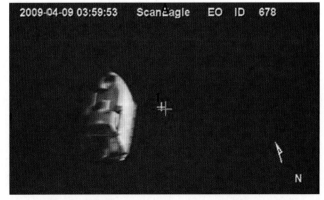

A 28-foot lifeboat from the American-flagged container ship Maersk Alabama *is shown in this still frame from a rare and now historic video taken by a ScanEagle flying over the Indian Ocean on 9 April 2009. Aboard the lifeboat was Captain Richard Phillips of the* Maersk Alabama, *who had been taken captive when his ship was hijacked by Somali pirates. Snipers from the U.S. Navy's SEAL Team 6 killed the pirates aboard the lifeboat on 12 April and Phillips was rescued after being held hostage for four days.* (U.S. Navy photo)

PREDATORS AND REAPERS OVER THE HINDU KUSH

Armed with smart bombs and AGM-114 Hellfire missiles, an MQ-9 Reaper taxis down a runway in Afghanistan. During operations on 15 July 2009 this Reaper released several weapons on possible improvised explosive devices located in a roadway near Qalat. According to the Air Force News Service, "this action eliminated any possible imminent threat to friendly forces and civilian forces." (U.S. Air Force photo by Staff Sergeant Brian Ferguson)

The mountains of central Asia have stymied Western armies since the time of Alexander the Great. They present an extremely rugged environment that is tailor-made for the Predator and Reaper. The ability of these unmanned aerial vehicles to fly high, slowly and quietly over this terrain has given American forces an offensive capability and flexibility that could barely have been imagined prior to 2001.

When the story of the twenty-first century war in the mountainous border regions of Afghanistan and Pakistan is eventually written, with full access to secret documents, we will learn the full extent of American covert operations, but in the meantime, we know that these operations are happening, and we know that both MQ-1 Predators and MQ-9 Reapers are helping to write that history.

It all began in Afghanistan with Operation Enduring Freedom in the difficult winter of 2001–2002.

We are reminded that success has many fathers, while failure is an orphan. Unclaimed by any service, the tactical failure of United States forces to defeat al-Qaeda decisively in these mountains that winter will be the object of spirited discussion in military circles indefinitely. Regardless of how or why it happened, much of al-Qaeda got away. To the singular vexation of American leaders was the fact that al-Qaeda's top leadership, especially Osama bin Laden and Ayman al-Zawahiri, were among the ones who got away.

The place to which they got away was of particular frustration for American planners, both from a diplomatic and military perspective. Pakistan became America's first twenty-first century conundrum. Diplomatically, there was a fragile "alliance" between the two nations that demanded a kid gloves approach. Though President Pervez Musharraf talked the talk when it came to supporting the United States in the Global War on Terror, he walked the walk on a narrow and tenuous tightrope.

President Musharraf and his government feared that if the United States forces had come across the border into the neighboring regions of Pakistan in 2001–2002, it would have invited a revolt against Musharraf by factions within his country who supported al-Qaeda and the Taliban. Therefore, the United States halted its offensive at the border.

The perilous diplomatic tightrope was matched by an equally formidable environment—from weather to topography. From a military perspective, the difficulty faced by the United States in 2002 was all about terrain. The area of Pakistan into which al-Qaeda and their Taliban allies got away is some of the most rugged country on earth. Military operations in these mountains by Western military forces—whether it be the British in the nineteenth century or the Americans in the twenty-first century—presented enormous logistical challenges.

Between them, Pakistan's North-West Frontier Province (NWFP) and Federally Administered Tribal Areas (FATA), the latter including North and South Waziristan, comprise a steep and mountainous area the size of Virginia, high in the Hindu Kush Mountains, with virtually no roads.

And then, there are the people who live in these places, people who supported and welcomed al-Qaeda and the Taliban as they came across from Afghanistan. Indeed, the people are ethnically similar and the Taliban are a dominant force on both sides of the border—a border they do not recognize.

Dressed in his general's uniform, a relaxed Pakistani President General Pervez Musharraf entertains Secretary of Defense Robert Gates over small dishes of mixed nuts in his Islamabad palace on 12 February 2007. (Defense Department photo by Cherie Thurlby)

Having hung up his uniform in favor of a civilian business suit, Pakistani President General Pervez Musharraf (right) sits down with Chairman of the Joint Chiefs of Staff Navy Admiral Mike Mullen (middle) and U.S. Ambassador to Pakistan Anne Peterson in his Islamabad palace on 9 February 2008. Musharraf was growing anxious over the rising tide of Taliban aggressiveness within his borders, audacious dissent within the Pakistani political establishment, and Mullins's unwillingness to provide the "Predator drones" that Musharraf demanded. By August, the cunning old strongman would be out of a job. (Defense Department photo by Mass Communication Specialist 1st Class Chad McNeeley, U.S. Navy)

The FATA are a lawless region that is claimed to be under the jurisdiction of Pakistan's central government, but which have essentially never been ruled by any outside entity. Here, as in the NWFP, there is essentially no law but that enforced by tribal warlords and local imams.

Effectively, bin Laden, al-Zawahiri, and their henchmen found themselves in the ultimate sanctuary, unreachable both by the Pakistani government, who feared the warlords, and by Americans, who bought into Musharraf's fear that the Pakistani government would be toppled if the Americans tried to enter the country. From their sanctuary, al-Qaeda and the Taliban could strike Coalition forces in Afghanistan with virtual impunity.

Though Pakistan was unwilling to grant the United States permission for offensive operations within its territory, they did grant access to Pakistani bases for "logistical" purposes. Around the time that Operation Enduring Freedom began in October 2001, air bases at Dalbadin, Jacobabad, Pasni, and Shamsi were all made available to the Americans. Located in a remote, mountainous region—about 190 miles southwest of the city of Quetta and 100 miles from Afghanistan—Shamsi had an interesting history, having been built for Arab sheiks on falconry excursions.

Jacobabad, meanwhile, became the primary American air base until Bagram in Afghanistan, near Kabul, was reconditioned and made available. It is still an important logistics base for United States forces. The others, such as Shamsi, garnered little publicity, even when a U.S. Marine Corps KC-130 crashed at Shamsi in January 2002, killing seven Marines on board.

In discussing air bases in Pakistan used by Americans for covert operations, it is worth recalling that the one at Peshawar was used in the 1950s and early 1960s to launch U-2 "spy planes" on clandestine flights over the Soviet Union. When Francis Gary Powers was shot down in May 1960 during such a mission, he had taken off that morning from Peshawar.

The rules of engagement that prevented American forces from crossing the Afghanistan-Pakistan border in the early days of the Global War on Terror also prevented operations here by armed UAVs—for a few years. By 2004, though, reports began coming out of Pakistan's NWFP and FATA of al-Qaeda and Taliban leaders and fighters getting blown up by missiles that could only have been launched by some whisper-quiet aircraft.

"It had to have been a Predator drone," speculated the defense analysts who were approached for comments by various news organizations. Soon, people on the ground—from Pakistani officials to local tribesmen—were tossing off the phrase "Predator drone."

One of the first warlords of note to feel the wrath of a Hellfire launched by a Predator was Nek Mohammad. Growing up in the FATA, Mohammad spent his teens engaged in stealing cars from rival tribes and other nefarious activities. He later decided on more serious mischief, moved to Afghanistan around the turn of the century,

and joined the Taliban. According to a Waziristan tribesman quoted in *Dawn*, Pakistan's most widely read English-language newspaper, his actions "catapulted him to a mid-level position in the Taliban military hierarchy, commanding 3,000 men at one time." He also made several videos exhorting militants to jihad.

At about 10:00 pm on the night of 18 June 2004, Nek Mohammad was lounging with some fellow militants, including Fakhar Zaman and Azmat Khan, at the village of Shah Nawaz Kot, near Wana in South Waziristan, when they came into the crosshairs of an MQ-1. This trio and two others died, although Nek reportedly survived for an hour or so.

According to reporters Ismail Khan and Dilawar Khan Wazir, writing in *Dawn*, "Witnesses said that a spy drone was seen flying overhead minutes before the missile attack. There were also reports that Nek Mohammad was speaking on a satellite phone when the missile struck, fuelling speculations that he might have been hit by a guided missile . . . The precision with which the missile landed right in the middle of the courtyard where Nek Mohammad and his colleagues were sitting, lent credence to the theory. Locals said that the missile created a six feet crater."

To cover up American involvement, Major General Shaukat Sultan of Pakistan's Inter-Services Public Relations agency insisted that a Pakistan missile had been fired, but "declined to speculate on how the militant had been killed."

As seen previously in Yemen, the attacking of jihadist leadership was destined to become a good use for the capabilities of the Predator.

Nearly a year later, in May 2005, high-value Haitham al-Yemeni died on the Afghanistan-Pakistan border in an attack that was credited by ABC News to a Hellfire-armed, CIA-operated Predator. ABC first reported that the attack happened in Pakistan near the Afghan border, but Pakistan Information Minister Sheikh Rashid Ahmad told CNN that the incident could not have occurred in Pakistan. ABC reported that al-Yemeni was in line to replace Abu Faraj al-Libbi as al-Qaeda's global operations chief. Al-Libbi, the number three man in the terror network's murky hierarchy, had been captured by Pakistani agents a week earlier inside Pakistan.

The man who next became bin Laden's number three, Abu Hamza Rabia, met his own death from above on 30 November 2005. As reported by *Dawn*, he and four others were killed when the mud-walled compound where they were staying in the village of Asoray near Miram Shah, the administrative capital of North Waziristan, was blown up around 1:45 am.

A few days later, Fox News reported, "Local residents found at least two pieces of shrapnel at the blast scene inscribed with the designation of the Hellfire missile, which is carried by the U.S. Air Force's unmanned, remote-controlled Predator aircraft. The metal pieces bore the designator 'AGM-114.'"

Quoting unnamed officials, NBC News said Rabia was killed by a missile launched from a Predator controlled by the Central Intelligence Agency, but "the CIA would not comment." The network added, "Tribal witnesses in Pakistan said a 'hail of missiles' struck the mud house . . . They also said they had heard six explosions, but it is uncertain how many of these were the result of missile attacks and how many may have been explosives detonating inside the house."

The Fox report quoted "a man who lives near the house," as saying that he heard "at least two detonations and saw a white streak of light before a missile hit the house, sparking a huge explosion."

Two explosions would imply a single Predator because an MQ-1 carries two Hellfires, while more blasts would imply that two MQ-1s were flying the mission.

Because neither the CIA nor the U.S. Central Command announce, discuss, or deny UAV operations inside Pakistani airspace, there would be no official version of such missions. What information about these operations that is available to the public must come from independent media reports. These usually begin with Pakistani military or intelligence personnel debriefing eyewitnesses. In turn, they are interviewed by reporters

An Air Force MQ-1 Predator prepares to land at Kandahar Air Base in Afghanistan, where the 62nd Expeditionary Reconnaissance Squadron provided the launch and recovery element for Predator missions in support of Operation Enduring Freedom. The door to the 62nd ERS command post featured a drawing of a Predator armed with Hellfire missiles underscored with the words "We're not drones—we fire back." (U.S. Air Force photo by Major David Kurle)

With Pakistan visible in the distance, soldiers from Charlie Company, 1st Battalion, 26th Infantry Regiment, 1st Infantry Division established a patrol base in the mountains surrounding the Korengal Valley of Afghanistan in April 2009. During Operation Viper Shake, these soldiers battled freezing temperatures while hiking to elevations above 8,200 feet. (U.S. Army photo by Sergeant Matthew Moeller)

A General Atomics MQ-1B Predator lands after a training flight, stateside at Creech AFB. The same pilots making the landings here, would be making landings across the globe, but they would still be doing it from the same building. (U.S. Air Force photo)

from Pakistani media, or by Pakistani stringers working for international media, especially Reuters and the BBC.

The next widely reported major attack credited to Predators came on 13 January 2006. It targeted al-Qaeda's number-two man, Ayman al-Zawahiri, but failed to nail him. Some reports indicated that the targeting was based on information given to the CIA by the captured Abu Faraj al-Libbi, who had earlier met with al-Zawahiri at this particular compound in Damadola, Pakistan.

Imtiaz Ali, reporting from Damadola for London's *Daily Telegraph*, said that the raid was "launched from four pilotless aircraft which intruded 30 miles into Pakistani air space from Afghanistan. But a senior American government official said that Pakistan would have been informed before an attack on a such high-profile target on its soil." He added, "Pakistani officials said [the compound] had been struck by as many as 10 missiles fired from the remote-controlled drones."

If the raid had involved four MQ-1s as reported, it would have involved one of the largest armadas of attack drones yet to have been launched on a coordinated mission in Southwest Asia.

Calling the meeting taking place at the site an "apparent terror summit," ABC News quoted Pakistani authorities in listing some of the high-value characters who were among the dead in the Damadola attack. These included Khalid Habib, the al-Qaeda operations chief for Pakistan and Afghanistan, as well as Abdul Rehmanal-

Magrabi, a senior operations commander for al-Qaeda and son-in-law of Ayman al-Zawahiri. ABC reported that Midhat Mursi al-Sayid Umar, also known as Abu Khabab al-Masri, al-Qaeda's master bomb maker and chemical weapons expert, was killed but this turned out not to have been the case. Al-Zawahiri himself had apparently not attended the "summit."

The *Daily Telegraph* noted, "Damadola is a stronghold of Gul Badin Hikmatyar—a mujahadin leader who is engaged in guerrilla warfare against American forces in neighboring Afghanistan."

With 18 dead in the attack, Pakistan moved quickly to establish plausible deniability. Reported the *Daily Telegraph*, "Pakistan is preparing to lodge a formal diplomatic protest over the attack . . . But a senior American government official said that Pakistan would have been informed before an attack on a such high-profile target on its soil."

After Damadola, few reports of air strikes by UAVs came out of Pakistan for more than a year, but on 26 April 2007 four people were reported killed in such a strike near the town of Saidgi in North Waziristan, just two miles from Afghanistan.

Bashirullah Khan of the Associated Press reported that a senior military official in the capital, Islamabad, said, "the dead and wounded were making bombs and had accidentally caused an explosion. But two local intelligence officials said it was a missile attack, and a government official said

Where the terrain makes surface travel arduous, the aerial option becomes a key part of battle doctrine. U.S. Army Sergeant 1st Class Steve Larocque, Charlie Company, 3rd Squadron, 61st Cavalry Regiment, looks back at Pfc. James Kelley during a patrol near Hajiabad, Afghanistan, just a few miles from the Pakistan border, in July 2009. (U.S. Army photo by Specialist Evan Marcy)

the projectiles were apparently fired from Afghanistan. The intelligence and government officials asked for anonymity because of the sensitive nature of the topic."

Khan was told by Habib Ullah, the owner of the destroyed house that five missiles hit the building and two empty madrasahs nearby. "The schools," reported Khan, "belonged to Maulana Noor Mohammad, a pro-Taliban cleric."

"Residents held up shards of metal that they said were remnants of the missiles," wrote Khan, "and pointed out the damaged roof of one of the schools. The metal pieces carried no identifying marks."

Nothing said "Hellfire" but the telltale craters.

On 2 November, it was a "school" established by Jalaluddin Haqqani, a Taliban commander with close ties to bin Laden, that took a hit attributed by *The New York Times* to "a missile fired from an unmanned aerial drone."

The paper quoted an unnamed Pakistani security official who said the strike took place in a village outside Miran Shah, the administrative center of North Waziristan, targeting a compound that "served as a safe house for Islamic fighters crossing between Afghanistan and Pakistan, and was owned by a militant leader from Waziristan."

As for all the Predators used over Pakistan having been based in Afghanistan, one is left to wonder. It was around the time of the Damadola strike that the satellite from which the Google Earth website would derive imagery of Pakistan, snapped a picture of Shamsi Air Base.

Parked on the ramp were three Predators.

Fear the Reaper

While "Predator drones" were filling both the skies over Southwest Asia and newspaper headlines around the globe, the General Atomics MQ-9 Reaper officially became an active combat asset of the U.S. Air Force during 2007.

Whereas Predators had entered service assigned to reconnaissance squadrons, the Reaper first went into action assigned to attack squadrons. As Air Force Chief of Staff Michael Moseley put it, "We've taken these aircraft from performing mainly as intelligence, surveillance, and reconnaissance platforms to carrying out true hunter-killer missions."

Said Air Force Lieutenant General Gary North, who commanded CENTCOM American and Coalition air power in the Middle East in October 2007, "It's a

An MQ-9 Reaper takes off on a mission on a hazy day in Afghanistan. Reapers, such as the one shown here, are routinely used to provide overwatch for Coalition forces during their missions. This photograph illustrated an Air Force News Service dispatch that reported on 12 August 2009 operations in which "an Air Force MQ-9A Reaper provided armed overwatch for friendly forces near Now Zad. Friendly forces reported and confirmed enemy action related to planting improvised explosive devices. The Reaper released precision guided munitions on the enemy position to deter the enemy action. The strike was deemed successful after the enemy position was destroyed." (U.S. Air Force photo)

tremendous increase in our capability that will allow us to keep UAVs over the airspace of Afghanistan and Iraq in the future for a very long time."

Speaking to the sensitivities of U.S. Army ground forces within CENTCOM, he called the Reaper an "evolutionary step where technology is helping commanders on the battlefield to integrate great effects from the air into the ground commander's scheme of maneuver."

Three MQ-1 Predators sit ready for launch in a hangar at a base in southern Afghanistan. The Predator is a multi-role attack reconnaissance unmanned aircraft system incorporating advanced surveillance capabilities with the offensive power of two AGM-114 Hellfire missiles. (U.S. Air Force photo by Staff Sergeant Samuel Morse)

American soldiers in the rugged mountains along the border between Afghanistan's Kunar Province and Pakistan's lawless North West Frontier Province, which is visible in the distance. U.S. Army Sergeant Levi Bradstream (foreground) provides security as Specialist Anthony Janda comes up an ancient trail over a mountain on 10 April 2009, during a patrol mission to search for caves and trails used by the Taliban to infiltrate from their nearby sanctuaries. Bradstream and Janda were both assigned to Charlie Troop, 6th Squadron, 4th Cavalry Regiment, 3rd Brigade Combat Team, 1st Infantry Division. (U.S. Army photo by Staff Sergeant David Hopkins)

In May 2007, the Air Force formally activated its 432nd Wing, soon redesignated as the 432nd Air Expeditionary Wing, an all-drone unit that would serve as an umbrella for existing Predator and Reaper squadrons, especially those which had been part of the 57th Operations Group, the overseer of training and flight operations at the Nellis AFB Range.

Headquartered at Creech AFB at the edge of the Nellis Range, near Las Vegas, Nevada, the unit would contain the 11th, 15th, and 17th Reconnaissance Squadrons, which had been activated at the base as part of the 57th in

Six successful strike missions are recorded on the side of this MQ-1B Predator, which is being stripped for maintenance by airmen assigned to the 432nd Aircraft Maintenance Squadron. (U.S. Air Force photo by Senior Airman Larry Reid, Jr.)

Activated at Creech AFB in May 2007, the 432nd Air Expeditionary Wing became the first U.S. Air Force wing dedicated solely to unmanned aerial vehicles. With dual reporting responsibilities to Ninth Air Force and the U.S. Air Forces Central Command, the 432nd became the umbrella organization for a number of pre-existing unmanned aerial vehicle units, including the 11th, 15th, and 17th Reconnaissance Squadrons and the 42nd Attack Squadron. The unit originated during World War II as 432nd Observation Group, and became 432nd Reconnaissance Group in April 1943. Deactivated later in 1943, it was reactivated between 1954 and 1958. In September 1966, it was reactivated as the 432nd Tactical Reconnaissance Wing at Udon RTAFB in Thailand. Equipped with RF-4C Phantom IIs, the Wing flew over 80 percent of all reconnaissance missions over North Vietnam. It operated Firebee drones in the 1970s, became a fighter wing in 1984, and was deactivated 10 years later. (U.S. Air Force)

1995, 1997, and 2002, respectively, as well as the 30th Reconnaissance Squadron activated in August 2005 at Tonopah Test Range Airport on the opposite end of the Nellis Range from Creech. Also part of the 432nd were the 19th and 42nd Attack Squadrons. It was to the 42nd Attack Squadron that the MQ-9s were assigned. Officially activated in November 2006, the 42nd had a lineage that went back to the 42nd Bomb Squadron in World War II. It would receive its first MQ-9 in March 2007.

"This is a monumental day for the Air Force," said Colonel Christopher Chambliss. The new wing commander of the 432nd, he had formerly been vice commander of the 366th Fighter Wing. "Having a wing dedicated to unmanned aircraft systems is a logical and important step in continuing the Air Force's role in being the world's greatest air and space power."

While Chambliss perceived the 432nd as part of a logical progression, his boss saw it as a landmark. Said Lieutenant General Norman Seip of the Twelfth Air Force, "although this standup is a landmark achievement for the Air Force . . . [the] transition of authority will seem transparent."

A parallel organization at Creech was Detachment 4 of the 53rd Test and Evaluation Group, an unmanned aerial vehicle test unit that had been flying Predators for some time. It was upgraded to squadron status in March 2008 because of the increasing workload and flying requirements, and the arrival of the Reaper in the arsenal. The detachment became the 556th Test and Evaluation Squadron, officially the Air Force's first operational test *squadron* for unmanned aircraft systems.

In the meantime, the U.S. Air Force was not alone in its acquisition of the Reaper. The United States Customs & Border Patrol also operated them, and as Stephen Trimble of Jane's Information Group reported in March 2006, so too did the U.S. Navy, although in announcing the acquisition, General Atomics "declined to elaborate on which naval organization has taken delivery of the MQ-9As and what purpose they will serve in operation."

Overseas, both Turkey and Italy placed Reaper orders. As reported by Italy's *Difesa News* in February 2008, the Aeronautica Militare, already a Predator customer, was flying Reapers out of Herat in Afghanistan. Italy had ordered the Reaper in 2004 and had deployed three with its 28th Gruppo at Herat. The same unit had flown UAVs of Tallil AB in Iraq in 2005–2006.

Another significant Reaper operator was Britain's Royal Air Force. Like the Aeronautica Militare, the RAF had also operated Predators.

The British acquisition of both Predators and Reapers was amusing in the context of a 2003 exchange between Tom Cassidy, president and CEO of General Atomics, and Lord William "Willy" Stephen Goulden Bach, then Britain's minister for defense procurement.

Cassidy had gone to the United Kingdom in the wake of the Predator's stellar performance in Iraq to interest Her Majesty's government in the company's products. Cassidy knew that the British were in the market for UAVs of this class, and he told Nick Cook of *Jane's Defence Weekly* that the Ministry of Defence "ought to buy a [General Atomics] system and use it," given that the "aircraft are available right now."

Lord Bach, meanwhile, insisted that the Ministry of Defence "buy European." He told the House of Commons Defence Select Committee that the

An MQ-9 Reaper goes through an engine check on a ramp at Kandahar Air Base in Afghanistan. (U.S. Air Force photo)

Watchkeeper UAV program, then in competitive evaluation in the United Kingdom, was a "generation ahead" of the Predator. As noted earlier, the Watchkeeper WK450 was a target acquisition and reconnaissance UAV based on the Israeli Elbit Hermes 450 UAV.

The General Atomics reaction to his lordship's "generation ahead" quip was a terse, "By any measure, that is untrue."

Even as the Ministry of Defence put more than a billion dollars worth of Watchkeeper into its budget, they also bought Predators and Reapers. Indeed, RAF personnel packed their bags for Creech AFB, as the U.S. Air Force and the RAF formed a Joint Predator Task Force. While the U.S. Army resisted placing its UAV assets under a joint command with those of the U.S. Air

Lucky Thirteen. An MQ-9 Reaper sits on a ramp in Afghanistan in October 2007, just after it was announced that the "new hunter-killer unmanned aerial vehicle" (as the Air Force described the Reaper) had completed a dozen successful missions. (U.S. Air Force photo)

Aircrews perform a preflight check on an MQ-9 Reaper before it takes off on a mission over Afghanistan on 1 October 2007. The MQ-9 had flown daily missions over Afghanistan since late September, supported by teams from the 658th Aeronautical Systems Squadron of the 303rd Aeronautical Systems Wing. The team was comprised of program managers, functional supporters, testers, and logisticians. (U.S. Air Force photo)

An aircrew member inspects the weapons loadout on an MQ-9 Reaper before it takes off on a mission over Afghanistan. (Defense Department photo)

Force, the British were willing to do so. When the RAF activated their first dedicated UAV unit, No.39 Squadron in early 2008, it was based at Creech.

The U.S. Air Force announced on 11 October 2007 that Reaper combat air patrols over Afghanistan had

An MQ-9A Reaper prepares to land after a mission over Afghanistan. The Reaper has the ability to carry both precision-guided bombs and air-to-ground missiles. This photo illustrated a July 2009 dispatch from Air Force News Service that reported "Coalition airpower integrated with Coalition ground forces in Iraq and the International Security Assistance Force in Afghanistan during operations 24 July, according to Combined Air and Space Operations Center officials here. At Sangin, an MQ-9A Reaper provided cover for Coalition forces taking small-arms fire from anti-Coalition forces entrenched on a ridgeline. The Reaper fired a missile which stopped the enemy action." (U.S. Air Force photo by Staff Sergeant Brian Ferguson)

begun on 25 September. As noted in a piece in the *Air Force Times*, datelined 29 October, the first air strike flown by a Reaper had occurred on 27 October when "an MQ-9 fired a Hellfire missile at Afghanistan insurgents in the Deh Rawood region of the mountainous Oruzgan province." According to the report, the strike was "successful."

Less than two weeks later, on 7 November, as reported by the U.S. Central Command, a Reaper dropped its first precision-guided bomb on an enemy force. This MQ-9 was operating over the Sangin region of Afghanistan on the hunt for enemy activity when its controllers at Creech AFB learned that friendly forces were taking fire from enemy combatants. The Reaper responded with two laser-guided GBU-12 bombs, which, in Central Command's pithy understatement, "eliminated" the enemy.

General Gary North was already delighted with his new bird. "The MQ-9 gives us an incredible addition to the arsenal," he enthused. "It's larger [than the Predator], carries an increased payload, and is able to fly longer, higher, and faster. It's an incredible addition to our attack capability in the CENTAF force lay-down."

The day after the Sangin strike, RAF No.39 Squadron operations began out of Kandahar. On 8 November, the Ministry of Defence officially announced that "the RAF's first Reaper Unmanned Aerial Vehicle, Britain's most sophisticated unmanned surveillance system, has taken to the air in Afghanistan."

This debut mission was flown in October by a Reaper, serial number ZZ200, that had just arrived in-country. The initial delivery of three Reapers to the RAF was seen as being part of an eventual dozen. As Air Chief Marshal Sir Glenn Torpy, Chief of the Air Staff, said, the Reaper would "significantly enhance the UK's surveillance and reconnaissance capability in Afghanistan."

Followed discretely by an Air Force Humvee and loaded with two bombs and four AGM-114 Hellfires, an MQ-9 Reaper taxis toward takeoff at Kandahar for a mission over Afghanistan. (U.S. Air Force photo)

Royal Air Force Flight Lieutenant Bert Weedon, along with honor guard members present the United Kingdom No.39 Reaper Squadron colors during an activation ceremony on 23 January 2008 at Creech AFB. Air Marshal Iain McNicholl, the RAF Operations Air Command deputy commander in chief, presided over the unveiling ceremony and RAF chaplain Pardre Lee blessed the new squadron. Prior to the squadron's activation, members of the RAF were completely embedded into U.S. Air Force 432nd Wing operations in all aspects of combat, training, maintenance, and mission support activities. They also assisted in standing up MQ-9 Reaper training at the U.S. Air Force 42nd Attack Squadron. (U.S. Air Force photo by Staff Sergeant Scottie McCord)

Royal Air Force Wing Commander Andy Jeffery hands off the flag during the activation ceremony of the United Kingdom's No.39 Reaper Squadron to Flight Lieutenant Bert Weedon on 23 January 2008 at Creech AFB. The squadron was the RAF's first unmanned aerial vehicle squadron, although the RAF had been operating UAVs at Creech AFB since 2004 as part of the Joint Predator Task Force. (U.S. Air Force photo by Staff Sergeant Scottie McCord)

A typical day in the course of Reaper operations. The Air Force News Service reported that on 27 May 2009, an Air Force MQ-9A Reaper like the one shown here, carried out a successful strike against Taliban wielding a rocket-propelled grenade launcher, obliterating them with a GBU-12. (U.S. Air Force photo by Tech. Sergeant Erik Gudmundson)

Added a ministry press release, "The [RAF] Reaper UAV is currently unarmed. It is capable of being armed and the Ministry of Defence is investigating arming options."

This was consistent with what Chief of the Air Staff, Air Chief Marshal Sir Glenn Torpy, told Tim Ripley of Jane's Information Group in an interview published on 4 May 2007.

"Predator B [Reaper] is coming later this year to give us a persistent striking capability, which is key to attacking the type of targets we need to attack," Torpy said to Ripley. "It is cleared for Hellfire. We will use the same weapons as the Americans at first because that is the quickest way to get capability...We will not need convincing of what [the Reapers] will deliver for us."

In March 2008, a "senior RAF source" told Richard Norton-Taylor of Britain's *Guardian* newspaper. "We need [people who are] air-minded and who know about dropping weapons."

A month later, Jonathan Barratt, who led the Ministry of Defence strategic unmanned air vehicles experiment integrated project team, confirmed to Robert

Another typical day in the course of Reaper operations. According to Air Force News Service reports, on 6 May 2009 an Air Force MQ-9 such as this one from the 62nd Expeditionary Reconnaissance Squadron seen taking off from Kandahar Air Base in Afghanistan, targeted a group of Taliban in the process of emplacing an improvised explosive device near Chahar Bagh, and took them out with a GBU-12. (U.S. Air Force photo by Staff Sergeant James Harper, Jr.)

An MQ-9 Reaper goes through an engine check on a ramp at Kandahar Air Base in Afghanistan. (U.S. Air Force photo)

Hewson of Jane's Information Group that the RAF Reaper would "be armed within a matter of weeks, with AGM-114P Hellfire missiles and GBU-12 Paveway bombs that we have acquired under a separate United States Foreign Military Sales [FMS] contract."

Hewson wrote that Barratt was aware that there had been "an 'ethical' issue over the employment of U.S. weapons on a UK platform that is active in a foreign theater but flown by UK crews from the U.S. The U.S. authorities wanted to make sure there were no legal obstacles to doing any of this, and there are not."

Germany, too, took an interest in the Reaper, and as Robert Wall reported in the 19 June 2007 issue of *Aviation Week*, General Atomics teamed with Diehl BGT Defense to develop the aircraft for the German market. However, like Britain, the Germans maintained that their eyes were on the aircraft for its reconnaissance capability rather than its ability to sling Hellfires.

Since Germany's armed forces were reconstituted a decade after World War II, there has been a powerful political reluctance to deploy German Bundeswehr combat assets beyond the country's borders. Although Germany is the third-largest contributor of forces to the International Security Assistance Force (ISAF) in Afghanistan, and leads Regional Command North, the Bundestag passed legislation prohibiting Bundeswehr troops to take part in combat operations against the Taliban in the east and south of the country.

"There is some concern in Germany because [the Reaper] can be armed," Robert Wall wrote. "That is not planned, though."

After the better part of a year of operations in Afghanistan, U.S. Air Force MQ-9 Reapers began operations out of Balad AB in Iraq began on 18 July 2008. They were flown by the 46th Expeditionary Reconnaissance and Attack Squadron of the 332nd Air Expeditionary Wing, which was already operating armed Predators.

As reported in a release by Staff Sergeant Don Branum of 332nd AEW public affairs, a "Reaper dropped a 500-pound bomb against an anti-Iraqi target 16 August in one of the first weapons engagements for the unmanned aircraft system . . . During an overwatch mission over southeast Iraq, Reaper operators from the 46th discovered a suspicious vehicle. The Airmen immediately relayed the information to personnel in a local ground unit . . . After the suspicious vehicle was confirmed to be a [Vehicle-Borne Improvised Explosive Device] a joint terminal attack controller cleared the Reaper to employ a GBU-12 laser-guided weapon against the vehicle."

"I'm looking at the opportunity to complement our manned airplanes with an increased amount of unmanned attack platforms—the Reaper," General North told Thom Shanker in an interview published in *The New York Times* on 29 July. "So that I get persistence overhead at a lower overall cost. The capability that I am providing [to ground troops] comes at less manpower on the ground."

As Shanker reported, "To a degree, the Air Force has become a victim of its own progress, having created a nearly insatiable desire for live video surveillance, especially as provided from remotely piloted vehicles like the Predator and now the Reaper.

On one average day over the past several weeks, senior ground commanders in Iraq requested more than 400 hours of video over a single 24-hour period. The combined surveillance efforts by the Army, Navy, and Air Force provided more than 95 percent of the hours requested. Almost 75 percent of the requested hours were supplied by aircraft under General North's Combined Air and Space Operations Center headquarters."

A few weeks later, on 11 August 2008, the 174th Fighter Wing of the New York Air National Guard also became active with MQ-9 Reapers. The wing, whose 138th Fighter Squadron had flown F-16s since 1988, became the first fighter unit to transition from manned fighters to drones, and the first all-Reaper wing in the Air Force.

Canada's Herons

In discussing the international units flying Predators and Reapers, it is worthwhile also to mention international forces running other unmanned aerial vehicles in Afghanistan. Of particular note are the Canadian Forces operating mainly in Kandahar Province. Beginning in 2003, Canada deployed the French-built CU-161 Sperwer, mainly for reconnaissance activities. In 2009, the Sperwer was phased out and replaced by the CU-170 Heron drone.

Manufactured by Israel Aerospace Industries, originators of the Pioneer and Hunter UAVs, the Heron had entered service in Israel in 2005. It was subsequently acquired by the United States Southern Command, and deployed from El Salvador for recon operations in the largely unheralded drug war in Central America.

Substantially larger than the Pioneer or Hunter, the Heron is 27 feet 10 inches long, with a wingspan of 54 feet 5 inches, making it larger than the Predator and just over three quarters the size of the Reaper. With a gross weight of 2,530 pounds and long endurance, it is certainly in the same generation of sophistication as the Predator and Reaper. Its potential as an offensive platform is limited, although it does have a payload capacity of around 550 pounds.

With its long range and its capability to carry a variety of sensors and information systems, it was destined to be an able complement to the surveillance and target acquisition capabilities of the Predator. Canadian Brigadier General Denis Thompson, the commander of Joint Task Force Afghanistan, announced the aircraft's having achieved initial operational capability on 21 January 2009, noting its "operational-level day or night video capability."

Canadian Forces were pleased with the marked improvement that the Heron demonstrated over the Sperwer, which was phased out four months later. Lieutenant Colonel Darrell Marleau, observed that

A Canadian Forces crew prepares an IAI CU-170 Heron medium altitude long endurance unmanned aerial vehicle for flight. Canada had made extensive use of the Heron for recon operations in Afghanistan. (Canadian Forces photo)

A Heron unmanned reconnaissance aircraft takes off from Comalapa International Airport in San Salvador, El Salvador, in May 2009, during a counter drug operations support mission. The Heron is part of an unmanned aircraft system deployed to El Salvador to support Project Monitoreo, a month-long evaluation initiative to assess the suitability of using unmanned aircraft for counterdrug missions in the United States Southern Command area. (U.S. Army photo by Jose Ruiz)

unlike Sperwer, "the Heron can fly in excess of 24 hours . . . the aircraft is two generations beyond the Sperwer . . . The product we're producing from the Heron is in high demand. In addition to providing data to the Army, several NATO countries . . . are now routinely requesting our assistance in gathering surveillance data."

The British Are Coming

At the same time that the United Kingdom was acquiring Predators and Reapers from General Atomics, British industry was working toward developing an

The BAE Systems HERTI XPA-1B in flight. The High Endurance Rapid Technology Insertion (HERTI) system captures, processes, and disseminates high quality imagery, which can be, as BAE describes, "relayed to ground stations, forward deployed units, and command centers in a variety of operational environments with very low network bandwidth demand." (BAE Systems)

indigenous armed UAV/UAS capability that went beyond the limited capability of the WK450 Watchkeeper that Lord Willy Bach once overstated as being a "generation ahead" of the Predator.

Indeed, the Ministry of Defence was very keen on unmanned warplanes. The UK's 2005 Defence Industrial Strategy stated that, "an essential part of future combat air capability, the UK is examining the balance between manned and uninhabited aerial vehicles." Could that mean that the balance could shift away from manned platforms?

Since the turn of the century, BAE Systems, the successor company to British Aerospace and the largest defense contractor in Europe, has had a number of such aircraft in the works. Part of the company's motivation in this initiative was to compete in the commercial marketplace with the Predator and Reaper by developing less expensive UAV/UAS aircraft. By the end of the first decade of the twenty-first century, several BAE types had been tested or deployed on a limited basis.

The BAE Systems High Endurance Rapid Technology Insertion (HERTI) program was developed at BAE's center at Warton in England, with substantial support from the company's BAE Systems Australia component. The latter had previously developed the

At the opposite end of the BAE Systems product spectrum from attack UAVs designed to compete with the Reaper are 2-inch stealthy and autonomous robotic dragonflies. They are being developed under the Micro Autonomous Systems and Technology (MAST) Collaborative Technology Alliance, which according to BAE, "will research and develop advanced robotic equipment for use in urban environments and complex terrain, such as mountains and caves." Said Steve Scalera, MAST program manager for BAE Systems in Merrimack, New Hampshire, "The technologies that will be developed under MAST represent capabilities and techniques that will influence nearly all of the products that BAE Systems will develop and produce in the future." (BAE Systems)

Mantis over Woomera. In November 2009, BAE Systems announced the successful debut flight of the Mantis at Woomera in South Australia. The largest fully autonomous unmanned aircraft ever built in the United Kingdom, it has a 66-foot wingspan and is BAE Systems' first all-electric aircraft. The Mantis completed a series of test flights demonstrating what the company described as "the capability of the system and the potential of large unmanned systems to support future UK Ministry of Defence operational needs . . . Mantis is designed to be a real workhorse with 'plug and play' elements in the mission system and the ability to carry a wide range of sensors." Said Air Vice-Marshal Simon Bollom, "These trials . . . have successfully demonstrated a number of key factors that have helped build confidence in the feasibility of a UK-derived medium-altitude long-endurance unmanned aerial system." (BAE Systems)

The BAE Systems High Endurance Rapid Technology Insertion (HERTI) unmanned aerial vehicle at Warton Aerodrome in Lancashire, England. According to BAE, the HERTI platform evolved from an extensive BAE Systems autonomous air vehicle and systems technology demonstration program. The system integrates world-leading autonomous systems and sensor technology with proven air vehicle expertise. (BAE Systems)

Kingfisher, a small, twin-boom surveillance UAV. The debut flight of the HERTI aircraft took place in December 2004 at the Woomera test range in Australia, where BAE predecessor companies had been conducting missile and other flight tests for half a century.

In 2005, several HERTI flights were made over Scotland, with the aircraft flying from Campbeltown Airport, formerly RAF Machrihanish. These reportedly made it the first UAV to fly in the UK with a Civil Aviation Authority certificate.

With an airframe based on a motorized glider designed in Poland by Jaroslaw Janowski of J&AS Aero Design, the HERTI prototype had a maximum takeoff weight of 990 pounds, and a payload of around 330 pounds, although *Flight International* reports that the operational HERTI weighs more than 1,600 pounds. Among the HERTI variants, grouped by engine type, are the HERTI-1A, powered by a BMW piston engine and equipped with the ICE (Image Collection and Exploitation) system; the HERTI-1B, powered by a Rotax piston engine and equipped with a more sophisticated autonomous ICE II system (payload) and the turbine-powered HERTI-1D.

In 2006, under Project Morrigan, the Royal Air Force leased HERTI for an evaluation deployment to Afghanistan, and BAE Systems flew missions from Camp Bastion. As reported by Craig Hoyle in *Flight Global* in November 2007, "BAE and the RAF decline to comment on the specific missions being performed, but sources indicate that the UAV could be useful for tasks such as monitoring border areas. Its payload's coherent change detection capability could also be to highlight the placement of improvised explosive devices . . . In addition to providing image intelligence, the deployment has also succeeded in demonstrating the system's ability to safely deconflict with other air traffic."

As with U.S. Air Force and Royal Air Force Predator and Reaper operations, where controllers were located in Nevada, the HERTI pilots were in Britain. Hoyle explained that HERTI operations "demonstrated a so-called 'reach-back' capability, where the team was able to relay imagery back to the UK via satellite . . . Operations are overseen from a ground control station housed within a 6.1-meter (20-foot) long ISO container, with work stations for a pilot, image analyst, and mission commander."

Andy Wilson, BAE's Military Autonomous Systems sales and marketing director, told Hoyle that this was "the first time that the RAF has fielded an autonomous system with certification."

As in the case of the Reaper, the idea of arming the HERTI was built in from the start. In June 2008, at the Farnborough International Air Show, BAE revealed the armed variant, which is known as Fury. Fitted with a stores management system, the Fury was designed to be armed with the Thales Lightweight Multi-role Missile (LMM). Initially introduced in the UK in 2007, the

LMM was created to provide a weapon with advanced precision to minimize collateral damage. Thales markets the LMM as having a "multi-function capability which allows it to engage static installations, wheeled or tracked vehicles, unmanned aerial vehicles, helicopters, and fast in-shore attack and landing craft."

Apparently, BAE hoped to capitalize on promoting the Fury as an inexpensive alternative to the Predator and Reaper. Said Chris Clarkson, BAE's project director for the Fury program, the new attack drone is "an affordable and reliable platform which has the ability to perform a number of military roles. With a high degree of autonomy, it combines many of the already proven elements of our other unmanned platforms, including a small logistic footprint and low operator workload with a reliable and highly accurate weapon system."

In March 2009, BAE unveiled yet another armed UAV type that was developed from the HERTI. This aircraft, known as Mantis, was debuted publicly at the Australian International Airshow and Aerospace and Defence Exposition in Avalon, Victoria. Funded jointly by BAE, the UK Ministry of Defence (MoD), and other industry partners, Mantis was an advanced technology demonstrator described officially as "an autonomous medium altitude long range (MALE) Unmanned Aircraft System providing deep and persistent ISTAR (Intelligence, Surveillance, Target Acquisition and Reconnaissance)."

BAE compared Mantis to HERTI, calling them "next-generation autonomous systems, with emphasis placed on the levels of autonomy designed into the system and the concept of operations developed for effective deployment and operation."

The role of BAE Systems Australia in the Mantis program had been, according to the company, "the design and integration of the real-time elements of the Ground System (through which the operator interface is achieved). The Mantis and HERTI ground environment is based on the ISR Management System concept developed by BAE Systems Australia through a three-year, internally funded R&D program . . . BAE Systems Australia has been responsible for the development, integration, and support of the Autonomous Vehicle Management System (VMS)—a significant element of the 'smart autonomy' capability."

With a wingspan in excess of 65 feet, Mantis was roughly the same size as the MQ-9 Reaper, and the armament with which the aircraft was posed when displayed also made it appear to be comparable to the Reaper in that respect. Indeed, the Mantis is designed for deep penetration, long-range intelligence gathering, and as BAE put it, the aircraft carries a significant payload in terms of sensors and potential weaponry."

While the HERTI had made its cameo appearance in the war zone, it remained to be seen when the Fury or the Mantis might be seen in active combat over the mountains of Afghanistan.

The Kid Gloves Come Off

By 2008, reports of armed UAV attacks within Pakistan had increased again against the backdrop of political turmoil in that country. At the end of 2007, Pakistan was emerging from the Musharraf era. Though he would not officially resign as president until 18 August 2008, Pervez Musharraf was already bowing to political pressure from within Pakistan, as well as from outside, to step aside in favor of new elections. These were scheduled for 8 January 2008, but postponed to 18 February after the assassination of front-runner Benazir Bhutto at the end of 2007. Yousaf Raza Gilani was elected as Prime Minister of Pakistan in February, and Asif Ali Zardari was elected president after Musharraf's resignation.

In the United States, the Bush Administration was also under pressure to show concrete results from a Global War on Terror that had already lasted half again longer than World War II. With all of these developments, the pressure on the Taliban and al-Qaeda sanctuaries—and the high-value targets who hid there—ratcheted up.

On 3 September 2008, less than two weeks after Musharraf's resignation and seven years after the start of the Global War on Terror, the United States first publicly acknowledged an American Special Forces operation within the Pakistani "Tribal Areas." As the BBC reported nine days later, "It has emerged that President Bush recently authorized U.S. raids against militants in Pakistan without prior approval from Islamabad."

Of course, this September milestone announcement was preceded by many months of barely covert strikes within the region by UAVs. At the time, the Pakistanis were apparently willing to sanction the UAV operations. As Pir Zubair Shah reported in *The New York Times*, the missile strikes were "conducted by the Central Intelligence Agency but are for the most part coordinated with Pakistan's government, according to American officials. But that cooperation does not extend to ground operations."

Interestingly, Shah added, "There have been few protests by people in the tribal region against the air strikes, apparently because those killed have mostly been Arab and Uzbek members of al-Qaeda, not Pakistanis."

The UAV attacks that began to intensify in 2008, had often borne fruit. The first senior al-Qaeda chief to feel the wrath of an American Hellfire within Pakistan during the year was Abu Laith al-Libi, killed in January, who some intelligence estimators suggested was Abu Hamza Rabia's successor as al-Qaeda's "number three." Laith al-Libi (not to confused with that earlier number three, Abu Faraj al-Libbi) was a Libyan who had fought the Soviets in Afghanistan. Later implicated in the 1996 Khobar Towers bombing that killed a number of U.S. Air Force personnel in Saudi Arabia, al-Libi was arrested but either escaped or was released by the Saudis. He went back to Afghanistan, where he appeared in a number of al-Qaeda propaganda videos. In 2007, he masterminded a suicide bombing that killed two dozen people near

An MQ-9 taxis out to the runway for a training mission. This Reaper was assigned to the 42nd Attack Squadron, part of 432nd Air Expeditionary Wing. (U.S. Air Force photo by Steve Huckvale)

Bagram Air Base in Afghanistan, while Vice President Dick Cheney was there.

The BBC reported the missile attack that killed al-Libi came on the night of 28–29 January near Mir Ali in North Waziristan, also killed seven Arabs and six Central Asians. The Italian news agency Adnkronos identified three of those killed as Abu Obeida Tawari al-Obeidi, Abu Adel al-Kuwaiti, and Abdel Ghaffar al-Darnawi, all of al-Qaeda. A witness told Reuters, "The missile appeared to have been fired by a drone."

Though the United States consistently declined to confirm or deny the UAV attacks, most of those on the ground had embraced the notion that unmanned aerial vehicles were responsible.

Reports in both Western and Middle Eastern media used the term "drone" as a matter of course when describing the incidents, and from these, we are able to piece together a history of significant operations.

On 27 February, the Arab television news network al-Jazeera reported that a building in South Waziristan had been blown up, noting that this house belonged to Sher Mohammad Malikkheil, "a Pashtun tribesman with known links to fighters in the area. . . [the] missile was believed to have been fired by a U.S. pilotless drone."

Dawn later reported that the 27 February attack, and another on 16 March, killed a number of al-Qaeda "trainees."

Al-Jazeera added that "neither U.S. nor Pakistani authorities officially confirm U.S. missile attacks on Pakistani territory. It can be considered an infringement of Pakistani sovereignty."

Not only Pakistani security officials, but "local tribesmen" were considered newsworthy sources for identifying UAVs. In reporting an 18 March attack near Shahnawaz Kheil Dhoog in South Waziristan, the *Daily Telegraph* quoted "Local tribesman Rahim Khan," saying, "at least two missiles from an unmanned drone hit and destroyed the home of a local militant leader and Taliban sympathizer who goes by the single name of Noorullah."

Khan may have seen the "drone," and perhaps he even squeezed off a couple of shots with his rifle.

In a 15 May piece in *Dawn*, reporter Anwarullah Khan (probably no relation) described an operation the day before in which he quoted "local residents and witnesses" in writing that "at least 12 people were killed in a Hellfire missile strike on Damadola . . . They said that a pilotless Predator fired two missiles on a two-story compound in Khaza, a small hamlet in the Damadola area at about 8:45 pm."

By 2008, the phrase "Predator drone" was fully entrenched in the lexicon of pop culture.

Damadola was, of course, the place where a January 2006 mass attack by four Predators had failed to kill Ayman al-Zawahri, but had taken out Abu Khabab al-Masri instead. In writing of the May 2008 strike for 1 June edition of *The Observer*, Jason Burke identified one of those killed as Abu Suleiman al-Jazairi, "a highly experienced Algerian militant . . . An al-Qaeda trainer and explosives specialist involved in a range of European terrorist networks."

In acknowledging that his agency was involved in the strike, CIA Director Michael Hayden said, "The ability to kill and capture key members of al-Qaeda continues, and keeps them off balance, even in their best safe haven along the Afghanistan-Pakistan border."

Meanwhile, Abu Khabab al-Masri, the al-Qaeda master bomb maker and chemical weapons expert, who was erroneously reported killed in the 2006 Damadola raid, had been surviving on borrowed time for two and a half years. Having earlier been the man who probably trained notorious "shoe-bomber" Richard Reid, al-Masri had spent those two and a half years working to revive the al-Qaeda effort to build an arsenal of weapons of mass destruction.

On 28 July 2008, just before dawn, the borrowed time ran out. As reported by the BBC, a missile struck a house often used by militants near a mosque in the village of Azam Warsak, 12 miles west of Wana in South Waziristan. "It was suspected to be a strike by U.S. forces, with residents saying they had heard U.S. drones, but this has not been confirmed," said the BBC. "The U.S. is reported to have carried out a number of drone missile attacks in the tribal regions."

Al-Masri had left the building for the last time.

In September, just as the United States first publicly conceded that its Special Forces were active within Pakistan, Jane Perlez and Pir Zubair Shah writing in the *International Herald Tribune* reported a series of attacks by UAVs. Among other operations, they reported that on 8 September, "Five missiles fired from an American pilotless aircraft on Monday hit a large compound in North Waziristan belonging to one of Pakistan's most prominent Taliban leaders."

As they reported, two Pakistani intelligence officials and a local resident said that a missile attack, at about 10:20 am, killed 23 people.

The strike hit the compound in the village of Daande Darpkhel, near Miranshah, that was run by Sirajuddin Haqqani. He was the son of Jalaluddin Haqqani, "whom the United States has accused of organizing some of the most serious recent attacks in Afghanistan against American and NATO forces and of masterminding a failed assassination attempt against the Afghan president, Hamid Karzai. It appeared that neither man was present at the compound during the attack."

Four days later, Miranshah was targeted in another strike. The BBC reported that missiles hit two buildings in the Tol Khel area on the outskirts of the town, adding that "the missiles were fired from a drone—an unmanned U.S. plane—local people said." A Pakistani army spokesman, Major Murad Khan, told the BBC that those killed included "foreign fighters."

The increasing tempo of UAV missile strikes in Pakistan had not only been taking a toll in blood, but it had gotten the al-Qaeda and Taliban to change their habits. Even as they did, however, constantly improving

American intelligence was starting to demonstrate the adage of their being able to run, but unable to hide.

A case in point was Khalid "Long Hair" Habib, an Egyptian who was described by the CIA as the "Number Four" in the al-Qaeda hierarchy and chief of operations in the Pakistani Tribal Areas. Known as "Zalfay," which literally means "long hair" in the Pashtun language, he had been feeling the heat in Wana, the capital of South Waziristan, where United States UAV attacks had been increasingly frequent. With this in mind, he moved to the village of Taparghai. On 16 October he was sitting in his Toyota station wagon, the vehicle of choice for Tribal Area jihadists, when it was blown up by a missile. This missile had been launched, according to witness accounts reported in various media, from a "drone."

From having been an ardently denied rarity in earlier years, the use of MQ-1 and MQ-9 UAVs in Pakistan became routine during the latter half of 2008. Incidents reported in the international media once drew headlines every few months, but were being reported several times a week after September. Targets were mentioned in the Tribal Areas of both North and South Waziristan. Locations in the vicinity of Miranshah and Wana were often on the target list.

In describing the events of September and October as "an unprecedented offensive," Chris Smyth of the *Times* of London wrote, "The U.S. is suspected of launching at least 17 missile strikes inside northwestern Pakistan since August. The strikes reflect U.S. frustration at what it says is Pakistani inaction against extremists blamed for planning attacks in Afghanistan and Pakistan and plotting to launch terror strikes in the West. Scores of foreign al-Qaeda members are believed to be hiding out in the lawless border area, which is considered a likely hiding place for Osama bin Laden."

Occasionally during one of these strikes, a high-value target made the transition from the headlines to the obituary page. On 26 October, it was Mohammad Omar, a henchman of the late Taliban commander Nek Mohammed, who was prey for Predator fire in 2004. Alas, this Omar was not the much sought Mullah Mohammed Omar, the reclusive leader of the Taliban of Afghanistan who had been Afghanistan's de facto head of state from 1996 to 2001. As the BBC reported, "Witnesses said that the missile strike completely destroyed Mohammed Omar's house, and partially damaged two neighboring houses. . . . Local officials confirmed that 20 bodies had been dug up from the debris of the compound."

A maintenance Airman inspects an MQ-9 Reaper during an engine run-up at Kandahar. Shortly before this picture was taken the Air Force reported that a Reaper "fired hellfire missiles in order to destroy enemy combatants engaging friendly forces with rocket propelled grenades. The JTAC reported that the mission was successful." (UASF photo)

A few days later, on 31 October, it was the turn of Abu Akash, described by a Pakistan intelligence source interviewed by Chris Smyth of the *Times* as a "mid-level al-Qaeda man who was leading a high-profile life in Mir Ali." Smyth reported two Halloween strikes, noting, "In the first attack two missiles hit a house in Mir Ali, a town in north Waziristan believed to be a sanctuary for Islamist militants Soon afterwards two more missiles, thought to have been fired from a U.S. drone, hit a house near Wana . . . thought to be a militant hideout and killed up to 12 suspected rebels. A Taliban commander, Mullah Nazir, was also reported wounded."

According to the report in the Pakistani daily *Dawn* about the incident, "local people" said "drones had been buzzing overhead throughout the day and residents had fired at them with light and heavy weapons."

"Two loud explosions were heard in Asori village while drones were flying over the area," said a villager.

Dawn also reported that Akash was al-Qaeda's "chief of financial affairs in the region," and quoted a Pakistan official who said, "he was involved in cross-border movement and attacks carried out with explosive devices."

Shortly before dawn on the morning of 22 November, a target of especially high value was hit by a UAV missile strike in the village of Ali Khel, close to the small town of Miram Shah in North Waziristan. Rashid Rauf, who held dual British and Pakistani citizenship, was at the compound of Khaliq Noor, described by Jason Burke, writing in *The Guardian*, as "a leader of the coalition of local extremist groups known as the Pakistan Taliban, [who] regularly sheltered foreign fighters."

Rauf was widely believed by the intelligence community to have been the mastermind of al-Qaeda's August 2006 plot to blow up transatlantic airliners departing Britain. Captured by Pakistani police, Rauf escaped from custody outside a Rawalpindi courthouse in December 2007. As Burke wrote, Pakistani officials said that the "missile strike, shortly before dawn, is thought to have killed several foreigners. At least one is believed to have been Egyptian, named as Abu Zubair al-Masri . . . the attack targeted a house in the village of Ali Khel, close to the small town of Miram Shah. The house belonged to Khaliq Noor, a leader of the coalition of local extremist groups known as the Pakistan Taliban, and he regularly sheltered foreign fighters."

Throughout 2008, as American UAVs struck targets inside Pakistan with increasing frequency, the Pakistani government came to repeatedly issuing perfunctory statements of protest. Despite these rhetorical condemnations of Predator attacks, they were quite happy to have someone keeping the Taliban off guard.

To quote Ayaz Gul, writing for the *Voice of America*, "Pakistan insists its security forces are engaged in successful anti-insurgent operations to secure the border with Afghanistan. But Pakistani leaders say U.S. drone attacks are undermining the country's sovereignty and efforts to win support of the local population against militant forces."

Pakistan had to have been especially pleased when a strike in South Waziristan on New Year's Day 2009 took out Usama al-Kini and Sheik Ahmed Salim Swedan. The two Kenyan nationals had been linked to the truck bombing of the Marriott Hotel in Islamabad in September 2008 that killed more than 50 people. Kini, a.k.a. Fahid Mohammed Ally Msalam, was also under a United States federal grand jury indictment for his role as a central planner in the attacks on the embassies in Kenya and Tanzania in 1998. In 2001, he headed al-Qaeda operations in Zabul Province, Afghanistan, and later moved his base of operations to Pakistan, where he was linked to numerous suicide attacks.

The timing of the escalation of the UAV attacks was seen as indicative of an unspoken understanding. It was suspected by many that there were secret "deals" between the United States and Pakistan immediately after Musharraf left power. As Ayaz Gul wrote on 22 December 2008 the Pakistan government "has long been under criticism from opposition parties for not taking a firm diplomatic stance against the missile attacks by U.S. drones. They say the strikes may be part of a secret deal between Islamabad and Washington, but the government denies the allegations."

If even the *Voice of America* voiced these suspicions, there had to be something to it. Right?

It was a secret that could not remain hidden. In the *Washington Post*, R. Jeffrey Smith, Candace Rondeaux and Joby Warrick reported on 24 January 2009 that "In September, U.S. and Pakistani officials reached a tacit agreement to allow such attacks to continue without Pakistani involvement, according to senior officials in both countries."

As reported in the media, notably by Eric Schmitt and Mark Mazzetti of *The New York Times*, the United States did compromise on the issue somewhat, by agreeing to give Pakistani officials advance notice of Predator strikes. However, the practice was quickly curtailed when it became apparent the Pakistanis were letting the information slip out, and times and dates were reaching the militants.

While the escalation of UAV operations over Pakistan began under the Bush administration, there was no interruption when the Obama administration took over in January 2009. On 23 January, just three days after Barak Obama moved into the White House, two separate strike missions were flown. According to the BBC, at least one missile hit a house in a village near the town of Mirali in North Waziristan, "a stronghold of al-Qaeda and Taliban militants." As reported, "four Arab militants were killed in the strikes . . . Their identities were not immediately clear but officials said one was a senior al-Qaeda operative."

As Smith, Rondeaux, and Warrick of the *Washington Post* observed, these strikes offered "the first tangible sign of President Obama's commitment to sustained military pressure on the terrorist groups there, even though Pakistanis broadly oppose such unilateral U.S. actions . . . members of Obama's new national security team have already telegraphed their intention to make firmer demands of Islamabad than the Bush Administration, and to back up those demands with a threatened curtailment of the plentiful military aid that has been at the heart of U.S.-Pakistani ties for the past three decades. . . . The Pakistani government, which has loudly protested some earlier strikes, was quiet."

Between August and December 2008 the total number of air strikes in the mountains of the Afghanistan-Pakistan border regions was double the total of the previous four years combined. Once the United States had treated the sovereignty of Pakistani air space with kid gloves, but the gloves had come off, and the incoming Obama administration would *keep* them off.

Shamsi Comes Out of the Cold

One of the most memorable lines from *Casablanca* (1942), a classic film with an overabundance of memorable lines, was uttered by Claude Rains in the character of Captain Renault. He is about to close down the establishment run by Humphrey Bogart, in the character of Rick Blaine.

"I'm shocked, shocked to find that gambling is going on in here!" Rains tells Bogart indignantly.

"Your winnings, sir," interrupts the croupier played by Marcel Dalio as he hands Rains a wad of cash.

"Oh, thank you very much," replies Rains, *sotto voce.*

"Pakistan has not allowed these drone attacks, there was no permission before nor is there any now," insisted Shah Mehmood Qureshi, the Pakistani Foreign Minister, as he stepped into the Claude Raines role on 15 February 2009. The news had just broken that the United States was not only flying armed UAV missions over Pakistan, but was basing them *inside* Pakistan at Shamsi Air Base.

"This is happening without any understanding and it is affecting our sovereignty, and we think that it is causing collateral damage."

"No. No. No. No. No. We unequivocally and emphatically can tell you that there is no basing of U.S. troops in Pakistan," an unnamed spokesman at the United States embassy in Islamabad told the *Times* of London. "There is no basing of U.S. Air Force, Navy, Marines, Army, none, on the record and emphatically. I want that to be very clear. And that is the answer any way you want to put it. There is no base here, no troops billeted. We do not operate here."

Both he and Qureshi were "shocked" at the suggestion.

The quote was published in the *Times* on 17 February 2009, by-lined by Tom Coghlan, Zahid [Zavid] Hussain, and Jeremy Page.

In this case, the croupier was played by Senator Dianne Feinstein of California, the chairwoman of the Senate Intelligence Committee. At a public hearing on 12 February, she had revealed in a public hearing—apparently

Shamsi or elsewhere? In May 2002, the U.S. Air Force released this photograph of Senior Master Sergeant Dale Neidigh (foreground). A Reconnaissance Systems Program Manager with Air Force Material Command, he is seen here guiding a support truss as a mobile expandable boom crane is used to construct a 68 x 40-foot mobile tensioned fabric shelter "at an undisclosed forward deployed location in Pakistan, during Operation Enduring Freedom. The shelter will be used to house the RQ-1B predator unmanned aerial vehicle." (U.S. Air Force photo by Tech Sergeant Joe Springfield)

by a slip of her tongue—that the United States was flying armed UAVs from Pakistani bases. "As I understand it," Feinstein said, speaking of the Predator missions, "these [operations] are flown out of a Pakistani base."

Indeed, a satellite image taken early in 2006 and posted on Google Earth had shown three Predators parked on the ramp at Shamsi. A February 2009 image of Shamsi showed no UAVs, but it did include a new hangar with clamshell doors which was large enough to accommodate several UAVs.

Safar Khan, a local journalist quoted in the *Times*, said that the outer perimeter of Shamsi was guarded by Pakistani troops, but the airfield itself was under the control of Americans. "We can see the planes flying from the base," he said "The area around the base is a high-security zone and no one is allowed there.

The battle doctrine involving the integration of armed UAVs—both Predators and Reapers—into ongoing tactical operations over Pakistan reached maturity in the latter half of 2008. This was apparent not only within military circles, but to the civilian mass media as well. Despite the official "shock" at the news about Shamsi, few people who had been following the ongoing war in the media were surprised.

Wrote Eric Schmitt in *The New York Times* on 8 January 2009, "Once largely reserved for missions to kill senior Arab al-Qaeda operatives, the Predator has since last summer been increasingly used to strike Pakistani militants and even trucks carrying rockets to resupply fighters in Afghanistan. Many of the Predator strikes are taking place as deep as 25 miles into Pakistani territory, not just along the border. . . . Senior military and counterterrorism officials say the increased Predator strikes have disrupted planning, pushed some insurgents deeper into Pakistan, prompted some militant commanders to post additional sentries, and forced the militants to use their cellphones and satellite phones, which American eavesdropping operations can monitor."

Redefining the War

The "Predator drone," the signature weapon of the Global War on Terror, had reached a total 100,000 hours in combat in October 2004 after three years, and passed the 250,000-hour milepost in June 2007. It is indicative of how ubiquitous the aircraft had become that the aircraft reached the half-million-hour mark just 20 months later in February 2009. It was against this backdrop that a new

Barack Obama is seen here on his first visit as President to the Pentagon on 28 January 2009. He came to office promising to focus the attention of American military strategy from Iraq to Afghanistan, and to link Afghanistan strategically with Pakistan. On his watch, the number of "Predator drone" strikes inside Pakistan, begun by his predecessor, increased dramatically. From left are Air Force Chief of Staff General Norton Schwartz, Army Chief of Staff General George W. Casey, Vice Chairman of the Joint Chiefs of Staff Marine General James Cartwright, and Chairman of the Joint Chiefs of Staff Navy Admiral Mike Mullen. (Defense Department photo by Mass Communication Specialist 1st Class Chad McNeeley)

administration came into Washington, and with them, a new perspective on the war itself.

As the pace of drone attacks against al-Qaeda and Taliban targets in Pakistan increased under the incoming Obama Administration in 2009, the American conception of the war was changing. When operations against these terrorist organizations began in 2001, it was under the worldwide umbrella of the "Global War on Terror," although this term was not an official Pentagon operational code name.

In March 2009, when the new administration stopped using the phrase "Global War on Terror," the media seized on this as a change in strategy as well as a change in conception. On 25 March, Scott Wilson and Al Kamen reported in the *Washington Post* that the "Obama Administration appears to be backing away from the phrase 'global war on terror,' a signature rhetorical legacy of its predecessor." they then went on to report that the International Commission of Jurists had "urged the Obama Administration to drop the phrase 'war on terror.'"

In their letter to the incoming administration asking for the change, the Geneva-based commission accused the outgoing Bush Administration of using it as "spurious justification to a range of human rights and humanitarian law violations."

Wilson and Kamen wrote that the change came subtly in a memo emailed two days earlier to Pentagon staff members. Reportedly this memo from the Defense Department's office of security review asserted that "this administration prefers to avoid using the term 'Long War' or 'Global War on Terror.' Please use 'Overseas Contingency Operation' . . . please pass this onto your speechwriters and try to catch this change before statements make it to OMB [Office of Management and Budget]."

The *Washington Post* reporters deduced that the memo was timed to be in circulation before upcoming congressional testimony by Marine Lieutenant General John Bergman. They went on to report discrepancies in the alleged source of the policy change. Though the memo said the instruction came from the OMB, Kenneth Baer, an OMB spokesman claimed on 24 March, "There was no memo, no guidance . . . I have no reason to believe that [the phrase] would be stricken" from testimony before Congress.

In their article, Wilson and Kamen suggested that the Pentagon had been using the phrase "overseas contingency operations" to describe the wars in Iraq and Afghanistan for a month, although the phrase, when lower-cased, has actually been used by the Pentagon for many years in discussing operations that take place overseas.

It may no longer have been a "war on terror," but on the same day that the *Washington Post* article appeared, an armed American UAV launched missiles at two vehicles in South Waziristan. The strike took out what the BBC reported as "seven militants" described by locals as being "of Arab and Uzbek origin."

Statistically, 50 percent of all armed UAV strikes were occurring in South Waziristan, while targets in North Waziristan received around 38 percent of the attacks.

While agencies such as the BBC and Reuters typically use the term "suspected U.S. drone," the *Agence France-Presse* went as far as to note the UAV type, although they lowercased the name, when quoting a Pakistani security official. He said, "a predator strike was carried out in Makeen area, [8 miles] northwest of Ladha." Makeen, in the northeastern part of South Waziristan, near North Waziristan is home to the Mehsud tribe, under the control of Taliban warlord Baitullah Mehsud, an al-Qaeda ally who was accused of plotting the 2007 assassination of former Pakistani Prime Minister Benazir Bhutto.

The war may have changed, but the "Predator drones" were still at work, and still alive and well in the global media.

The next day, the *Agence France-Presse* reported another strike, this time in quoting a "local security official," who told them that "two missiles fired from a suspected U.S. drone hit the compound of a local pro-militant tribal elder Malik Gulab Khan, killing four residents." Five days later, Mehsud struck back, not against the CIA who had flown the drone, but against the police of the country that sheltered him. On Tuesday, Mehsud sent a dozen gunmen to attack the Manawan Police Academy in Lahore with automatic weapons and grenades or rockets. Five trainees, two instructors, and a passer-by were killed.

The "contingency operation" continued unabated into April, with armed UAVs flying against targets in Pakistani tribal areas from either Shamsi or from within Afghanistan. On the first day of the month, the BBC reported that a missile "fired by a suspected U.S. drone" killed at least 14 in the Orakzai area of Pakistan's FATA, close to the Afghan border. The news service also reported that "residents in the area say that the missile struck a house being used by the Taliban which was completely destroyed." The BBC's Syed Shoaib Hasan in Islamabad said that this strike was the first drone attack in Orakzai and "another sign that the U.S. is expanding the zones of attack."

On 4 April, when another "drone" attack killed what Pakistani intelligence reported as 13 "foreign militants," Mehsud claimed responsibility for killing 13 people at an immigration services center in Binghamton, New York, the same day. It was entirely bravado, tailored for his followers who didn't know better. In fact, the suspect in the Binghamton incident was Jiverly Wong, an immigrant from Vietnam. According to Binghamton's police chief, he was upset when "people were making fun of him . . . because of his inability to speak English."

Under the Contingency Operation, the number of UAV attacks conducted inside Pakistan and reported in the media during March and April alone, was greater than all such attacks reported in the first nine months of 2008. Because neither the CIA nor the U.S. Central Command discusses such missions, the information

Members of the 380th Expeditionary Aircraft Maintenance Squadron back an RQ-4 Global Hawk into a hangar at Al Dhafra AB in the United Arab Emirates after an 11 March 2008 mission over Southwest Asia. (U.S. Air Force photo by Senior Airman Levi Riendeau)

The insignia of the 380th Air Expeditionary Wing (380 AEW). Based at Al Dhafra AB in the United Arab Emirates the 380th operates KC-10A Extenders, U-2 Dragon Ladies, and E-3 Sentry AWACS aircraft as well as RQ-4 Global Hawks. The unit was constituted as the 380th Bombardment Group (Heavy) on 28 October 1942, and activated on 3 November 1942. During World War II, it deployed to the Pacific Theater with the Fifth Air Force V Bomber Command. (U.S. Air Force)

General Donald Hoffman, commander of the Air Force Materiel Command, is briefed on RQ-4 Global Hawk operations during a visit with the 380th Air Expeditionary Wing in the UAE in early 2009. The AFMC and Northrop Grumman were then about to roll out the first Block 40 version of Global Hawk with the Multi-platform Radar Technology Insertion Program (MP-RTIP) enhanced sensor suite. (U.S. Air Force photo by Senior Airman Brian Ellis)

is derived entirely from independent media outlets that get their information from stringers on the ground within Pakistan.

Though the United States released no official statistics, there was little doubting the widespread media reports of a significant escalation in the armed UAV offensive in both Pakistan and Afghanistan. An overview of publicly available data on the U.S. air campaign in Pakistan compiled by Bill Roggio and Alexander Mayer for the *Long War Journal* observed both a "marked increase" in frequency, and noted that attacks were also "becoming increasingly lethal." They noted that more than one in five of the strikes had killed a high-value target.

They also noted that training camps used by al-Qaeda's external operations branch had been a primary target, adding that this branch "is tasked with carrying out attacks in the U.S., Europe, and India, and against other allies of the West outside the Afghan-Pakistan region. Al-Qaeda operatives known to have lived in the West and holding foreign passports have been killed in several Predator strikes."

As under the Global War on Terror, Pakistan had continued to condemn each of these strikes in routine fashion. However, when Pakistan "decried" the "contingency" missions, the fact was not that they opposed them, but that they wanted to be part of them.

Augustine Anthony of Reuters reported on 14 June 2009, the Obama Administration maintained that "the missile strikes are carried out under an agreement with Islamabad which allows Pakistani leaders to decry the attacks in public." He went on to add, "the United States had given Pakistan data on militants in the Afghan border area gathered by surveillance drones in Pakistani airspace under an agreement with Pakistan."

As Husain Haqqani, Pakistan's ambassador to the United States once told *The New York Times*, "Pakistan's concerns about the drones do not relate to their ability to take out bad guys, they relate to . . . concerns about national sovereignty."

Having been cut out on a joint mission scenario by the Bush Administration in 2008, the Pakistanis were brought somewhat into the intel-sharing loop as of a new agreement that was made in March 2009. As described by Eric Schmitt and Mark Mazzetti in *The New York Times* on 13 May, "the offer to give Pakistan a much larger amount of imagery, including real-time video feeds and communications intercepts gleaned by remotely piloted aircraft, was intended to help defuse a growing dispute over how to use the drones and which country should control the secret missions flown in Pakistani airspace."

The article went on to say "the American military in Afghanistan flew a demonstration mission of a Predator drone along a stretch of the Afghanistan-Pakistan border [in March] to show the kind of imagery and communications information the Predator could provide. The Americans transmitted the information to a border coordination center near the Khyber Pass operated by American, Pakistani, and Afghan personnel, and the information was sent through Pakistani security databases."

Apparently this "test run" went so well that Pakistan then asked for more Predator flights to support their own operations in the tribal areas.

Nevertheless, Pakistan continued to play the game of annoyed denial. During 2009, the Claude Rains character from *Casablanca* was being played by foreign ministry spokesman Abdul Basit. Five months after the cooperative agreement was stuck, Basit puffed indignantly, "We want drone attacks stopped. We are taking up this matter with America again and again. Pakistan has the capability to do this operation itself."

One can almost imagine the croupier played by Marcel Dalio stepping in from offstage to hand Basit his "winnings." In this case, a sheaf of Predator datalink downloads.

Basit's words were dutifully reported by the media as Pakistani forces moved ahead with their own offensive against the Taliban, and their own hunt for Mehsud. For the Pakistanis, he was a sort of "public enemy number one." Indeed, the Jane's Information Group described him as "Pakistan's most wanted." In addition to the assassination, Mehsud's gang of thugs and starry-eyed suicide bombers had harassed and terrorized major cities for years. He was also a thorn in the side of American efforts because, as Jane's pointed out, he was understood to have granted al-Qaeda carte blanche to "use his swathe of territory as a sanctuary."

In their report, Schmitt and Mazzetti also described meetings held in early May between President Obama and Pakistan President Asif Ali Zardari in which the latter repeated his earlier requests by his country for Predators of their own. Pakistan had long been making increased back channel requests to be supplied with Predators of its own. Though both Britain and Italy operated Predators, and Turkey's request had been approved, the Pakistani overture was repeatedly declined.

The reporters quoted anonymous Pakistani officials as saying that Zardari wanted to have armed UAV technology "partly to tamp down anger inside Pakistan over the campaign of CIA air strikes inside the country . . . If Pakistan had its own Predators . . . the government in Islamabad could make a more plausible case to the public that Pakistani missiles, not American missiles, were being used to kill militants."

Mohammad Aqil Nadeem, the Pakistani Consul General in Houston, Texas, went a step further by indicating that the war could be lost if Pakistan did not get control of the unmanned aerial vehicles. "Do we want to lose the war on terror or do we want to keep those weapons classified?" Nadeem asked Sig Christenson of the *San Antonio Express-News* after a 28 April speech before the local World Affairs Council. "If the American government insists on our true cooperation, then they should also be helping us in fighting those terrorists."

Zardari also continued to press Obama for true joint UAV operations, not just a share of the intel. However, the people who operate the unmanned aerial vehicles over Pakistan pointed to past failures, and insisted that the operational missions remain under American control. "We're going after terrorists plotting directly against the United States and its interests," one American countert-errorism official told Schmitt and Mazzetti. "Nobody wants to gamble with those kinds of targets. We tried a joint approach before, and it didn't work. Those are facts that can't be ignored."

Rebuffed by the Americans, the Pakistani military finally went shopping, looking not only to buy UAVs of its own, but also to acquire the capability to manufacture

First Lieutenant Jorden Smith operates an MQ-1 Predator during a training mission with the 11th Reconnaissance Squadron in April 2009. (U.S. Air Force photo by Senior Airman Nadine Barclay)

The unassuming front gate at Creech AFB, home to the people who fly Predator and Reaper missions worldwide. Known as Indian Springs Air Force Auxiliary Field before 2005, the base is located on U.S. Highway 95, north of the small town of Indian Springs, Nevada, about 65 miles northwest of the Las Vegas Strip and about 45 miles northwest of Nellis AFB. (U.S. Air Force photo)

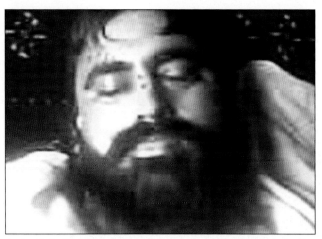

Baitullah Mehsud, the notorious Taliban warlord who terrorized Pakistan for years and planned the 2007 assassination of former Prime Minister Benazir Bhutto, was hunted by American drones throughout the summer of 2009. He was finally killed or fatally wounded in an attack, probably by a CIA Predator, on 5 August. This image is from a video taken shortly after his death and released at the end of September. (Taliban Video Image)

them within Pakistan. It finally cut a deal with the Italian joint venture firms SELEX (Sensors and Airborne Systems Limited) and Galileo Avionica SpA, major defense electronics companies owned by Finmeccanica.

The deal called for the manufacture of the company's Falco UAV at the Pakistan Aeronautical Complex in Kamra. A twin-boom, pusher-prop aircraft, with an endurance of up to 14 hours, the Falco is similar in configuration and almost the same size as the RQ-5 Hunter. By the autumn of 2009, it was reported that the first of two dozen Falcos had been deployed with Pakistani forces in their operations against the Taliban in the Swat Valley, although only in a surveillance and target acquisition role.

With the onset of the summer of 2009, the effort to target Baitullah Mehsud continued, with both American and Pakistani forces in the hunt. It was not the sort of joint operation that Zardari craved, but rather a case of two armies operating independently against the same foe.

On 23 June, as the Pakistani Army and Air Force were underway with a large-scale operation against the Taliban in South Waziristan, Mehsud ordered a hit on a rival gang boss, Qari Zainuddin. It had been with this warlord that the Pakistani government had hoped to cut a deal in an effort to checkmate Mehsud's Taliban gangsters.

In an article in *The New York Times*, Pir Zubair Shah and Salman Masood, wrote that "in recent months, Mr. Zainuddin and his group had helped the government by denying Baitullah Mehsud and his fighters the ability to operate in the region, killing about 30 of Mr. Mehsud's fighters. When he was in his 30s, Mr. Zainuddin was part of Mr. Mehsud's tribe. However, Mr. Zainuddin split with Mr. Mehsud and joined forces with Turkestan Bhaitani, an older Taliban fighter who had switched sides to ally with the government . . . Officially, the Pakistani military denies supporting the effort."

Mehsud's hit would soon backfire.

As with motion picture mobsters, funerals of gang bosses in Pakistan's tribal areas are apparently attended by rival gang bosses. Such was the case on the afternoon of 23 June, as a funeral procession formed near the town of Makeen. Overhead and unbeknownst to the mourners, was what the news media from the BBC to al-Jazeera described as an "American drone."

Reports of the death toll from the missile attack ranged from 45 mentioned by al-Jazeera to 60 reported in *The New York Times*. This made it the deadliest known hit by an armed UAV in the campaign against the Taliban and al-Qaeda leadership in Pakistan to date. As in March, however, Mehsud was not among the casualties. As reported in *The New York Times* and the Geo Television Network, quoting unnamed sources, "the dead included a trainer of suicide bombers named Qari Hussain as well as a Taliban commander named Sangeen, though there was no way to immediately verify the report."

Less than two weeks later, on 8 July, as reported by the BBC, "American drones" killed approximately 50 militants in two nearly simultaneous strikes. Targeted were a convoy on the main road between Ladha and Sararogha, and a Taliban "hideout" in the thickly forested and mountainous Karwan Manza area 6 miles southeast of Ladha. The BBC's Syed Shoaib Hasan in Islamabad reported that "the militants targeted in the double strike were loyal to Baitullah Mehsud." However, he was not among them. The report did add that "our correspondent says the increased number of drone attacks has caused a great deal of insecurity among the Pakistan Taliban commander's fighters."

Pakistani officials who spoke to the BBC reported that six missiles were fired in the forest camp attack, and five in the convoy strike. If the attacking UAVs had been Predators, this would suggest that three aircraft were flown as a multi-plane strike package in each of the missions. At the time, coordinated missions by multiple aircraft were a rare occurrence for operations by Predators, which typically operated solo.

On 5 August, Predators were again hunting Mehsud, and the crosshairs were on a house in the Zangarha area of South Waziristan about 9 miles northeast of Ladha. According to what locals later told the BBC, Baitullah Mehsud's father-in-law, Malik Ikramuddin, owned the house. According to the BBC, two missiles were fired by a "suspected U.S. drone," killing one of the wives in the licentious gang boss's harem. On the day of the attack Mohammad Iqbal Mehsud, a nephew of Malik Ikramuddin, told Dilawar Khan of the BBC Urdu Service's that at least 40 people were present in the house when the missiles hit.

Initial reports out of Pakistan said that Baitullah Mehsud hadn't been there, but rumors soon began to surface suggesting that he had been mortally wounded. Within a few days, Pakistan's Interior Minister Rehman Malik remarked that he had "credible information" that the warlord had been killed. Jim Jones, the U.S. National Security Adviser told NBC's "Meet the Press" that evidence of Mehsud's death "is pretty conclusive," defining this as a "90 percent" certainty.

On 25 August, the BBC reported that the Taliban had finally confirmed his death, adding that his henchmen, Hakimullah Mehsud and Waliur Rehman, confirmed "he had died of injuries sustained in a U.S. missile strike" but had survived for more than two weeks after being hit. At the end of September, the Taliban released a video that apparently showed Mehsud's corpse. By then, Hakimullah was widely reported to have been acclaimed as Baitullah's successor as the leader of the Taliban in Pakistan.

The war against al-Qaeda and the Taliban was a war against a many-headed snake, but one by one, heads were rolling.

The concept of using quiet, unmanned aircraft to hunt small, high-value targets was certainly an idea whose time had come. By 2009, some were suggesting that this tactic should become, not just a component of overall strategy, but the very cornerstone of future United States strategy in Afghanistan, as well as in Pakistan.

Flying Those Drones

Out at Creech AFB in the Nevada desert, so close to Las Vegas that you can almost smell the cologne on the Elvis impersonators, American and British pilots go to work each day controlling the Predators and Reapers flying over that other desert half a world away. Once they were on the fringes of the world of combat pilots, but by 2009, this had quietly changed as more and more pilots arrived to become part of the fastest growing pilot community within the U.S. Air Force.

By the end of 2008, with monthly UAV/UAS flying hour totals running into the five figures, and with demand increasing, the Air Force instigated a broad program to expand capabilities. This especially meant getting more warm bodies into the control stations at Creech. Indeed, the Air Force had announced plans to increase the number of UAV pilots and air operations staffers from 450 to 1,100 over four years. As observed by Brigadier General Lyn Sherlock, the director of air operations for the Air Staff's directorate of operations, UAV pilots would then outnumber pilots flying any other type of aircraft except F-16s.

Lieutenant Colonel Lawrence Spinetta, commander of the Predator-operating 11th Reconnaissance Squadron at Creech, and himself a former F-15 pilot, observed that the Air Force was beginning to head down a road of buying "more unmanned than manned platforms" for the first time.

Until 2009, pilots who came to Creech to fly drones had previously flown conventional aircraft types, the kinds that are flown by actually sitting in the cockpit. They were rotated into the UAV world on temporary duty assignments, and then rotated back into the cockpit. However, a radical paradigm shift in pilot training had begun in the fall of 2008 as the Air Force Air Education and Training Command began training non-pilots to fly unmanned aerial vehicles, and to make flying UAVs a permanent duty assignment.

As Anna Mulrine wrote in the January 2009 issue of *Air Force Magazine*, "in a series of firsts, freshly minted pilots are being sent directly to UAVs for their initial assignments, nonpilots are being trained as unmanned aircraft pilots, and UAV operators will soon have their own distinct career field . . . The buildup is an acknowledgement that UAVs and the pilots who fly them are going to be in critical demand in the years to come."

In October 2008, Lieutenant Patrick Lebow had become the first graduate of the Joint Specialized Undergraduate Pilot Training assigned as a UAV pilot. The following month, unmanned aerial vehicle fundamentals training began at Randolph AFB in Texas for around 100 undergraduate pilots—out of about 700 applicants—destined for unmanned aerial vehicles.

The unmanned aerial vehicle training course was formalized to include introductory flight training at Pueblo, Colorado, the UAS fundamentals course at Randolph; Joint Air-to-Ground Operations School at Nellis AFB in Nevada; and finally the Initial Qualification Training Course at Creech. The first group of Undergraduate Pilot Training (UPT) students emerged from the course in April 2009.

"We want to go to a dedicated career field because we can see this as a force that we're going to need in the future," Sherlock told Mulrine, explaining why the Air Force was embarking on such an expansion of UAV pilot numbers. "We want to look at someone who can learn to operate an unmanned system and teach them how . . . We want to be able to show that we can take someone through an Air Force training program and teach him how to get air sense, and to fly in the United States as well as in a combat zone . . . We want to make sure that the test is good for someone who has little or no aviation experience right now."

At Creech, the pilots passed through what were referred to as "schoolhouses." Colonel Spinetta of the 11th Reconnaissance Squadron presided over the Predator Schoolhouse, while Lieutenant Colonel Christopher Gough, commander of the 42nd Attack Squadron and a former F-16 pilot, was the schoolmaster at the Reaper Schoolhouse.

The schoolhouse curriculum consisted of basic aircraft handling, instruction in the basics of finding and exploiting an intelligence target, and "basic surface attack." In the latter, students learned how to fire an AGM-114 Hellfire missile and how to coordinate with other airborne strike aircraft in support of ground forces.

Colonel Gough told Anna Mulrine, "We also get deep into who is able to provide that clearance authority, and how we coax that out of them," and that schoolteachers work "with guys on the ground to develop that awareness of friendly locations, and [positive identification]."

In July 2009, a second location for Predator and Reaper training was opened at Holloman AFB in New Mexico, formerly home to the F-117 stealth fighters. As at Creech, Holloman offered a good environment of flying weather, and plenty of open space. While Creech is located adjacent to the air space of the Nellis AFB Range, Holloman is next to the White Sands Missile Range.

Also in July, to complement the pilot training, the Air Force initiated the Basic Sensor Operator Training (BSOT) course at Randolph AFB. As announced by the 12th Flying Training Wing, the first group of sensor operators consisted of "cross-trainees from other career fields," while a second group arrived in September directly from basic training. While the Air Force continued to insist on its pilots being officers, the BSOT was open to enlisted personnel. After graduating from the course, the sensor operators joined the pilots to complete their training jointly.

At the same time, non-pilot Air Force officers were also being brought in for UAV flight training. The first 10 of these, selected from 40 prescreened applicants, arrived at Pueblo in January 2009. According to Colonel Charles Armentrout, chief of the military force policy division, "the Air Force Personnel Center received hundreds of calls . . . The criteria for this first ten were fairly narrow. We plan to open up the process to take advantage of the high interest in the program, particularly among our younger officers who will help posture us for long-term success."

Meanwhile, the Air Force was dispersing its UAV operations to bases other than Creech. Coordinated by the 432nd Air Expeditionary Wing at Creech, these missions were flown from secure locations at Air National Guard facilities throughout the United States. By the beginning of 2009, the Guard had activated three Predator units in Arizona, California, North Dakota, and Texas.

Colonel Robert Becklund, commander for the 119th Wing in North Dakota, observed that more than two thirds of the wing's F-16 pilots chose to retrain for the Predator when the 119th's F-16s were replaced by C-21

General Norton Schwartz, Air Force Chief of Staff, greets Airman 1st Class Michael Garlich during an inspection trip to the 432nd Air Expeditionary Wing at Creech AFB in 2008. During his visit, Schwartz described unmanned aerial systems as "a game-changing capability and vital to the global war on terrorism and it is no surprise that these systems are in such high demand with the combatant commanders." (U.S. Air Force photo by Staff Sergeant Kenneth Kennemer)

Learjet executive transports in 2006. California Air Guard pilots at March ARB retrained to Predators from KC-135 Stratotankers. As the F-16s of the New York Air Guard's 174th Fighter Wing returned to Hancock Field from a tour in Iraq early in 2009, the wing began the transition to becoming the first Air Guard MQ-9 Reaper squadron.

In an article in the June 2009 issue of *Fly RC* magazine, Colonel Spinetta went inside the "cockpit" of the armed UAV/UAS pilots to explain the technical challenges of flying these aircraft, from what he describes as the comfort of a leather chair that resembles Captain Kirk's command chair on "Star Trek." The audience of the publication are people who are experts at flying aircraft, albeit smaller aircraft, remotely.

The chair in the Ground Control Station (GCS) at Creech may be comfortable, but the Predator pilots have their work cut out, managing banks of computers, as well as the standard stick, throttle, and rudder. "Manipulating two keyboards and monitoring five video screens keeps you extremely busy," explained Predator pilot Lieutenant Colonel Deb Lee, in a conversation with Spinetta. "When you throw in a complex mission such as providing support to a special forces raid on a suspected terrorist hideout, you definitely need to bring your A game!"

As with flying a remotely controlled model aircraft that you can see, Predator pilots are able to "exercise instantaneous control" of a vehicle 7,000 miles away despite that distance and a datalink that passes back and forth through a communications satellite in geostationary orbit 22,000 miles above the earth.

If anything, flying a UAV/UAS is more challenging for someone used to conventional aircraft than RC aircraft. As Spinetta explains, when flying an unmanned aircraft via remote control, pilots "do not have the luxury of being able to look outside the cockpit window . . . There are no external cues to help you fly by the seat of your pants. For example, you cannot hear adjustments in engine rpm or the sound of wind rushing by the cockpit to alert you to an increase in your airspeed . . . With a strong crosswind, you have to point the aircraft so far away from the runway that it is no longer visible in your video field of view. You can only sneak an occasional peek at the runway; otherwise, the aircraft will drift too far from the runway centerline to permit a safe landing. The inability to see beyond a two-dimensional computer screen makes landing the Predator one of the most difficult feats in aviation."

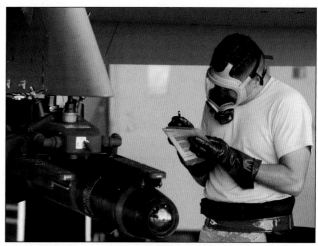

Staff Sergeant Bobby Domanski, a Reaper weapons loader assigned to the 432nd Aircraft Maintenance Squadron, double checks an AGM-114 Hellfire II air-to-ground missile during weapons load training. (U.S. Air Force photo by Senior Airman Nadine Barclay)

A wide-angle view of airmen from the 432nd Aircraft Maintenance Squadron working on a Predator at Creech AFB. Senior Airman Ignacio Reyes (right), ensures the Rotax engine for the MQ-1 Predator is sealed before boxing the engine for storage. Lester Sylvester shows Senior Airman Michael Osmun, how to the remove an oil line union, while Staff Sergeant Michael Rushing works on the union from inside the fuselage. Osmun is with Air Force Engineering and Technical Service. Staff Sergeant Alyssa Burns (second from left) shows structural maintenance technical data to Airman 1st Class Rex Leavitte. (U.S. Air Force photo by Lance Cheung)

Colonel James Gear, a former F/A-18 pilot and Navy Top Gun graduate, agrees, saying, "It can be very nerve-racking. When the wind picks up, it's way more challenging even than landing on a carrier!"

By the time that Gear made this observation, a tide was beginning to turn in which those in the "Captain Kirk's command chairs" would no longer have carrier landing experience, nor experience landing real aircraft of any kind.

A decade earlier, it was a page from science fiction that unmanned aerial vehicles could fly combat missions at all. Now a day was coming in which many—and perhaps eventually *most*—combat missions would be flown by people who were detached by thousands of miles from both their aircraft and their targets.

As the war in the cold heights of the Hindu Kush dragged on, there were many in the media, far outside the military community, who suggested that the entire war could be carried out by "Predator drones." Perhaps they were closer to being right than they might have appeared.

Staff Sergeant Steve Fraser, a crew chief deployed to the 62nd Expeditionary Reconnaissance Squadron, attaches a brace to the tail of an MQ-1 Predator at Kandahar Air Base in Afghanistan. (U.S. Air Force photo by Major David Kurle)

Lieutenant Colonel Debra Lee, commander of the 46th Expeditionary Reconnaissance and Attack Squadron, flies an MQ-1 Predator from Creech AFB in February 2009. (U.S. Air Force photo by Senior Airman Tiffany Trojca)

Airman 1st Class Caleb Force assists 1st Lieutenant Jorden Smith in locating simulated targets during an MQ-1 Predator training mission. Force is a Predator sensor operator and Smith is a Predator pilot. (U.S. Air Force photo by Senior Airman Nadine Barclay)

Jonathon Johnson, an air interdiction agent for the U.S. Customs and Border Protection, pilots a Reaper in April 2009 from Grand Forks AFB in North Dakota. The aircraft had been flying and observing flood dangers along the Red River. (Defense Department photo by Senior Master Sergeant David Lipp, U.S. Air Force)

While operational missions are flown from Creech AFB, landings and takeoffs are handed off to controllers located in-country. At Kandahar Air Base in Afghanistan, Captain Ryan Jodoi (rear) flies an MQ-9 Reaper while Airman 1st Class Patrick Snyder controls a full motion video. (U.S. Air Force photo by Staff Sergeant James Harper, Jr.)

CHAPTER SIX

THE STORY CONTINUES

The General Atomics Predator C Avenger made its first flight on 4 April 2009 from the company's Gray Butte Flight Operations Facility in Palmdale, California. As stated by the company, it was designed and developed "to provide the U.S. Air Force and other potential customers with an expanded quick-response armed reconnaissance capability." (General Atomics)

From anomaly to mainstream, the use of unmanned aerial vehicles in combat had become the trend to watch, though the direction of that trend was as hard to follow as a Predator at 25,000 feet. Early in the twenty-first century, when this writer first chronicled the use of drones as offensive weapons, the Predator was just about the only game in town and the UCAV program, just redesignated as J-UCAS, was the well mapped road to the future of unmanned aerial combat. By the end of the decade, the ambitious J-UCAS had been terminated, but armed tactical drones were cropping up from many unexpected corners of the aerospace world.

So too has there been many changes in the doctrine of deploying such craft. As noted in the previous chapter, the notion that unmanned air combat could ever be the centerpiece of a tactical doctrine once seemed absurd — but those days are gone.

Lieutenant Colonel Lawrence Spinetta of the 11th Reconnaissance Squadron had characterized the armed Predator, "only the first step in the transformation of the Air Force into a UAS-centric force . . . We have reached a tipping point in this technological revolution."

He is probably right about its being a first step, with the more heavily armed and more capable Reaper probably representing a second step. He is correct also that the armed Predator brought the technology of air combat to a tipping point. Whether or not the U.S. Air Force will evolve into a "UAS-centric force" remains to be seen.

Given the way that J-UCAS went away so abruptly in 2006, and how so many armed UAV/UAS concepts have emerged, the best thing that can be said about the future turns is that anything is possible. Indeed, in 2009, the Boeing X-45C program, which evaporated along with J-UCAS, was reborn several years later as the Phantom Ray concept.

As we can see through the example of the arming of the Predator, virtually any UAV/UAS can potentially be adapted to carry a weapon. A century ago, even before World War I, military biplanes fluttered into the sky to snoop on enemy troop movements. Just as it didn't take long to figure out that projectiles could be dropped from an open cockpit, it didn't take long to hang a Hellfire on a Predator.

In the present century, there will be sophisticated successors to the J-UCAS idea, but the future may best be seen in the creativity involved in the deployment of smaller and more varied aircraft.

Unpredictable Deployments

The future story of unmanned aerial vehicles in combat is one of the "what" of technology, but it is also one of the "where" and "why" of deployments. Who, for example, could have imagined in August 2001 that the ensuing decade would so consume the American and NATO armed forces in a "where" such as Afghanistan?

It is a growth industry. Customers mingle with the industry at the Association for Unmanned Vehicle Systems International and Unmanned Systems North America Convention in August 2009. More than 5,000 people attended the four-day conference and exhibit to see the more than 320 unmanned aerial, maritime and ground systems that were on display. (Defense Department photo by Army Sergeant 1st Class Michael Carden)

Major General Blair Hansen addresses an audience of unmanned systems developers and industry professionals during the Unmanned Vehicle Systems Convention at the Washington, D.C., Convention Center. General Hansen was the Air Force deputy chief of staff for intelligence, surveillance, and reconnaissance. (Defense Department photo by Army Sergeant 1st Class Michael Carden)

By 2009, another unimagined "why" intruded upon our popular conception of military action as the world's navies found themselves battling the pirates of the Somali coast, and battling them at sea in the Indian Ocean. Just as the ScanEagle aboard the USS *Bainbridge* became the signature recon drone of America's first well-publicized battle with piracy in generations, so too would armed drones soon enter the theater.

On 29 August of that year, Mark Abramson reported in an article in *Stars and Stripes* that the United States was deploying MQ-9 Reapers under a U.S. Africa Command (AFRICOM) operation called Ocean Look. The purpose of the operation, according to U.S. Navy Captain John Moore of Combined Task Force 67, who stated the obvious, was "maritime security and counter-piracy operations."

Indeed, around 75 American military and civilian personnel were already packing their bags for Mahé

Potential customers can glimpse the future at the Unmanned Vehicle Systems Convention. Here, an unmanned maritime surveillance system is displayed. (Defense Department photo by Army Sergeant 1st Class Michael Carden)

Airport in the Indian Ocean island nation of Seychelles, about 1,000 miles off the African east coast. The base had recently been used by U.S. Navy P-3 Orion patrol planes assigned to Patrol Squadron VP-10, based in Djibouti.

"It is a very strategic location," Vince Crawley, an AFRICOM spokesman, told Abramson. "We will get it up and running and see."

"Traditionally what we are seeing this time of year, the monsoon season will end," Lieutenant Nathan Christiansen of the Navy's Fifth Fleet, interjected. "Last August, right about this time, we saw 12 attacks in one day."

The U.S. Navy had been using ship-based drones like the ScanEagle for this work in the Indian Ocean for some time, but the land-based Reapers obviously brought greater range, longer endurance, and weapons to the equation.

As Mark Thompson wrote in *Time* magazine on 4 September, "It's not firepower but endurance that is needed to prevail over pirates. Ships can survey only a tiny swath of the sea, and previous ship-launched drones and land-based manned aircraft lack the Reaper's capacity to remain aloft for up to 14 hours . . . The Reaper, with its unblinking eye, could help capture pirates who too often have been able to slip away."

He went on to cite the case of a 20,000-ton German cargo ship, from which pirates managed to escape with a $2.7 million ransom even though the German frigate *Brandenburg* arrived on the scene within 12 minutes of the pirates' departure from the cargo vessel.

Writing in an article about the deployment that was datelined Nairobi and widely published in the east African media, writer Alisha Ryu reminded readers that "since March, two Seychelles-flagged vessels have been hijacked and several others attacked in waters near the Seychelles and the Comoros Islands."

She reported that the "lack of naval patrols in the area are tempting some pirates to expand their operations further east. The Indian Ocean is considered a safer hunting ground than the Gulf of Aden, a narrow shipping lane to the north that is heavily patrolled by warships from more than a dozen countries . . . For nearly a year, the international armada has been successful in keeping many ships from being hijacked. But it has done little to deter pirates from targeting ships."

The Reapers provided the potential to change this.

The Future of Small Tactical Drones

Since the turn of the century, small unmanned aerial vehicles like the Shadow from AAI (now part of Textron) and the ScanEagle from Insitu (now part of Boeing) have been both integrated into the tactical routine, and have proven themselves as valuable assets to small units operating where extensive infrastructure is not available.

Among those aircraft that were emerging as part of a successor generation were aircraft from both AAI and Insitu. In the case of AAI, the aircraft was the Aerosonde,

originally developed by the company of the same name in Australia that had been the originator of the SeaScan fish-tracking system developed by Insitu some years earlier. Since 2005, when an Aerosonde was flown into Hurricane Ophelia, the American National Oceanic & Atmospheric Administration (NOAA) had been using this UAV to track and monitor tropical storms.

Meanwhile, by 2009, Insitu was testing its Integrator, a newer unmanned aerial vehicle that was half again larger than the ScanEagle. A twin-boomed aircraft, the Integrator had two fuselage payload bays with a total capacity of 50 pounds, and underwing hardpoints each rated with a capacity for 15 pounds of payload.

Both the Aerosonde and the Integrator were UAVs that had been included in evaluations that took place under the Small Tactical Unmanned Aircraft System (STUAS)/Tier II program. Originally a U.S. Navy and Marine Corps program, STUAS was expanded in 2007 to include the U.S. Air Force, who was looking for a new aircraft for base security operations. In October 2009, the U.S. Army also announced an interest in the STUAS program, having identified "a gap" in battalion-level UAV/UAS capability.

As for the "Tier II" appellation, it means different things to different services. For the Air Force, the Predator and Reaper are Tier II, but for the Army, Tier II describes the much smaller RQ-7 Shadow. For the other services, small aircraft such as the ScanEagle are classified under Tier II. Whatever the Tier definition, the emphasis under STUAS is on "Small."

According to the official Pentagon release on the subject, the catalyst for STUAS came when "during combat operations in the Global War on Terror, the Marine Corps has identified a significant gap in its Intelligence, Surveillance, and Reconnaissance (ISR) capability and . . . confirmed the need for organic, tactical UAS coverage in order to enhance Situational Awareness (SA) and enable timely decision making by its battlefield commanders . . . The STUAS/Tier II UAS will be a persistent, multi-sensor, easily maintained and operated expeditionary system with ties to the Global Information Grid (GIG). The system will be operated from austere forward bases and from ships using a minimum of personnel, equipment and unique support equipment."

To meet the STUAS requirements, AAI decided in 2009 to scale up its Aerosonde Mark 4.7 aircraft from 38.5 pounds to 55 pounds. This compares to a maximum takeoff weight for the ScanEagle of 44 pounds. Also in 2009, AAI made the first flight of its Aerosonde 5 unmanned aerial vehicle.

In addition to the Aerosonde and Integrator, other STUAS unmanned aerial vehicles include the KillerBee, developed by Raytheon and race car developer Swift Engineering, and the Storm, an unmanned aerial vehicle under development by UAS Dynamics, a joint venture formed in 2009 by the American subsidiary of Israel-based Elbit and General Dynamics. In forming this

The Aurora GoldenEye 50 makes the transition from vertical to horizontal flight. (Aurora Flight Sciences)

In vertical flight, the Aurora GoldenEye 80 climbs to a higher altitude during a test flight. (Aurora Flight Sciences)

This photo of the vehicle being deployed by troops in the field provides an idea of the size and scale of the GoldenEye 80. (Aurora Flight Sciences)

The Aurora GoldenEye 80 is seen here climbing out on vertical takeoff. (Aurora Flight Sciences)

The Aurora GoldenEye 50 shown during its vertical takeoff. (Aurora Flight Sciences)

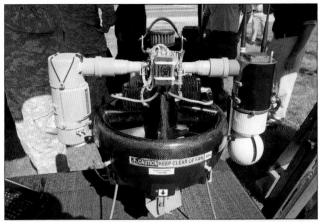

A close-up view of the Class 1 Unmanned Aerial Vehicle, an element of the U.S. Army's Future Combat Systems (FCS) tool kit. (U.S. Army photo by Todd Lopez)

A test launch of the KillerBee at the Yuma Proving Ground. As Raytheon points out, the aircraft "offers 5,800-ci payload capacity, low operation cost, continuous battlespace intelligence, surveillance, and reconnaissance (ISR)" capabilities. (Raytheon)

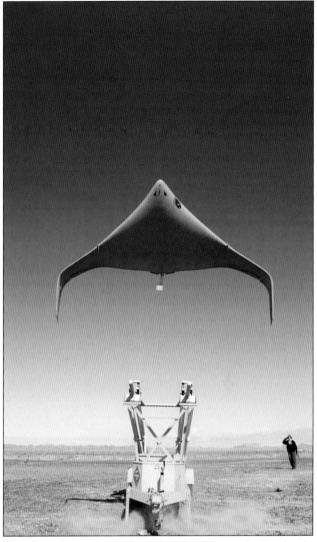

The KillerBee was designed with a blended wing-body design that sets this unique system apart from unmanned aerial vehicles of similar size. (Raytheon)

venture, Elbit provided the experience of the "combat-proven Hermes and Skylark systems," and General Dynamics brought a half century of experience as a top-tier American defense contractor.

While many of the small unmanned aerial vehicles in this class conform to the straight wing, twin-boom fuselage design pioneered by such UAVs as the IAI Pioneer, the KillerBee uses a blended wing-body design. As with the earlier aircraft types, it can be both launched and recovered on land and at sea. In initial testing, the KillerBee operated at an altitude of 4,500 feet and relayed video to a ground station about 60 miles away.

In September of 2008 Raytheon took the KillerBee down to the Yuma Proving Ground for a "Simulated Combat Environment" demonstration. In this, a company flight operations crew simulated a combat environment by delivering the aircraft system to a remote location via Humvees, setting up and launching the KillerBee in less than 45 minutes. During the four-hour test flight, the

aircraft communicated with both Navy and Marine Corps computer systems using a Raytheon Universal Control System. According to a company after action report, the KillerBee system "received target input from a Javelin Command Launch Unit and an Improved Target Acquisition System from Raytheon's TOW (Tube-Launched, Optically Tracked, Wire-Guided) missile."

As explained by Bob Francois, head of Raytheon's Advanced Missiles and Unmanned Systems component, at the 2009 Paris Air Show, "With a common datalink and an open architecture system, KillerBee can communicate with any sensor or shooter on the network . . . This provides incredible flexibility, allowing the warfighter to share information with anyone who needs it."

Aurora Flight Sciences of Manassas, Virginia, has produced the GoldenEye series of ducted fan, vertical takeoff unmanned aerial vehicles, the first of which debuted in 2003. Barrel-shaped with stubby wings, the GoldenEye series aircraft have an appearance in

The Austrian army flew the Schiebel S-100 Camcopter as part of its maneuvers at Allensteig military training area near Vienna in December 2008. (Schiebel Corporation)

The Schiebel S-100 Camcopter was the first unmanned aerial vehicle to fly as part of the official flight displays at the Paris Air Show. (Schiebel Corporation)

flight that one my easily be inspired to use the phrase "flying saucer."

Funded by the U.S. Army, GoldenEyes are designed to fly quiet, clandestine surveillance missions in very tight spaces requiring a VTOL capability, as well as the ability to transition to high-speed wingborne flight. The company also proposes the GoldenEyes for missions such as "providing maritime law enforcement teams with a hover and stare capability during boarding operations and helping first responders assess post-disaster situations."

First flown in 2006, the GoldenEye 50 had a ceiling of 5,000 feet and an endurance of one hour. Debuted in March 2009, the GoldenEye 80 has a ceiling twice that of its predecessor and an endurance of eight hours. Its payload capacity is 16 pounds, and it has a top speed of 140 mph in horizontal flight.

As the size and payload capacity of this class of small drones increases, so too will the inclination of operators to try to figure out ways to arm them, and to turn KillerBees into killers. As small UAVs become an accepted and *expected* part of surface operations on the twenty-first century battlefield, nothing less will do.

The Future of Unmanned Tactical Rotorcraft

With the MQ-8 Fire Scout and MQ-18 Hummingbird transitioning from development to deployment, they have paved the way for other innovative rotary wing unmanned aerial vehicles. As such aircraft have become practical, they attracted plenty of interest from customers because, unlike fixed wing UAV/UAS aircraft, they do not require specialized launch and recovery equipment. This is especially attractive to navies, where space aboard ships is at a premium.

Notable among the subsequent generation of rotorcraft was the Schiebel S-100 Camcopter, which, in 2009, became the first unmanned aerial vehicle ever to fly as part of the official flight displays at the Paris Air Show.

Headquartered in Vienna, Austria, and dating back to 1951, Schiebel cut its teeth on small electronic components for appliances. Beginning in the 1980s, the company became the world's leading producer of mine detecting equipment—with the customer roster including the U.S. Army.

In the 1990s, Schiebel branched into unmanned aerial vehicles, with its Camcopter program starting out as a stabilized camera platform for aerial photography and motion picture filming. Again, the U.S. Army took an interest, with the company's Camcopter Model 5.1 being acquired by the Night Vision and Electronic Sensors Directorate for research and development in the area of airborne land mine detection. It was the U.S. Coast Guard that first successfully operated a Camcopter 5.1 from the deck of a ship.

The S-100 Camcopter unmanned rotorcraft, a substantially larger aircraft than the 5.1, was developed between 2003 to 2005. Like many twenty-first century UAV/UAS aircraft, it can be operated manually using

A Schiebel S-100 Camcopter over the sea. In addition to its being considered by various navies, the vehicle was also evaluated at sea by Spain's Guardia Civil. (Schiebel Corporation)

daylight or infrared cameras, or programmed to fly an autonomous mission profile using a triple-redundant flight computer. As Schiebel points out, in both scenarios the S-100 is automatically stabilized via redundant Inertial Navigation Systems (INS), with navigation accomplished using redundant Global Positioning System (GPS) receivers.

A Schiebel S-100 Camcopter during shipboard trials. The aircraft has been evaluated by several navies, including those of France and Germany. (Schiebel Corporation)

The S-100 is designed with two fuselage payload bays, hardpoints on the side, and an internal auxiliary electronics and avionics bay. The primary bay, located directly beneath the main rotor shaft, is capable of carrying payloads weighing up to 100 pounds, or 75 pounds on missions over six hours. Schiebel markets the S-100 for tactical surveillance and reconnaissance, artillery support, and maritime surveillance and amphibious support, as well as civil applications.

The first customer for the S-100 was the army of the United Arab Emirates, who bought 40 aircraft. The German Navy became the first maritime force to acquire the aircraft, buying them for use aboard K130 Braunschweig Class corvettes. Sea trials took place in the Baltic Sea in the summer of 2008. Also in 2008, the French Navy conducted sea trials aboard the frigate *Montcalm* in the Mediterranean off Toulon, and with the Spanish Guardia Civil in the Atlantic off the Canary Islands. In the latter trials, the S-100 was able to use an emergency helipad measuring just 35 feet on its longest dimension.

Ashore, the armies of both Austria and Germany have also evaluated the S-100.

In August 2009, Schiebel signed a "teaming agreement" with the Boeing Company to, as the press release stated, "pursue marketing and support opportunities" for the S-100. Boeing clearly saw potential in the aircraft as it had with the ScanEagle when it partnered with Insitu in 2002, or with the Hummingbird when it acquired Frontier Systems in 2004.

With both the Hummingbird and the S-100 in its marketing portfolio, Boeing was poised to be an important competitor for Northrop Grumman, even though the Fire Hawk was already being stowed aboard the USS *McInerney* as news of the "teaming agreement" landed on the business page.

The Future of Very Long Endurance Drones

During the first decade of the twenty-first century, as the Predator became the signature weapon of unmanned air combat, the Northrop Grumman RQ-4 Global Hawk became the signature aircraft in the High-Altitude, Long-Endurance (HALE) category for the U.S. Air Force. By the end of the decade, the huge aircraft with the intercontinental range was also entering service with the U.S. Navy and the German Luftwaffe, and being considered by other potential users, including Australia. While the HALE acronym is still used in describing the aircraft, the term "Tier II Plus" that was originally coined for the Global Hawk in the 1990s is rarely mentioned by the Air Force.

Having been selected in April 2008 for the Navy's Broad Area Maritime Surveillance (BAMS) program, the first naval Global Hawks, designated as RQ-4Ns, entered service less than a year later. Technically, the RQ-4N is derived from the RQ-4B Block 30 Global Hawk operated by the U.S. Air Force. Though the two aircraft are virtually identical to the untrained eye, differences in missions have made for differences in equipment. The U.S. Air Force flies its Global Hawk missions mainly at high altitude, while the Navy requires its Global Hawks to fly beneath the clouds to observe shipping and such details as deck cargo.

Operationally, the BAMS aircraft operate in conjunction with other long range patrol aircraft such as the P-3 Orion and its successor, the Boeing P-8. While these aircraft have an attack capability, including the ability to drop torpedoes, the Navy has been mum on whether or not to arm it Global Hawks. Certainly, with provisions for stores on each wing, this is a potential.

"You have hundreds of other airplanes that can drop bombs, so it doesn't make sense to put that system in," Tom Twomey of Northrop Grumman told Stephen Trimble of *Flight Global*. "It just adds cost and weight. [The RQ-4N] is there to be an intelligence, surveillance, and reconnaissance sensor."

In detailing operational differences, Trimble went on to say that "the array of communications channels on board the RQ-4N easily dwarfs those on the USAF system. The USAF controls the RQ-4B from the ground using a commercial Ku-band satellite link. Although expedient for the service's overland patrol mission, commercial satellite links for the over-water mission are impractical. Instead, the USN will use Ka-band Wideband Gapfiller satellites for the control link, which provides superior communications coverage over the oceans."

As Twomey explains, this "changes the paradigm of maritime surveillance from going out and surveying an area and coming back and distilling the data and getting it to the people who essentially use it, to a real-time data feed. You know exactly where ships are at all times . . . Because now they'll be getting data real time, they won't be waiting for the airplane to land. The airplane will be over the target and they'll be analyzing the information real time."

As the U.S. Air Force Global Hawks are controlled remotely from Beale AFB in California, the BAMS Global Hawks are controlled from a similar mission control element at Naval Air Station Patuxent River in Maryland. Writing in the June 2009 issue of *SeaPower* magazine, Aviation Warfare Specialist Jake Reithi, a BAMS sensor operator and former P-3 crewman, described the operations center as being like an aircraft flight deck.

"You have to work as a team [so] I think it's smart to keep the actual crew integrity even though it's an unmanned aircraft," he wrote. "That's how everybody's trained, so just because we're not actually physically in the aircraft, we'd want to keep that same dynamic. Missions can last eight to 12 hours. The aircraft is going to be taking the images whether you're sitting in that terminal or not, so you're able to go take a short break, come back and then process the images as you go through that. The missions are quite different from P-3 missions, which now are mostly over land. Our Global Hawk missions are mostly over international waters."

He admits, "Sometimes, operating an unmanned vehicle thousands of miles away seems like cheating. But if you look at the actual product that we're giving to the fleet, then you kind of lose that feeling because we're giving them the intelligence that they need to do their

An artist's concept of a U.S. Navy Broad Area Maritime Surveillance (BAMS) Global Hawk on patrol. (Northrop Grumman)

A U.S. Navy Global Hawk arrives at its hangar at Al Dhafra AB in the United Arab Emirates in February 2009 as part of the first operational deployment for the Navy's Broad Area Maritime Surveillance (BAMS) program. Personnel from the BAMS maintenance detachment tend to the aircraft. (U.S. Air Force photo by Staff Sergeant Mike Andriacco)

An artist's conception of a pair of EuroHawks in Luftwaffe markings in flight over an alpine European landscape. (Northrop Grumman)

The U.S. Navy's first operational Global Hawk aircraft takes off from Naval Air Station Patuxent River in Maryland on its flight to Al Dhafra AB in the United Arab Emirates. The Navy Global Hawks in Southwest Asia would be co-located with the Global Hawks of the U.S. Air Force 380th Air Expeditionary Wing, and would conduct operational Broad Area Maritime Surveillance missions over the Persian Gulf and Indian Ocean. (Defense Department photo)

The first EuroHawk, the international configuration of the RQ-4 Global Hawk, rolled out at Northrop Grumman's Palmdale, California, facility on 9 October 2009. More than 300 employees from Northrop Grumman and EADS Defence & Security (DS), as well as officials from the Luftwaffe and the German Bundesministerium der Verteidigung (Ministry of Defense) gathered for the ceremony, which concluded in what the press release called "a dramatic curtain drop" revealing the distinctively different aircraft that will be equipped with German sensors. Based on the Block 20 Global Hawk, EuroHawk was equipped with a new signals intelligence (SIGINT) mission system developed in Europe by DS. (Northrop Grumman)

missions. We're able to help them. Without us, they would not be able to do their mission."

In February 2009, the BAMS Global Hawks went overseas on their first operational deployment, based at Al Dhafra AB in the United Arab Emirates, alongside the Air Force RQ-4s assigned to the 380th Air Expeditionary Wing. This came after more than five months of joint effort to stand up a maritime surveillance presence in Southwest Asia. According to an official Pentagon statement, the basing choice came when the Navy "answered a Department of Defense call for increased intelligence, surveillance, and reconnaissance assets in Southwest Asia."

"It's a good feeling to finally get the aircraft here," Navy Lieutenant Commander John McLellan, a BAMS detachment officer, told Sergeant Mike Andriacco of the 380th AEW Public Affairs. "We have really been made to feel at home and a part of the team . . . Now that we have the launch and recovery element and mission asset, we can finally bring this capability to the fight."

Andriacco went on to write in a news release that the Navy and the Air Force benefitted from co-locating Global Hawk operations, adding that Navy personnel leveraged Air Force expertise and proficiency with the Global Hawk "to step into a program that has been proven in an operational environment, virtually eliminating the learning curve that usually comes with a new program . . . Experts in the two services have been able to come together to develop a process that will ensure

The first RQ-4 Block 40 Global Hawk aircraft was formally unveiled on 25 June 2009 at Air Force Plant 42 in Palmdale, California. (Northrop Grumman)

The Block 40 Global Hawk incorporates the Multi-Platform Radar Technology Insertion Program or MP-RTIP radar, which provides high fidelity ground moving target indication and high quality radar imagery. The Electronic Systems Center at Hanscom AFB in Massachusetts oversees MP-RTIP sensor suite development, while the Aeronautical Systems Center at Wright-Patterson AFB in Ohio manages the overall RQ-4 Global Hawk program. (Northrop Grumman)

An artist's conception of the Lockheed Martin proposal for DARPA's Vulture program, a project aimed at developing an unmanned aircraft capable of remaining on-station uninterrupted for over five years. (Lockheed Martin via DARPA)

differences in operational and maintenance rules and standards are identified and resolved quickly."

Colonel Kyle Garland, commander of the 380th Expeditionary Operations Group explained that the similarities between the Air Force and Navy Global Hawk launch and recovery elements "provide enhanced mission capability by allowing each service to use the other's [landing and recovery equipment] as a back-up in the event of a malfunction."

A few months later, in June 2009, Northrop Grumman rolled out the Block 40 RQ-4B Global Hawk for the U.S. Air Force at Plant 42 in Palmdale, California. The Block 40 aircraft introduced the Multi-platform Radar Technology Insertion Program (MP-RTIP) enhanced sensor suite, which was developed by Northrop Grumman itself. According to Dr. Yvette Weber, engineering director with the 303rd Aeronautical Systems Group at Wright-Patterson AB, the Global Hawk system manager, the Block 40 weapon system primarily supports "the battle management command and control (BMC2) mission while also supporting the Intelligence, Surveillance, and Reconnaissance mission. Its multi-mode MP-RTIP radar provides enhanced ground moving target indication and high quality radar imagery."

On 9 October 2009, also at Palmdale, came the roll-out of the first EuroHawk, the Global Hawk variant that had been produced for the German Luftwaffe. Developed jointly by Northrop Grumman and EADS Defence & Security (DS), the EuroHawk was based on the Block 20 Global Hawk.

Organizationally, the EuroHawk was developed, tested, and supported by a DS subsidiary entity called EuroHawk GmbH that would also provide aircraft modifications, mission control, and launch and recovery ground segments, as well as flight test and logistics support. According to EuroHawk CEO, Heinz-Juergen Rommel, this entity would function as "national prime contractor" to the German Federal Ministry of Defense (Bundesministerium der Verteidigung) "through the entire life cycle of the EuroHawk."

The aircraft was equipped with a new signals intelligence (SIGINT) mission system developed by DS. Nicolas Chamussy, the senior vice president of Mission Air Systems for DS, explained that this system would provide "standoff capability to detect electronic and communications emitters . . . the German Armed Forces will be able to independently cover their needs for SIGINT data collection and analysis . . . contributing to NATO, EU, and UN peacekeeping operations."

Joe Pappalardo of *Popular Mechanics* wrote, "EuroHawk is a symbol that Europe is finally equipping its military with modern equipment, which might help bridge a chasm within NATO. European countries watched as the United States poured money into a host of new systems for use in Afghanistan and Iraq."

Indeed, the capability presented by the EuroHawk was long overdue. At the time, Germany's maritime surveillance capability consisted of a pair of Breguet Atlantique aircraft that had been in service for nearly 40 years.

Whether the EuroHawk would actually see service in support of Germany's NATO commitment in Afghanistan was yet to be seen.

Even as the Global Hawk was dominating headlines as the poster child for long endurance UAV operations, other aircraft with fantastically longer endurance were taking shape, at least conceptually.

With aircraft such as Helios, NASA had demonstrated the potential for very large, very high flying, solar-powered aircraft. As the first decade of the twenty-first century came to a close, the Defense Advanced Research Projects Agency (DARPA) was undertaking a program which underscored the agency's interest in the extreme.

As DARPA describes its Vulture program, the objective is "to develop an aircraft capable of remaining on-station uninterrupted for over *five years* [our italics] to perform intelligence, surveillance, reconnaissance (ISR), and communication missions over an area of interest. The technology challenges include development of energy management and reliability technologies capable of allowing the aircraft to operate continuously for five years. Vulture, in effect, will be a retaskable, persistent pseudo-satellite capability, in an aircraft package."

The term "infinite endurance" has even been used at DARPA in discussing the project.

Jim Hodges, in a September 2008 article in *Air Force Times* wrote, "Derek Bye, who designs airplanes for Lockheed Martin, remembers the titter that ran through the audience when [DARPA] held an industry day in Arlington, Virginia, to announce Vulture . . . But such a thing wasn't completely out of the blue. Seven years earlier, a strange-looking, unmanned solar-powered plane called Helios set an altitude record for propeller-driven craft of 96,863 feet."

The QinetiQ Zephyr in flight at the U.S. Army's Yuma Proving Ground in Arizona. The company proudly touts the Zephyr as "the world's leading solar powered high-altitude long-endurance (HALE) Unmanned Aerial Vehicle (UAV)." (QinetiQ photo)

The Zephyr UAV, developed by QinetiQ (pronounced "kinetic"), takes off on a test flight. In August 2008, the aircraft flew for 82 hours and 37 minutes, exceeding the official world record for unmanned flight. (QinetiQ photo)

"We want to completely change the paradigm of how we think of aircraft," said Daniel Newman, DARPA's Vulture program manager. "Aviation has a perfect record—we've never left one up there [in the air]. We will attempt to break that record."

The name "Vulture" is suggested by the fact that Rüppell's Vulture is the highest flying bird known to science, having been observed above 37,000 feet. It is also the unwieldy acronym, Very high altitude, Ultra-endurance, Loitering Theater Unmanned Reconnaissance Element.

Like Helios, another precedent for Vulture technology is the Zephyr, a 75-pound unmanned aerial vehicle with a 59-foot wingspan that flew for 82 hours 37 minutes in July 2008, exceeding the then-current official world endurance record for unmanned flight. The Zephyr was a product of the British firm QinetiQ (pronounced "kinetic"), a defense technology spinoff of the former British government organization, Defence Evaluation and Research Agency (DERA). Built of lightweight carbon fiber, the solar-powered Zephyr used solar-charged lithium-sulphur batteries for nighttime power.

Though QinetiQ was not, Lockheed Martin was among the firms contracted with by DARPA to submit proposals. So too were Boeing and Aurora Flight Sciences, who proposed its Z-winged Odysseus concept, developed in conjunction with BAE Systems, as a candidate for the Vulture program.

Meanwhile, under another project called Rapid Eye, the Pentagon is also looking at a reconnaissance aircraft that could be delivered anywhere in the world within an hour by means of a ballistic missile, then deployed into flight remotely. Such a capability had been studied back in the 1960s, and was one of the intended capabilities of the never-flown X-20 Dyna-Soar program.

Odysseus, the Aurora Flight Sciences proposal for the DARPA Vulture program, would involve a folding, Z-shaped wing structure. Using solar energy to power the aircraft during the day, and stored solar energy to power the aircraft at night, Odysseus would fly in the stratosphere throughout its five-year mission. (Aurora Flight Sciences)

DARPA is also looking at a way of combining the capabilities of Vulture and Rapid Eye. As Larry Greenemeier reported in *Scientific American* in 2007, "an unmanned surveillance aircraft packed into the nose of a missile would be launched over suspicious areas to gather more intelligence; if the threat were confirmed, it would be replaced by another aircraft that could perform low-flying surveillance for up to five years without returning to Earth to refuel."

The Vulture would be large, with a wingspan of up to 500 feet, but would probably weigh only around half a ton.

"We're not talking about big, thick structures that we want to keep an eye on like in the Cold War," DARPA's Wade Pulliam told Greenemeier. "Threats today are more fluid right now, and military responses are more likely to be low-level and long-term, rather than fast and sharp. So endurance of all the assets involved is important."

As Greenemeier wrote, one problem in the development of the Vulture would be "sturdy components that will last at least five years. One option is to make the aircraft modular, so that components can break off and fly home via remote control when necessary and new modules can be flown up and remotely attached. Another option is to use a second aircraft to refuel the Vulture and repair it while in flight."

Another issue is the batteries used for nighttime electricity storage. As Craig Nickol, an engineer at NASA's Langley Research Center told Jim Hodges, "If you're flying near the summer solstice, when the days are really long and the nights are short, then it looks pretty good, but if you're trying to fly missions at northern latitudes during the winter, when the days are very short and the nights are very long, at that point, it becomes a challenge."

"It could be positioned over the battle, at 65,000 feet versus 260 miles," Wade Pulliam says, comparing Vulture to satellites. He also went on to note that operating in the stratosphere rather than Low-Earth Orbit would improve both communications capability and onboard sensor resolution.

Whether or not Vulture is deployed as it was originally imagined, the study of such a machine will certainly result in technology and data that will spawn unpredictable machines in the later twenty-first century.

In the meantime, there will be

Global Hawks, with their endurance routinely running for more than a day. It is a capability that is very attractive to strategic planners.

"This is the future of aviation," writes BAMS crewman Reithi. "Essentially taking the risk away for the crews that are actually flying. A piece of machinery lost is better than losing a life. It's the best of both worlds."

The Future of the Unmanned Combat Air Vehicle

The UCAV acronym for "Unmanned Combat Air Vehicle" was superseded in 2003 as the United States Department Defense began conceptualizing its unmanned warfare in a "system of systems" context under the Joint Unmanned Combat Air Systems (J-UCAS) concept. When J-UCAS also ended as a program in the United States in 2006, neither the idea of a UCAV or the idea of a UCAS went away. Indeed, UCAV still best describes the aircraft of the future that will be the centerpiece of Colonel Lawrence Spinetta's conceptual "UAS-centric force."

The BAE Systems' Raven unmanned aerial vehicle lifting off from a runway at the company's Warton, England, facility. (BAE Systems)

The stealthy Corax unmanned aerial vehicle, developed by BAE Systems for the United Kingdom government, was first revealed to the public in January 2006. (BAE Systems)

Not only the U.S. Air Force, but Britain's Royal Air Force, are seriously pursuing prototypes of the UCAVs of the future. As the Mantis could be loosely described as the BAE Systems equivalent of the General Atomics Reaper, BAE had also been working on another armed unmanned aerial vehicle that could be seen roughly as an equivalent of the American J-UCAS X-planes, X-45 and X-47.

Like the J-UCAS, the BAE Corax (Raven) incorporated stealth technology, and the appearance of the aircraft was somewhat like that of the Lockheed Martin RQ-3 DarkStar. First flown in 2004, Corax was kept under wraps for two years. According to Bill Sweetman of *Jane's International Defence Review*, the Corax aircraft that made the initial flights appeared to have been a small-scale demonstrator with a wingspan between 16 and 19 feet that was built to investigate the stability, control, and performance of the design.

As Sweetman told BBC News science reporter Paul Rincon, "if you look at that Corax shape, it's very reminiscent of something that's designed to fly fairly high, fairly slow, and have quite a long endurance. It looks rather typical for a surveillance aircraft . . . But if you take those long outer wings off and put on shorter swept wings [like the X-45], you have a somewhat faster aircraft that would be more of a penetrating strike platform."

Meanwhile, beginning in 2008, BAE Systems was also building an armed UAV similar to the American J-UCAS aircraft, named Taranis, for the Celtic god of thunder. Developed under the United Kingdom Strategic Unmanned Air Vehicle (Experimental) program (SUAV[E]), Taranis had BAE Systems as lead contractor, with the former Smiths Aerospace component of GE Aviation Systems providing electrical subsystems, and QinetiQ accountable for "UCAV flight autonomy." Major carbon fiber fuselage components were made in the Special Engineering Composite Facility (SECF) at BAE Systems at Samlesbury.

"It is the first time the UK has built an unmanned air vehicle on this scale with this level of capability," said Chris Allam, the BAE project director. As he pointed out, a Rolls-Royce Adour Mk.951 turbofan engine was specified for Taranis.

Taranis was briefly at the center of a reported UFO event. On 9 January 2009, Britain's *Telegraph* newspaper reported, "UFOs have been widely blamed for the destruction of a wind turbine in Lincolnshire," adding that "Lincolnshire has many air force bases and other airfields, and RAF Scampton, where the Red Arrows are based, is close to the wind farm. But experts say the plane would have come off worse in any collision, and no wreckage was found at the site. No local planes have been reported damaged or missing. The MoD has denied earlier reports that any testing of new Taranis unmanned stealth aircraft was taking place and confirmed that the nearby Donna Nook test range was closed to any low flying aircraft over Christmas until the January 6."

At the time, Taranis had not yet made its first flight.

Meanwhile, in continental Europe, there were several other equivalents to the American J-UCAS under development. Notably, there was the Barracuda (also spelled Barrakuda), a joint German-Spanish effort, and the Neuron (also spelled nEUROn), which was a French-Swedish-Italian effort. The lead contractor for Barracuda was the multinational European Aeronautic Defence and Space Company (EADS), while France's Dassault Aviation took the lead on Neuron.

Barracuda was developed in relative secrecy, although in 2006 it came out of the cold, and was widely reported in the aviation enthusiast press, and in the mainstream German newsmagazine, *Der Spiegel*. As discussed in the media, it was apparently a technology demonstrator for an aircraft that was primarily intended as a reconnaissance platform, but which could incorporate an offensive attack capability. Dr. Rolf Wirtz, head of operations at EADS Military Air Systems, said the experimental aircraft was powered by a Pratt & Whitney Canada turbofan engine. He described it as being about 25 feet long, with a wingspan of more than 23 feet, and a maximum takeoff weight of about 6,600 pounds.

An artist's concept of the BAE Systems Taranis unmanned air vehicle technology demonstrator. Developed as part of the Ministry of Defence Strategic Unmanned Air Vehicle (experimental) (SUAV[E]) programme, the aircraft was designed to, as the company put it, "explore and demonstrate how emerging technologies and systems can deliver battle-winning capabilities for the UK Armed Forces." (BAE Systems)

Developed jointly by Germany and Spain, the largely secret EADS Barracuda was built in Germany, and flight tested at a remote location on the Iberian Peninsula in 2006. The first prototype was lost in 2006, but a second prototype was flying out of Goose Bay, Labrador, in 2009. (EADS photo)

The aircraft was built and initially tested at the facilities of the former Deutsche Aerospace (an EADS predecessor) in Germany near Munich. Early photographs showed the Barracuda (serial 99+80) in Luftwaffe markings, but with both German and Spanish flags on the tail.

Beginning in April 2006, flight testing was conducted at a remote facility in Spain. Said Dr. Stefan Zoller of EADS, "With the first flight of our technology demonstrator for unmanned high performance military systems we have thrust the door wide open to one of the most promising future global markets in our branch. We now have an additional, more powerful test platform at our disposal for the further development of our core technological competencies in this extremely important field."

In September 2006, the Barracuda demonstrator was lost in a landing crash at San Javier AB in Spain, reportedly due to a software glitch. Despite initial EADS statements to the contrary, the company resumed the project in 2008. In July 2009, the flight test program for a second Barracuda aircraft (serial 99+81) was underway at Canadian Forces Base Goose Bay in Labrador.

The Neuron, widely described as an unmanned combat air vehicle, evolved primarily from the Logiduc (LOGIDUC), program undertaken by Dassault in 1999. Logique de Développement d'UCAV (Unmanned Combat Aerial Vehicle development solution) was an internal initiative by the company that evolved through a series of aircraft, beginning with the AVE-D Petit Duc, said to be the first stealth UAV in Europe, which first flew in July 2000. Subsequent, larger variants were the AVE-C Moyen Duc of 2001, and the Grand Duc, a full size variant of the Moyen Duc, that was renamed Neuron in 2003.

The Swedish aerospace firm Saab joined the program in 2005, having earlier developed its own swept wing, high performance UAV, known as SHARC (for Swedish Highly Advanced Research Configuration). The SHARC demonstrator had flown and demonstrated capabilities such as autonomous takeoffs and landings, and, according to Saab, "autonomous decisions."

Dassault is the 50 percent prime contractor for Neuron, responsible for overall architectures and design, flight control systems, and final assembly. Saab is a 25 percent subcontractor, accountable for the equipped

An artist's conception of a Dassault nEUROn stealthy unmanned combat air vehicle in flight over the French Alps. (Dassault Aviation)

In this artist's conception, a Dassault nEUROn releases ordnance over a live target. (Dassault Aviation)

A mock-up of the Dassault nEUROn experimental unmanned combat air vehicle on display at the Paris Air Show. (Dassault Aviation)

The future of unmanned combat air vehicles in the twenty-first century is suggested in this artist's conception of an air strike being conducted by a pair of Northrop Grumman QSPs. DARPA's Quiet Supersonic Platform test program involved the modification of a manned F-5E aircraft, but had the QSP concept evolved into an unmanned combat aircraft, it might have taken the form similar to this notional aircraft. (Northrop Grumman)

Technician conducts a preflight check of the Aurora Excalibur half-scale demonstrator aircraft prior to its debut at the Aberdeen Proving Grounds in Maryland. The full scale aircraft was intended for quick response armed air support of surface forces. (Aurora Flight Sciences)

The first flight of the Aurora Excalibur demonstrator occurred on 24 June 2009. Its configuration enables vertical takeoff and landing as well as transition to high-speed forward flight. Said Aurora President, John Langford, "It was a flawless first flight with a crisp takeoff and perfect landing. In flight, the hover stability and heading control performance were excellent." (Aurora Flight Sciences)

fuselage and avionics. Italy's Alenia Aeronautica, which joined the program in 2006, has a 22 percent share, and is responsible for electrical systems, the weapons firing system, and the integrated weapons bay. All three have a share in flight testing. Other subcontractors include EADS CASA in Spain, Hellenic Aerospace in Greece, RUAG in Switzerland, and Thales in France.

In the United States, Aurora Flight Sciences, developer of the Odysseus HALE aircraft in DARPA's Vulture program, has proposed its Excalibur high-speed, vertical takeoff aircraft, which the company describes as "a purpose-built armed tactical UAV" designed to "provide tactical air support." Armament for this mission includes the AGM-114 Hellfire missile, the GBU-41 Viper Strike laser-guided smart bomb, and the Advanced Precision-Kill Weapon System (APKWS), or a mix of weapons up to the 4,400-pound payload capacity.

Developed under contract for both the U.S. Army Aviation Applied Technology Directorate and the Office of Naval Research, a half-scale Excalibur "proof-of-concept" vehicle made its debut flight autonomously at the U.S. Army's Aberdeen Proving Grounds in Maryland on 24 June 2009. According to Aurora, the aircraft combines "jet-borne vertical lift with three electric lift fans" to provide "attitude control and a significant fraction of hover thrust."

With this turbine-electric hybrid propulsion system, the full scale aircraft has VTOL capability, and can achieve a forward speed in excess of 500 mph in horizontal flight. The ceiling is 40,000 feet, better than the MQ-1B Predator or MQ-1C Warrior, and the same as what was specified for the X-45 or X-47.

Out of the experience garnered by Boeing and Northrop Grumman beneath the official umbrella of UCAV and J-UCAS, many aircraft will eventually evolve. Of special note is the Boeing Phantom Ray program.

Phantom Ray is essentially a development of the Boeing X-45C, the first of which was nearly completed when J-UCAS was terminated in 2006. "We will incorporate the

The new capabilities of the jet-propelled Predator C Avenger are seen by General Atomics as a complement to the operational flexibility of MQ-1 Predators and MQ-9 Reapers "by expanding the operational envelope of this series of aircraft, Predator C rounds out the flexibility of these aircraft systems with quick response armed reconnaissance." (General Atomics)

latest technologies into the superb X-45C airframe design," said Dave Koopersmith, vice president of Boeing Advanced Military Aircraft, a division of Phantom Works. "Phantom Ray will pick up where the UCAS program left off in 2006 by further demonstrating Boeing's unmanned systems development capabilities in a fighter-sized, state-of-the-art aerospace system."

As Graham Warwick of *Aviation Week* wrote in May 2009, "if the [Phantom Ray] aircraft looks familiar, that's because it is—it's the X-45C that was completed, but never flown, when the [J-UCAS] program was canceled back in 2006 . . . Unveiling of the Phantom Ray comes hard on the heels of U.S. defense secretary Robert Gates' April 7 announcement that the [Next Generation Bomber] program is to be deferred and his comments that perhaps the next Air Force bomber could be unmanned. In effect, we are back to where we were before March 2006, when the J-UCAS program was planning to demonstrate technology for future unmanned strike/surveillance platforms."

Meanwhile, the UCAV/J-UCAS concept also lives on in the U.S. Navy's Naval Unmanned Combat Air System (UCAV-N) aircraft carrier demonstrator program, under which the Northrop Grumman X-47B will be the first stealthy, armed unmanned aerial vehicle to conduct autonomous operations aboard a carrier.

However, for all the buzz about stealthy armed UCAVs, it has been General Atomics that has consistently led the way in the first decade of the twenty-first century when it comes to operationally deployable armed drones. The MQ-1B Predator, MQ-1C Warrior, and MQ-9 Reaper have all been flying routine missions and killing real threats while a myriad of other concepts live only on drawing boards and test fields.

The General Atomics Avenger, a jet-propelled sibling to the Predator and Reaper, made its first flight on 4 April 2009. Originally called Predator C, the Avenger is powered by a Pratt & Whitney Canada PW545B delivering 4,800 pounds of thrust, with its exhaust shielded by a radar deflecting V-tail.

The Avenger airframe design incorporates many other features to reduce its radar signature, not the least of these being that it does not have a propeller. Especially notable in reducing signature is an internal weapons bay that is capable of carrying 500 pounds of the total 3,000 pounds of payload capacity. As Tom Cassidy of General Atomics adds, the bay doors could be removed to accommodate a surveillance pod, or extra fuel tanks.

As David Fulghum and Bill Sweetman pointed out in the 20 April 2009 issue of *Aviation Week*, Pratt & Whitney "has been developing an S-shaped exhaust that offers protection from radar observation and cooling to

A Predator C Avenger in flight, sporting the two-tone gray camouflage pattern shared with manned tactical aircraft today. Although no weapons are visible on external racks or pylons, the aircraft does have an internal weapons bay, unlike either the Predator or Reaper. (General Atomics)

As viewed from slightly below, the Predator C Avenger clearly has a few design features in common with its piston-powered predecessors. Quite apparent are the bulbous forward fuselage of both the Predator and Reaper, and the outward-canted tail surfaces reminiscent of those of the Reaper. (General Atomics)

reduce the IR signature . . . The humpbacked design of the engine compartment offers room enough for a serpentine exhaust that eliminates radar observation of the engine . . . The [Avenger's] cranked trailing edge provides the aerodynamic and structural benefits of a tapered wing and helps shield the engine inlet from radar. Canted upper and power body sides meet at a sharp chine line, continuous from nose to tail, thereby avoiding the radar cross-section hot spot caused by a curved side."

Also important is the fact that General Atomics designed the Avenger so the wings can be folded for storage in hangars or aboard aircraft carriers, and that the aircraft is also equipped with a tailhook. Thus the potential array of customers would be wider even than that of the Predator and Reaper.

Fulghum and Sweetman have written that the poten-tial for the Avenger has raised the eyebrows of those who fear that it may be a serious competitor on Capitol Hill for combat aircraft funding. They cite a decision made by Defense Secretary Robert Gates and Marine Corps General James Cartwright, vice chairman of the Joint Chiefs of Staff, to include armed UAVs within the fighter force structure. As they wrote in *Aviation Week*, "Critics view this as a first, false step driven by economic rather than military considerations that will lead to the substitution of 'Reapers, and later Predator Cs, for F-35 Joint Strike Fighters.'"

Could this be another milepost on the road to the "UAS-centric force?"

For the foreseeable future, the only way to conclude any discussion of both the technology and tactical doctrine related to unmanned combat air vehicles will be to include the phrase, "to be continued."

Boeing officially rolled out its Phantom Ray prototype aircraft on May 10, 2010. Funded internally, this unmanned warplane is derived from Boeing's X-45C J-UCAS demonstrator aircraft. (Courtesy of Chris Haddox, Boeing Phantom Works Communications)

An artist conception of the Boeing Phantom Ray in flight. (Courtesy of Chris Haddox, Boeing Phantom Works Communications)

APPENDIX A: SPECIFICATIONS FOR SELECTED UNMANNED AERIAL VEHICLES

Note: Data is drawn from various sources, should be considered approximate, and is provided for comparison purposes only.

MQ-1B Predator

Manufacturer:	General Atomics Aeronautical Systems Inc.
User classification:	U.S. Air Force Tier II, Medium Altitude, Long Endurance (MALE)
Powerplant:	Rotax 914F four-cylinder engine (115 hp)
Wingspan:	48.7 feet (14.8 m)
Length:	27 feet (8.22 m)
Height:	6.9 feet (2.1 m)
Weight:	1,130 pounds (512 kg)
Max takeoff weight:	2,250 pounds (1,020 kg)
Payload:	450 pounds (204 kg)
Speed:	Cruise, 84 mph (135 km/h); top, 135 mph (215 km/h)
Ceiling:	25,000 feet (7,620 m)
Range:	454 miles (730 km)
Endurance:	40 hours (maximum)
Armament:	2 laser-guided AGM-114 Hellfire missiles

MQ-1C Sky Warrior

Manufacturer:	General Atomics Aeronautical Systems
User classification:	U.S. Army Tier III, Extended Range, Multi-Purpose (ERMP)
Powerplant:	Thielert Heavy-Fuel Engine (135 hp)
Wingspan:	56 feet (17 m)
Length:	28 feet (8 m)
Height:	6.9 feet (2.1 m)
Max takeoff weight:	3,200 pounds (1,451 kg)
Speed:	155 mph (250 km/h)
Ceiling:	29,000 feet (8,800 m)
Armament:	Four AGM-114 Hellfire missiles

MQ-18A Hummingbird

Manufacturer:	Boeing (Originated with Frontier Aircraft)
Powerplant:	Pratt & Whitney PW207D turboshaft (710 hp)
Main rotor diameter:	36 feet (11 m)
Length:	35 feet (10.7 m)
Empty weight:	2,500 pounds (1,134 kg)
Gross weight:	6,500 pounds (2,948 kg)
Speed:	160 mph (258 km/h)
Ceiling:	20,000-30,000 feet (6,100-9,150 m)
Endurance:	20 hours plus
Armament:	None specified

RQ-4 Global Hawk

Manufacturer:	Northrop Grumman (primary), Raytheon, and L3 Comm
User classification:	U.S. Air Force Tier II Plus, High Altitude, Long Endurance (HALE)
Powerplant:	Rolls-Royce-North American AE 3007H turbofan (7,600 pounds thrust)
Wingspan (Block 10):	116.2 feet (35.4 m)
Wingspan (Block 20/30/40):	130.9 feet (39.9 m)
Length (Block 10):	44.4 feet (13.5 m)
Length (Block 20/30/40):	47.6 feet (14.5 m)
Height (Block 10):	14.6 (4.2 m)
Height (Block 20/30/40):	15.4 feet (4.7 m)
Weight (Block 10):	26,700 pounds (12,111 kg)
Weight (Block 20/30/40):	14,950 pounds (6,781 kg)
Maximum takeoff weight (Block 10):	26,750 pounds (12,133 kg)
Maximum takeoff weight (Block 20/30/40):	32,250 pounds (14,628 kg)
Payload (Block 10):	2,000 pounds (907 kg)
Payload (Block 20/30/40):	3,000 pounds (1,360 kg)
Speed (Loiter Velocity) (Block 10):	395 mph (635 km/h)
Speed (Loiter Velocity) (Block 20/30/40):	357 mph (575 km/h)
Ceiling:	65,000 feet (19,800 m)
Ferry Range (Block 10):	13,817 miles (22,236 km)
Ferry Range (Block 20/30/40):	14,155 miles (22,780 km)
Endurance:	Over 42 hrs. maximum (on-station endurance, 24 hours)
Armament:	None specified

X-47B Pegasus

Manufacturer:	Northrop Grumman
Powerplant:	Pratt & Whitney F100-PW-220U turbofan (16,000 pounds thrust)
Wingspan:	62.1 feet (18.92 m)
Length:	38.2 feet (11.63 m)
Height:	10.4 feet (3.10 m)
Weight:	14,000 pounds (6,350 kg)
Max takeoff weight:	44,567 pounds (20,215 kg)
Payload:	4,500 pounds (2,040 kg)
Speed:	High subsonic
Ceiling:	40,000 feet (12,190 m)
Range:	4,000 miles (6,500 km)
Armament:	Two GBU-31 Joint Direct Attack Munition guided bombs

RQ-7 Shadow

Manufacturer:	AAI Corporation (An operating unit of Textron)
User classification:	U.S. Army and U.S. Marine Corps Tier II
Powerplant:	Wankel UAV Engine 741 (38 hp)
Wingspan:	11.2 feet (3.41 m)
Length:	14 feet (3.87 m)
Height:	3.3 feet (1 meter)
Weight:	186 pounds (77 kg)
Payload:	60 pounds (27 kg)
Ceiling:	15,000 feet (4,600 m)
Range:	27 miles (50 km)
Endurance:	6.1 hours
Armament:	None specified

X-47A Pegasus

Manufacturer:	Northrop Grumman
Powerplant:	Pratt & Whitney F100-PW-220U turbofan (16,000 pounds thrust)
Wingspan:	27.8 feet (8.47 m)
Length:	27.9 feet (8.50 m)
Weight:	3,836 pounds (1,740 kg)
Maximum takeoff weight:	5,500 pounds (2,500 kg)
Speed:	Subsonic
Ceiling:	40,000 feet (12,192 m)
Range:	1,726 miles (2,778 km)
Armament:	None specified

X-45C Unmanned Combat Air System

Manufacturer:	Boeing Company
Powerplant:	General Electric F404-GE-102D turbofan (7,000 pounds thrust)
Wingspan:	49 feet (14.9 m)
Length:	39 feet (11.9 m)
Height:	4 feet (1.2 m)
Maximum takeoff weight:	36,500 pounds (16,600 kg)
Payload:	4,500 pounds (2,040 kg)
Speed:	Mach 0.85
Ceiling:	40,000 feet (12,200 m)
Mission Radius:	1,500 miles (2,400 km)
Armament:	Two GBU-31 Joint Direct Attack Munition guided bombs

X-45A Unmanned Combat Air Vehicle

Manufacturer:	Boeing Company
Powerplant:	Honeywell F124-GA-100 turbofan engine (6,300 pounds thrust)
Wingspan:	26 feet 6 inches (8.08 m)
Length:	33 feet 10 inches (10.3 m)
Height:	3.7 feet (1.13 m)
Weight:	8,000 pounds (3,630 kg)
Maximum takeoff weight:	12,190 pounds (5,528 kg)
Payload:	1,500 pounds (680 kg)
Speed:	Mach 0.75
Ceiling:	35,000 feet (10,700 m)
Mission Radius:	570 miles (920 km)
Armament:	1,500 pounds (680 kg) of test ordnance

MQ-9 Reaper

Manufacturer:	General Atomics Aeronautical Systems
User classification:	U.S. Air Force Tier II, Medium Altitude, Long Endurance (MALE)
Powerplant:	Honeywell TPE331-10GD turboprop (900 shaft hp)
Wingspan:	66 feet (20.1 m)
Length:	36 feet (11 m)
Height:	12.5 feet (3.8 m)
Weight:	4,900 pounds (2,223 kg) empty
Max takeoff weight:	10,500 pounds (4,760 kg)
Payload:	3,750 pounds (1,701 kg)
Speed:	Cruise, 230 mph (370 km/h)
Ceiling:	50,000 feet (15,240 m)
Range:	3,682 miles (3,200 nautical miles)
Endurance:	40 hours (14 hours when fully armed)
Armament:	Combination of AGM-114 Hellfire missiles, GBU-12 Paveway II and GBU-38 Joint Direct Attack Munitions

Excalibur

Manufacturer:	Aurora Flight Sciences
Powerplant:	Williams F415 turbofan (700 lb. thrust)/Three 12-kilowatt battery-powered lift fans
Wingspan:	30 feet (9.1 m)
Wingspan (with lift fans retracted):	21 feet (6.4 m)
Length:	26 feet (8 m)
Max takeoff weight:	2,600 pounds (1,180 kg)
Payload:	400 pounds (182 kg)
Speed:	500 mph (800 km/h)
Ceiling:	40,000 feet (12,200 m)
Endurance:	3 hours
Armament:	AGM-114 Hellfire missile, GBU-41 Viper Strike laser-guided smart bomb, Advanced Precision-Kill Weapon System (APKWS)

MQ-8B Fire Scout

Manufacturer:	Northrop Grumman
Powerplant:	Rolls-Royce 250-C20 turboshaft (900 shaft hp)
Main rotor diameter:	27 feet 6 inches (8.4 m)
Length (folded):	22.87 feet (6.97 m)
Height:	9.42 feet (2.9 m)
Gross weight:	3,150 pounds (1,430 kg)
Payload:	600 pounds (270 kg)
Speed:	125 mph (200 km/h)
Ceiling:	20,000 feet (6,100 m)
Endurance:	8 hours with a 200-pound payload
Armament:	2.75-inch Advanced Precision-Kill Weapon System (APKWS) rockets

CQ-10A SnowGoose

Manufacturer:	Mist Mobility Integrated Systems Technology (MMIST).
Powerplant:	Rotax 914 piston engine (110 hp)
Length:	9 feet 6 in (2.9 m)
Weight empty:	600 pounds (270 kg)
Gross weight:	1,400 pounds (635 kg)
Speed:	38 mph (61 km/h)
Range:	185 miles (300 km) (with 75 pounds payload)
Ceiling:	Above 18,000 feet (5,500 m)
Armament:	None specified

ScanEagle

Manufacturer:	Insitu, Inc./Boeing Company
User classification:	U.S. Navy and U.S. Marine Corps Tier II
Powerplant:	Sonex Research (1.9 hp)
Wingspan:	10.2 feet (3.11 m)
Length:	4.5 feet (1.37 m)
Weight:	28.8 pounds (13.1 kg)
Max takeoff weight:	44 pounds (20 kg)
Ceiling:	19,500 feet (5,944 m)
Speed:	90 mph (150 km/h)
Endurance:	24 hours plus
Armament:	None specified

CU-170 Heron

Manufacturer:	Israel Aerospace Industries
Powerplant:	Rotax 914 (115 hp)
Wingspan:	54 feet 5 inches (16.60 m)
Length:	27 feet 10 inches (8.5 m)
Max takeoff weight:	2,530 pounds (1,150 kg)
Payload:	550 pounds (250 kg)
Speed:	130 mph (207 km/h)
Ceiling:	32,800 feet (10,000 m)
Range:	217 miles (350 km)
Endurance:	40 hours
Armament:	None specified

Falco

Manufacturer:	SELEX Galileo (Co-Producer Pakistan Aeronautical Complex)
Powerplant:	UAV Engines Ltd. gasoline engine (65 hp)
Wingspan:	23.6 feet (7.20 m)
Length:	17.2 feet (5.25 m)
Height:	6 feet (1.80 m)
Max takeoff weight:	926 pounds (420 kg)
Payload:	155 pounds (70 kg)
Ceiling:	21,325 feet (6,500 m)
Speed:	135 mph (217 km/h)
Endurance:	Less than 14 hours
Armament:	None specified

S-100 Camcopter

Manufacturer:	Schiebel Group
Powerplant:	Diamond engine (55 hp)
Main rotor diameter:	133.9 feet (34 m)
Length:	122 feet (31.1 m)
Height:	44 feet (11.2 m)
Max takeoff weight:	440 pounds (200 kg)
Payload:	110 pounds (50 kg)
Speed:	140 mph (220 km/h)
Range (maximum):	112 miles (180 km)
Ceiling:	18,000 feet (5,500 m)
Endurance:	6 hours with 75 pounds (34 kg) payload
Armament:	None specified

Avenger (Predator C)

Manufacturer:	General Atomics Aeronautical Systems, Inc.
Powerplant:	Pratt & Whitney Canada PW545B turbofan (4,800 pounds thrust)
Wingspan:	66 feet (20.12 m),
Length:	41 feet (12.50 m)
Payload:	3,000 pounds (1,360.78 kg)
Speed:	460 mph (740 km/h)
Operational altitude:	60,000 feet (18,288 m)
Endurance:	20 hrs (extra 2 hours with bomb bay fuel tank)
Armament:	AGM-114 Hellfire, GBU-24 Paveway III, GBU-31 JDAM, GBU-38 Small Dia. Bomb

APPENDIX B: CHECKLIST OF AMERICAN MILITARY UNMANNED AERIAL VEHICLES

As Designated Under the Post-1997 "Q" Designation System

RQ-1A/B	General Atomics Predator
MQ-1B	General Atomics Predator
MQ-1C	General Atomics Warrior
RQ-2A/B/C	IAI Pioneer
RQ-3A	Lockheed Martin DarkStar
RQ-4A/B	Northrop Grumman (Teledyne Ryan) Global Hawk
RQ-5A and MQ-5A/B (formerly BQM-155A)	Northrop Grumman (TRW/IAI) Hunter
RQ-6A	Alliant Techsystems Outrider
RQ-7A/B	AAI Shadow 200
RQ-8A/MQ-8B	Northrop Grumman Fire Scout
MQ-9A	General Atomics Reaper
CQ-10A	MMIST SnowGoose
RQ-11A/B	AeroVironment Raven
Q-12	(Designation not yet assigned)
Q-13	(Designation not yet assigned)
RQ-14A	AeroVironment Dragon Eye
RQ-14B	AeroVironment Swift
RQ-15A	DRS Neptune
YRQ-16A	Honeywell Micro Air Vehicle (MAV)
XMQ-17A	MTC Technologies SpyHawk
YMQ-18A	Boeing A160T Hummingbird

Note: Some operational UAVs, such as the Boeing/Insitu ScanEagle had not received official designations in this series when this book went to press.

INDEX

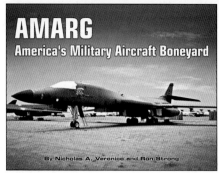
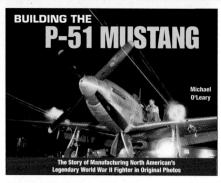
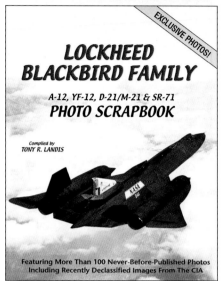

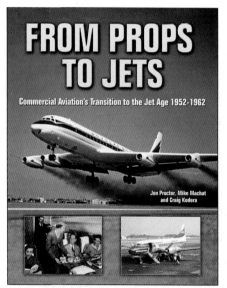
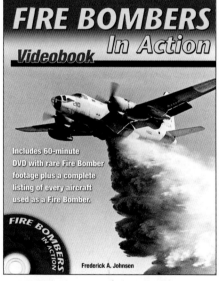